A POETICAL RHAPSODY

LONDON : HUMPHREY MILFORD

OXFORD UNIVERSITY PRESS

A POETICAL RHAPSODY
1602–1621

EDITED BY

HYDER EDWARD ROLLINS

VOLUME I

HARVARD · UNIVERSITY · PRESS

CAMBRIDGE · MASSACHUSETTS : 1931

PRINTED AT THE HARVARD UNIVERSITY PRESS

CAMBRIDGE, MASS., U.S.A.

To

MY TEACHER AND FRIEND

MORGAN CALLAWAY, JR.

CONTENTS

A
POETICAL RAPSODY

Containing,

*Diuerſe Sonnets, Odes, Elegies, Madrigalls,
and other Poeſies, both in Rime, and
Meaſured Verſe.*

Neuer yet publiſhed.

*The Bee and Spider by a diuerſe power,
Sucke Hony & Poyſon from the ſelfe ſame flower.*

*Printed at London by V.S. for Iohn Baily, and
are to be ſolde at his Shoppe in Chancerie lane,
neere to the Office of the ſix Clarkes.*
1 6 0 2.

To the most Noble, Honorable, and Worthy Lord, William Earle of Pembroke, Lord Herbert of *Caerdiffe, Marmion, and Saint Quintine.*

5

GReat Earle, whose high and noble minde, is higher
And nobler, then thy noble high Degree:
Whose outward shape, though it most louely bee,
Doth in faire Robes a fairer Soule attier:
Who Rich in fading Wealth, in endlesse Treasure   10
Of Vertue, Valour, Learning, richer art:
Whose present greatnes, men esteeme but part
Of what by line of future Hope they measure.
Thou Worthy Sonne, vnto a peerelesse MOTHER,
Thou Nephew to great SIDNEY of renowne,   15
Thou that deseru'st thy CORONET to crowne
With Lawrell Crowne, a Crowne excelling t'other;
I consecrate these Rimes to thy great NAME,
Which if thou like, they seeke no other fame.

The deuoted Admirer of your Lord-   20
ships noble virtues,

FRA: DAVISON

humbly dedicates, his owne, his Brothers, and *Anomos* Poems, both in
his owne, and their names.   25

[3]

EING induced, by fome priuate reafons, and by the inftant intrea- tie of fpeciall friendes, to fuffer fome of my worthleffe Poems to be publifhed, I defired to make fome written by my deere friend *Anomos*, and my deerer *Brother*, to beare them company: Both without their confent, the latter being in the low Country Warres, and the former vtterly ignorant thereof. My friendes name I concealed, mine owne, and my brothers, I willed the Printer to fuppreffe, as well as I had concealed the other: which he hauing put in, without my pri- uity, we muft both now vndergoe a fharper cenfure perhaps then our nameles works fhould haue done, & I efpecially. For if their Poems be liked, the praife is due to their inuention, if difliked, the blame both by them, and all men will be deriued vppon me, for publifhing that which they meant to fuppreffe.

If thou thinke wee affeſt fame by thefe kindes of writings, though I thinke them no difparagement e- uen to the beſt iudgements, yet I anfwere in all our behalfes, with the Princely Shepheard *Dorus*;

Our hearts doe feeke another eſtimation.

If thou condemne Poetry in generall, and af- firme, that it doth intoxicate the braine, and make

men

5

10

15

20

25

men vtterly vnfit,either for more ferious ftudies, or
for any actiue courfe of life,I only fay, *Iubeo te ftultum
effe libenter*: Since experience proues by examples of
many, both dead and liuing, that diuers delighted   5
and excelling herein, being Princes or States-men,
haue gouerned and counceled as wifely,being Soul-
diers,haue commanded armies as fortunately,being
Lawyers,haue pleaded as iudicially and eloquent-
ly,being Diuines, haue written and taught as pro-   10
foundly, and being of any other Profeffion, haue
difcharged it as fufficiently as any other men what-
foeuer: If liking other kindes, thou miflike the Lyri-
call, becaufe the chiefeft fubiect thereof is Loue;
I reply,that Loue being virtuoufly intended,& wor-   15
thily placed,is the Whetftone of witt, and Spurre to
all generous actions: and that many excellent fpi-
rits with great fame of witt, and no ftaine of iudgement,haue written excellently in this kind,and fpe-
cially the euer-praife worthy *Sidney*: So as if thou   20
will needs make it a fault, for mine owne part,

> *Haud timeo, fi iam nequeo defendere crimen*
> *Cum tanto commune viro.*

If any except againft the mixing (both at the beginning and ende of this booke) of diuerfe thinges   25
written by great and learned Perfonages, with our
meane and worthles Scriblings, I vtterly difclaime
it, as being done by the Printer, either to grace the
forefront with Sir *Ph. Sidneys*,and others names , or
to make the booke grow to a competent volume.   30

For thefe Poems in particular,I could aledge thefe
excufes;that thofe vnder the Name of *Anomos*,were
                                                       writ-

written (as appeareth by diuers things to Syr *Philip
Sidney* liuing, and of him dead) almoſt twentie yeers
ſince, when Poetry was farre from that perfection, to
which it hath now attained; that my Brother is by   5
profeſſion a Souldier, and was not 18. yeeres olde
when hee writt theſe Toyes: that mine owne were
made moſt of them ſixe or ſeuen yeeres ſince, at idle
times as I iourneyed vp and downe during my Tra-
uails. But to leaue their workes to iuſtifie them-   10
ſelues, or the Authors to iuſtifie their workes, and
to ſpeake of myne owne; thy miſlikes I contemne,
thy prayſes (which I neither deſerue, nor expect), I
eſteeme not, as hoping (God willing) ere long, to
regaine thy good Opinion, if loſt, or more deſer-   15
uedly to continue it, if already obtained, by ſome
grauer Worke. *Farewell.*

FRA: DAVISON.

[6]

Two Paſtoralls, made by Sir *Philip Sid-*
ney, neuer yet publiſhed.

[1] *Vpon his meeting with his two worthy Friends*
   and fellow-Poets, Sir Edward Dier,
   and Maiſter Fulke Greuill.   5

IOyne Mates in mirth to me,
Graunt pleaſure to our meeting:
Let *Pan* our good God ſee,
How gratefull is our greeting.
 Ioyne hearts and hands, ſo let it be,   10
 Make but one Minde in Bodies three.

Ye Hymnes, and ſinging ſkill
Of God *Apolloes* giuing,
Be preſt our reedes to fill,
With ſound of muſicke liuing.   15
 Ioyne hearts and hands,&c.

Sweete *Orpheus* Harpe, whoſe ſound
The ſtedfaſt mountaynes moued,
Let heere thy ſkill abound,
To ioyne ſweete friends beloued.   20
 Ioyne hearts and hands,&c.
    B   My

My two and I be met,
A happy bleſſed Trinitie;
As three moſt ioyntly ſet,
In firmeſt band of Vnitie.   5
   Ioyne hands,&c.

Welcome my two to me,   E.D. F.G. P.*S*.
The number beſt beloued,
Within my heart you be
In friendſhip vnremoued.   10
   Ioyne hands,&c.

Giue leaue your flockes to range,
Let vs the while be playing,
Within the Elmy grange,
Your flockes will not be ſtraying.   15
   Ioyne hands,&c.

Cauſe all the mirth you can,
Since I am now come hether,
Who neuer ioy, but when
I am with you together.   20
   Ioyne hands,&c.

Like Louers do their Loue,
So ioy I,in you ſeeing;
Let nothing mee remoue
From alwayes with you beeing.   25
   Ioyne hands,&c.

                      And

And as the Turtle-Doue
To mate with whom he liueth,
Such comfort, feruent loue
Of you, to my hart giueth.   5
 Ioyne hands,&c.

Now ioyned be our hands,
Let them be ne'r a funder,
But linkt in binding bands
By metamorphoz'd wonder.   10
 So fhould our feuer'd bodies three
 As one for euer ioyned bee.
       Sir Ph. Sidney.

<hr>

[2] *Difprayfe of a Courtly life.*

WALKING in bright *Phœbus* blaze   15
 Where with heate oppreft I was,
 I got to a fhady wood,
Where greene leaues did newly bud.
And of graffe was plenty dwelling,
Deckt with pyde flowers fweetely fmelling.   20

In this wood a man I met,
On lamenting wholy fet:
Rewing change of wonted ftate,
Whence he was transformed late,
Once to Shepheards God retayning,   25
Now in feruile Court remayning.
    B 2   There

<hr>

There he wandring malecontent,
Vp and downe perplexed went,
Daring not to tell to mee,
Spake vnto a fenceleffe tree,   5
One among the reft electing
Thefe fame words, or this effecting:

My old mates I grieue to fee,
Voyde of me in field to bee,
Where we once our louely fheepe,   10
Louingly like friends did keepe,
Oft each others friendfhip prouing,
Neuer ftriuing, but in louing.

But may Loue abiding bee
In poore fhepheards bafe degree?   15
It belongs to fuch alone
To whom arte of Loue is knowne:
Seely fhepheards are not witting
What in art of Loue is fitting.

Nay, what neede the Arte to thofe,   20
To whom we our loue difclofe?
It is to be vfed then,
When we doe but flatter men:
Friendfhip true in hart affured,
Is by natures giftes procured.   25

Therefore fhepheardes wanting skill,
Can Loues duties beft fulfill:
Since they know not how to faine,

                              Nor

Nor with Loue to cloake Diſdaine,
Like the wiſer ſorte, whoſe learning,
Hides their inward will of harming.

Well was I, while vnderſhade   5
Oten Reedes me muſicke made,
Striuing with my Mates in Song,
Mixing mirth our Songs among,
Greater was that ſhepheards treaſure,
Then this falſe,fine,Courtly pleaſure.   10

Where,how many Creatures be,
So many pufft in minde I ſee,
Like to *Iunoes* birdes of pride,
Scarce each other can abide,
Friends like to blacke Swannes appearing,   15
Sooner theſe than thoſe in hearing.

Therefore *Pan*, if thou mayſt be
Made to liſten vnto me,
Grant, I ſay (if ſeely man
May make treaty to god *Pan*)   20
That I,without thy denying,
May be ſtill to thee relying.

Only for my two loues ſake,   *Sir Ed.D. and M.F.G.*
In whoſe loue I pleaſure take,
Only two do me delight   25
With their euer-pleaſing ſight,
Of all men to thee retaining,
Grant me with thoſe two remaining.

B 3   So

So shall I to thee alwayes,
With my reedes, sound mighty praise;
And first Lambe that shall befall,
Yearely decke thine Altar shall: 5
If it please thee be reflected,
And I from thee not reiected.

So I left him in that place,
Taking pitty on his case,
Learning this among the rest,   10
That the meane estate is best,
Better filled with contenting,
Voyde of wishing and repenting.

                    Sir Ph. Sidney.

[3] *Fiction how* Cupid *made a Nymph wound her selfe*   15
          with his Arrowes.

IT chaunst of late a Shepheards swaine,
   That went to seeke a strayed sheepe,
Within a thicket on the plaine,
Espide a daintie Nymph asleepe.   20

Her golden Haire ore-spread her face,
Her carelesse Armes abroad were cast,
Her Quiuer had her Pillowes place,
Her breast lay bare to euery blast.

                                              The

The Shepheard ſtood and gazde his fill,
Nought durſt hee doo,nought durſt he ſay:
When Chance or elſe perhaps his Will,
Did guide the God of Loue that way.   5

The crafty boy that ſees her ſleep,
Whom if ſhee wakte, he durſt not ſee,
Behinde her cloſely ſeekes to creepe,
Before her nap ſhould ended bee.

There come,he ſteales her ſhaftes away,   10
And puttes his owne into their place,
Ne dares he any longer ſtay,
But ere ſhe wakes, hies thence apace.

Scarce was hee gone,when ſhee awakes,
And ſpies the Shepheard ſtanding by;   15
Her bended Bowe in haſte ſhee takes,
And at the ſimple Swaine let fly.

Foorth flew the ſhafte,and pierſt his hart,
That to the ground hee fell with paine:
Yet vp againe forthwith hee ſtart,   20
And to the Nymphe hee ran amaine:

Amaz'de to ſee ſo ſtrange a ſight,
She ſhot, and ſhot, but all in vaine,
The more his wounds, the more his might,
Loue yeeldeth ſtrength in midſt of paine.   25

B 4   Her

Her angry Eyes are great with teares,
She blames her hands, she blames her skill;
The bluntneſſe of her Shaftes ſhe feares,
And try them on her ſelfe ſhe will.   5

Take heed, ſweet Nimph, try not the ſhaft,
Eache little touch will pricke the harte,
Alas, thou knoweſt not *Cupids* craft,
Reuenge is ioy, the End is ſmart.

Yet try ſhe wil, and prick ſome bare,   10
Her Hands were glou'd, and next to hand
Was that faire Breaſt, that breaſt ſo rare,
That made the ſhepheard ſenceleſſe ſtand.

That breſt ſhe prickt, and through that breſt,
Loue findes an entry to her hart: 15
At feeling of this new-come Gueſt,
Lord how the gentle Nimph doth ſtart!

Shee runnes not now, ſhe ſhootes no more,
Away ſhe throwes both ſhaftes and bowe,
Shee ſeekes for that ſhe ſhun'd before,   20
She thinks the Shepheards haſte too ſlowe.

Though mountaines meet not, Louers may:
So others doo, and ſo doo they.
The God of Loue ſittes on a tree,
And laughes that pleaſant ſight to ſee.   25

Anomos.

[4] *A* DIALOGVE *betweene two shepheards,* Thenot,
and Piers, *in praise of* ASTREA, *made by the excellent Lady, the Lady* Mary *Countesse of* Pembrook,
at the Queenes Maiesties being at her house at   5
Anno 15 .

Then. I Sing diuine ASTREAS praise,
        O Muses! help my wittes to raise,
          And heaue my Verses higher.
Piers. Thou needst the truth, but plainly tell,   10
        Which much I doubt thou canst not well,
          Thou art so oft a lier.

Then. If in my Song no more I show,
        Than Heau'n, and Earth, and Sea do know,
          Then truely I haue spoken.   15
Piers. Sufficeth not no more to name,
        But being no lesse, the like, the same,
          Else lawes of truth be broken.

Then. Then say, she is so good, so faire,
        With all the earth she may compare,   20
          Not *Momus* selfe denying.
Piers. Compare may thinke where likenesse holds,
        Nought like to her the earth enfoldes,
          I lookt to finde you lying.

                    B 5   *Then.*

Then. ASTREA ſees with Wiſedoms ſight,
    Aſtrea workes by Vertues might,
      And ioyntly both do ſtay in her.
Piers. Nay take from them, her hand, her minde,   5
    The one is lame, the other blinde,
      Shall ſtill your lying ſtaine her?

Then. Soone as ASTREA ſhewes her face,
    Strait euery ill auoides the place,
      And euery good aboundeth.   10
Piers. Nay long before her face doth ſhowe,
    The laſt doth come, the firſt doth goe,
      How lowde this lie reſoundeth!

Then. ASTREA is our chiefeſt ioy,
    Our chiefeſt guarde againſt annoy,   15
      Our chiefeſt wealth, our treaſure.
Piers. Where chiefeſt are, three others bee,
    To vs none elſe but only ſhee;
      When wilt thou ſpeake in meaſure?

Then. ASTREA may be iuſtly ſayd,   20
    A field in flowry Roabe arrayd,
      In Seaſon freſhly ſpringing.
Piers. That Spring indures but ſhorteſt time,
    This neuer leaues *Aſtreas* clime,
      Thou lieſt, inſtead of ſinging.   25

Then. As heauenly light that guides the day,
    Right ſo doth thine each louely Ray,
      That from *Aſtrea* flyeth.

                      Piers.

Piers. Nay, darknes oft that light enclowdes,
   Aſtreas beames no darknes ſhrowdes;
   How lowdly *Thenot* lyeth!

Then. ASTREA rightly terme I may,   5
   A manly Palme,a Maiden Bay,
   Her verdure neuer dying.
Piers. Palme oft is crooked,Bay is lowe,
   Shee ſtill vpright,ſtill high doth growe,
   Good *Thenot* leaue thy lying.   10

Then. Then *Piers*, of friendſhip tell me why,
   My meaning true,my words ſhould ly,
   And ſtriue in vaine to raiſe her.
Piers. Words from conceit do only riſe,
   Aboue conceit her honour flies;   15
   But ſilence,nought can praiſe her.

         Mary Counteſſe of Pembroke.

A

[5] ¶ *A Roun-de-lay in inuerted Rimes, betweene the two*
friendly Riuals, Strephon *and* Klaius, *in the presence*
of VRANIA, *Mistris to them both.*

Strephon.   5

O Whither shall I turne mee,
          From thine eies sight,
          Whose sparkling light
With quenchles flames, present, & absent burne me?
          For I burne whenas I view them,   10
          And I burne when I eschew them.

Klaius.

Since I cannot eschew them,
          But that their light
          Is in my sight,   15
Both when I view them not, and when I view them,
          Ere their flames will cease to burne me,
          From my selfe my selfe must turne me.

Strephon.

When none are present by you,   20
          I feele their might,
          And your eies bright
Appeare more glorious, others being nie you.
          So alone, or else compared,
          Wretch, I am by them ensnared.   25

                                        Klaius.

Klaius.

Since that I am infnared
   By your eies bright,
   And feele their might,   5
Whether alone they be,or elfe compared,
  Wherefoeuer I am nie you,
  Loue I muft, if I be by you.

Strephon.

When you looke kindely on me,   10
   They loue incite:
   And fpite of Spite
I loue them likewife,when you frowne vpon me.
  So,how e're your lookes are framed,
  By your lookes I am inflamed.   15

Klaius.

Since that I am inflamed,
   Ee'n by their fpite;
   And they incite
Soul-warming flames whẽ they are mildly framed,   20
  Howfoe're you looke vpon me,
  Loue I muft, if you looke on me.

Strephon.

O when fhall I them banifh,
   Since againft right,   25
   Nor day nor night,
Though abfent from me,from me they do vanifh?
  So no refpite Time doth graunt me,
  But inceffantly they haunt me.
          Klaius.

Klaius.

Since they (alas) do haunt me
　　Both day and night.
　　And wonted right　　　　　　　　　5
Obtain'd by abſence, abſence doth not grant me:
　　Night and day may ſooner vaniſh,
　　Then from mee I can them baniſh.

Strephon.

They, when the Day doth leaue mee,　　　10
　　Lodge in my ſpirite;
　　And of their ſight,
No ſight by day diſcerned can bereaue mee.
　　So, nor Day ought elſe reuealeth,
　　Nor the Night the ſame concealeth.　　15

Klaius.

Since Day, like Night concealeth
　　Each other ſight,
　　And to my ſpirite
Concealing Darknes, them like Day reuealeth.　　20
　　Time of time muſt quite bereaue mee,
　　Ere your lookes, ſweet lookes, will leaue mee.

Walter Dauiſon.

[6] STREPHONS PALINODE.

Strephon, vpon some vnkindenes conceiued, hauing made
shew to leaue VRANIA, *and make loue to another*
Nymph, was at the next solemne assembly of shepheards, 5
not onely frowned vpon by VRANIA, *but commanded*
with great bitternesse out of her presence: Whereuppon,
sory for his offence, and desirous to regaine her grace
whom he neuer had forsaken, but in shew, vpon his knees
he in this Song humbly craues pardon: and VRANIA 10
finding his true penitence, and vnwilling to loose so wor-
thy a seruant, receiues him againe into greater grace
and fauour than before.

S WEETE, I doe not pardon craue,
    Till I haue, 15
By deserts, this fault amended:
This, I onely this desire,
    That your ire
May with penance be suspended.

Not my Wil, but Fate did fetch 20
    Me poore wretch,
Into this vnhappy error.
Which to plague, no Tyrants minde
    Paine can finde,
Like my hearts selfe-guiltie terror. 25
            Then

Then, O then! let that fuffize;
  your deare Eies
Need not, need not more afflict me.
Nor your fweet Tongue dipt in gall,   5
  Need at all
From your prefence interdict me.

Vnto him that Hell fuftaines,
  No new paines
Need be fought for his tormenting.
O my paines helles paines furpas: 10
  Yet, alas,
You are ftill new paines inuenting.

By my Loue, long firme and true,
  Borne to you.   15
By thefe teares my greefe expreffing.
By this Pipe which nights and daies
  Sounds your praife,
Pitty mee my fault confeffing.

Or if I may not defire,   20
  That their yre
May with pennance bee fufpended;
Yet let me full pardon craue,
  When I haue,
With foone death my fault amended.   25

VRANIAES

===

[7] VRANIAES *Answer in inuerted*
Rimes, Staffe for Staffe.

SInce true pennance hath fufpended
    Fained yre,   5
  More Ile grant then you defire.
Faults confeft are halfe amended,
    And I haue,
In this halfe, al that I craue.

Therefore banifh now the terror,   10
    Which you finde
In your guiltleffe grieued minde.
For though you haue made an Error,
    From mee wretch
Firft beginning it did fetch.   15

Ne're my fight Ile interdict thee
    More at all.
Ne're fpeake words more dipt in gall.
Ne're ne're will I more afflict thee
    With thefe Eies,   20
What is paft, fhal now fuffize.

Now new Ioyes Ile be inuenting,
    Which (alas)
May thy paffed woes furpas.

                    Too

===

Too long thou haſt felt tormenting,
      Too great paines
So great Loue and Faith ſuſtaines.

Let theſe Eies (by thy confeſſing   5
      worthy praiſe)
Neuer ſee more nights nor daies.
Let my woes be paſt expreſſing,
      when to you
I ceaſe to be kind and true.   10

Thus are both our States amended,
      For you haue
Fuller pardon then you craue,
And my feare is quite ſuſpended,
      Since mine ire   15
Wrought th'effect I moſt deſire.

                        Fra:Dauiſon.

[8] I. Eglogve.

A Shepheard poore, *Eubulus* call'd he was,
(Poore now alas, but erft had iolly beene)
One pleafant morne whenas the Sunne did paffe   5
The fiery hornes of raging Bull betweene,
 His little Flocke into a Meade did bring,
 As foone as day-light did begin to fpring.

Frefh was the Meade, in Aprils liuerie dight,
Deckt with green Trees,bedewd with filuer Brooks,   10
But ah!all other was the fhepheards plight,
All other were both fheepe and fhepheards lookes.
 For both did fhew by their dull heauy cheere,
 They tooke no pleafure of the pleafant yeere.

He weeping went, ay me that he fhould weepe!   15
They hung their heads as they to weep would learn.
His heauy Heart did fend forth fighings deepe.
They in their bleating voyce did feeme to yearne.
 He leane and pale, their fleece was rough & rent:
 They pinde with paine,and he with dolors fpent.   20

His pleafant Pipe was broke,(alas the while)
And former meriment was banifht quite.
His fhepheards Crooke that him vpheld ere-while,
He erft had throwne away with great defpite.
 Tho leaning gainft a fhrubbe that him fuftained,   25
 To th'earth,fun,birds,trees,Eccho thus he plained
        Thou

Thou all-forth-bringing earth, though winter chill,
With boyftrous blafts blow off thy Mantle greene,
And with his Snowe and hoary Frofts doe fpill,
Thy *Flora*-pleafing flowers, and kill them cleene: 5
    Yet foone as Spring returnes againe
    To driue away thy Winters paine,
        Thy Froft and Snowe
        Away doe goe.
Sweete *Zephyres* breath cold *Boreas* doth difplace,   10
        And fruitfull fhowers
        Reuiue thy flowers,
And nought but Ioy is feene in euery place.

But ah! how long, alas, how long doth laft
My endleffe Winter without hope of Spring?   15
How haue my fighes, my bluftring fighes, defafte
The flowers and buds which erft my youth did
    Alas the tops that did afpire,   (bring.
    Lie troaden now in filthy mire.
        Alas! my head   20
        Is all befpread
With too vntimely fnow: and eke my hart
        Al fence hath loft,
        Through hardned froft,
Of colde Defpaire, that long hath bred my fmart.   25

What though Soone-rifing Torrents ouerflow
With nought-regarding ftreams thy pleafant green,
And with their furious force do lay full lowe,
Thy drowned flowers, how euer fweet they been!
    Soone fall thofe flouds, as foone they rofe,   30
           (For

(For fury foone his force doth lofe;)
　　And then full eath
　　　Apolloes breath,
The cold, yet drying North-wind, fo doth warme,　　5
　　　That by and by
　　　Thy Meades be dry,
And grow more fruitfull by their former harme.

O would the teares that Torrent-like do flowe
Adowne my hollow cheekes with reftleffe force,　　10
Would once(O that they could once)calmer grow!
Would like to thine, once ceafe their ceafles courfe!
　　Thine laft not long, mine ftill endure:
　　Thine cold,and fo thy wealth procure:
　　　Hot mine are ftill,　　15
　　　And fo do kill
Both flower and roote, with moft vnkindely dew.
　　　What Sun or Winde
　　　A way can finde,
The roote once dead, the flowers to renew?　　20

Thou,though the fcorching heate of Summer Sun,
(While ill-breath'd Dog the raging Lyon chaceth)
Thy peckled flower do make of colour dun,
And pride of all thy greeny haire defaceth;
　　And in thy moyfture-wanting fide　　25
　　Deepe wounds do make,and gafhes wide:
　　　Yet as thy weate,
　　　By *Phœbus* heate,
To turne to wholfome dryneffe is procured.
　　　So *Phœbus* heate　　30

　　　　　　By

By ſouth-winds weate,
Is ſoone aſſwaged, and all thy wounds recured.

Such heate as *Phœbus* hath me almoſt ſlaine.
As *Phœbus* heate? ah no,farre worſe then his.   5
It is *Aſtreas* burning-hot Diſdaine
That parched hath the roote of all my blis:
  That hath (alas) my youth defaced,
  That in my face deep wounds hath placed.
   Ah that no Heate   10
   Can dry the weate
The flowing weate of my ſtill-weeping Eies!
   Ah that no weate
   Can quench the heate,
The burning heate within my Hart that lies!   15

Thou doſt,poor Earth, beare many a bitter ſtound,
While greedy Swaines forgetting former neede,
With crooked plowes thy tender backe do wound,
With harrowes biting teeth do make thee bleede.
  But earth (ſo may thoſe greedy Swaines   20
  With pitteous Eye behold thy paines)
   O Earth, tel mee,
   When thou doſt ſee,
Thy fruitfull Back with golden Eares beſet,
   Doth not that ioy   25
   Kil all annoy,
And make thee all thy former wounds forget?

And I,if once my tired Hart might gaine
The Harueſt faire that to my faith is due:

         If

If once I might A S T R E A S grace regaine:
If once her hart would on my ſorrows rue,
   Alas,I could theſe plaints forgo,
   And quite forget my former wo.   5
       But(O! to ſpeake
       My Hart doth breake)
For all my ſeruice,faith,and patient minde,
      A crop of greefe,
      Without releeſe,   10
A crop of ſcorne,and of contempt, I finde.

Soone as the Shepheards Star abroad doth wend
(Nights harbinger) to ſhut in bright-ſome Day;
And gloomy Night, on whom black clouds attend,
Doth Tirant-like through skie vſurpe the ſway,   15
   Thou art (poore Earth)of Sunne depriued
   Whoſe beames to thee all Ioy deriued:
      But when *Aurore*
      Doth ope her Dore,
Her purple dore to let in *Phœbus* waine,   20
      The night giues place
      Vnto his race,
And then, with ioy,thy Sun returnes againe.

O would my Sunne would once returne againe!
Returne and driue away th'infernall night,   25
In which I die,ſince ſhe did firſt refraine
Her heauenly beames, which were mine only light.
   In her alone all my light ſhinde,
   And ſince ſhe ſhinde not, I am blinde.
      Alas, on all,   30
             Her

Her beames doe fall,
Saue wretched me, whome ſhe doth them deny.
And bleſſed day
She giues alway, 5
To all, but me, who ſtill in darkeneſſe lie.

In mournefull darkeneſſe I alone doe lie,
And wiſh, but ſcarcely hope, bright day to ſee,
For hop'd ſo long, and wiſht ſo long haue I,
As hopes and wiſhes both are gone from mee. 10
My night hath laſted fifteene yeeres,
And yet no glimpſe of day appeeres.
O do not let,
Him that hath ſet,
His ioy, his light, his life in your ſweete Grace! 15
Be vnrelieu'd,
And quite depriu'd
Of your deere ſight, which may this night diſplace.

Phœbus, although with firy-hoofed ſteedes,
Thou daily doe the ſteepy Welkin beate, 20
And from this painefull taske art neuer freed,
But daily bound to lend the world thy heate:
Though thou in fiery Chariot ride,
And burning heate thereof abide,
Yet ſoone as night 25
Doth dim the light,
And hale her ſable Cloake through vaulted skie,
Thy iournie's ceaſt,
And thou dooſt reſt,
In cooling waues of *Tethis* ſoueraigntie. 30

Thrice

Thrice happy Sun, whofe pains are eas'de by night,
O hapleffe I,whofe woes laft night and day.
My paines by day do make me wifh for night,
My woes by night do make me cry for day.   5
  By day I turmoyle vp and downe,
  By night in Seas of teares I drowne.
    O painefull plight!
    O wretched night,
Which neuer findes a morne of ioyfull light!   10
    O fad decay,
    O wretched day,
That neuer feeles the eafe of filent night!

Ye chirping Birds,whofe notes might ioy my minde,
(If to my minde one drop of ioy could finke,)   15
Who erft,through Winters rage were almoft pinde,
And kept through barren froft from meat or drinke,
  A bleffed change yee now haue feene,
  That changed hath your woefull teene.
    By day you fing,   20
    And make to ring
The neighbour groues with Eccho of your Song:
    In filent night,
    Full clofely dight,
You foundly fleepe the bufhes greene among.   25

But I,who erft (ah woefull worde to fay)
Enioy'd the pleafant fpring of her fweete grace,
And then could fing and dance, and fporte & play;
Since her fierce anger did my Spring difplace,
  My nightly reft haue turn'd to detriment,   30
     C   To

[31]

To plaints haue turn'd my wonted meriment.
      The Songs I sing
      While day doth spring,
Are bootlesse plaints till I can plaine no more.   5
      The rest I taste,
      While night doth last,
Is broken sighes, til they my hart make sore.

Thou flowret of the field that erst didst fade,
And nipt with Northerne cold didst hang the head.   10
Yee Trees whose bared bowes had lost their shade,
Whose with'red leaues by western blasts were shed
      Yee gin to bud and spring againe,
      Winter is gone that did you straine.
        But I, that late   15
        With vpright gate
Bare vp my head, while happy fauour lasted;
        Now olde am growne,
        Now ouerthrowne,
With wo, with griefe, with wailing now am wasted.   20

Your springing stalke with kindly iuice doth sprout,
My fainting legs do waste and fall away:
Your stretched armes are clad with leaues about,
My griefe-consumed armes do fast decay.
      Yee gin againe your tops lift vp;   25
      I downe to earth-ward gin to stoope.
        Each bowe and twig
        Doth waxe so big,
That scarce the rinde is able it to hide;
        I so do faint,   30
               And

And pine with plaint,
That flops and Hofe,and Galage wax too wide.

Eccho, how wel may fhe that makes me mone,
By thy example learne to rue my paine?   5
Thou hear'ft my plaintes when as I waile alone,
And wailing accents anfwereft againe.
  When as my breft through greefe I beate,
  That wofull found thou doft repeate.
    When as I fob,   10
    And hartly throb,
A dolefull fobbing found againe thou fendeft:
    And when I weep,
    And figh full deep,
A weepy fighing Voice againe thou lendeft.   15

But ah! how oft haue my fad plaints affaide
To pierce her Eares,deafe only vnto mee?
How oft my Woes in mournfull inke arraide
Haue tride to make her Eies my griefe to fee?
  And you,my Sighs and Teares,how often   20
  Haue ye fought her hard hart to foften?
    And yet her Eye,
    Doth ftill denie
For all my Woes,one bitter teare to fhed.
    And yet her Hart   25
    Will not impart,
One harty figh,for griefe her felf hath bred.

Nor I,alas,do wifh that her faire Eyes,
Her bleffed-making Eies fhould fhed a teare,
    C 2   Nor

Nor that one figh from her deere Breaft fhould rife,
For all the paines,the woes,the wrongs I beare.
   Firft let this weight oppreffe me ftill,
   Ere fhee,through mee tafte any ill. 5
      Ah if I might
      But gaine her fight,
And fhew hir,e're I die,my wretched cafe!
      O then fhould I
      Contented dy; 10
But ah I dy,and hope not fo much grace.

With that his fainting legs to fhrinke,begun,
And let him finke with gaftly look to ground
And there he lay as though his life were don,
Till that his Dog,feeing that wofull ftound, 15
   With pitteous howling, kiffing & with fcraping.
   Brought him again from that fweet-fowre efca-
                    (ping.

Then gan his Teares fo fwiftly for to flow,
As forft his Ey-lids for to giue them way.
Then bluft'ring fighes too boyft'roufly gan blow, 20
As his weake lips could not their fury ftay.
   And inward griefe withall fo hugely fweld,
   As tears,fighes, griefe had foon al words expeld.

                          At

At laſt,whenas his teares began to ceaſe,
And weary ſighes more calmely for to blowe:
As he began with words his griefe to eaſe,
And remnant of his broken plaint to ſhow: 5
   He ſpide the skie o're-ſpread with nightly clouds,
   So home he went,his flocke and him to ſhrowde.

Eubulus his Embleme.

VNI MIHI PERGAMA RESTANT.

Francis Dauiſon.   10

C 3   III.

[9] III. EGLOGVE.

Made long since vpon the death of Sir
Phillip Sidney.

Thenot.   *Perin.*   5

PERIN, arreed what new mifchance betide,
Hath raft thee of thy wonted meriment?
Faire feeds thy flock this pleafant fpring befide,
Nor Loue, I ween, hath made thee difcontent,
Sild Age and Loue, to meet in one, confent.   10

Perin.
Ah *Thenot*, where the Ioy of hart doth faile,
   What maruaile there, if mirth & mufick quaile?
See how the flowrets of the field do fpring,
The Purple Rofe, the Lilly white as Snow;   15
With fmell and colour for an Harueft King,
May ferue to make vs yong againe, I trow.
Yet all this pride is quickly laid full low,
   Soon as the root is nipt with northerne cold,
   What fmell, or beauty, can we then behold?   20

Thenot.
As good not heare, as heard, not vnderftand,
My borrell braines through eld beene all too dull,
                                                  Sike

Sike miſter meaning nill by mee be ſcand,
All as my Face,ſo wrinckled is my skull:
Then ſay me *Perin*,by thy hope of wull,
   And by thine Ewes blown bags and bagpipes   5
   So not one Aneling in thy flock be found,(found,

Perin.

Ah *Thenot*,by thine alderliefeſt Laſſe,
Or whatſoeuer is more deere to thee;
No Bagpipe name,let ſong and ſollace paſſe,   10
Death hath vndon my flock,my pipe,and mee.
Dead is the Sheeps delight,and Shepheards glee,
   Broke is my Pipe,and I my ſelfe forlorne,
   My Sheep vnfed,their fleeces rent and torne.

Thenot.   15

I mickle muz'de ſuch vncouth change to ſee,
My flockes refuz'de to feed,yet hale they weare:
The tender Birds ſate drooping on the tree,
The careleſſe Lambs went wandring here & there:
My ſelfe vnknowne a part of griefe did beare,   20
   Ne wiſt I why,yet heauy was my hart,
   Vntimely Death was cauſe of all this ſmart.

Vp *Perin*,vp,aduaunce thy mournfull layes,
Sound loud thy pipe,but ſound in dolefull wiſe.

Perin.   25

Who elſe, but *Thenot*, can the Muſes raiſe,
And teach them ſing and dance in mournfull guiſe?
My fingers ſtiffe,my voice doth hoarſely riſe.
          C 4   *Thenot.*

Thenot.
Ah,where is *Collin*, and his paffing skill?
For him it fits our forrow to fulfill.

Perin.   5
Tway fore extreames our *Collin* preffe fo neere,
(Alas that fuch extreames fhould preffe him fo)
The want of wealth, and loffe of loue fo deere,
Scarfe can he breathe from vnder heapes of woe,
He that beares heau'n,beares no fuch weight I trow.   10

Thenot.
Hath he fuch skill in making all aboue,
And hath no skill to get, or Wealth,or Loue?

Perin.
Praife is the greateft prife that Poets gaine,   15
A fimple gaine that feeds them ne're a whit.
The wanton laffe for whom he bare fuch paine,
Like running water loues to change and flit.
But if thee lift to heare a forry fit,
    Which *Cuddy* could in dolefull verfe endite,   20
    Blow thou thy Pipe while I the fame recite.

Thenot.
Ginne when thou lift,all-be my skill but fmall,
My forward minde fhall make amends for all.

Perin.   25
YEe Nimphs that bathe your bodies in this fpring:
    Your tender bodies white as driuen Snow:
                                            Ye

Yee Virgins chaſte which in this Groue doe ſing,
Which neither griefe of Loue, nor Death do know:
   So may your ſtreames runne cleere for ay,
   So may your trees giue ſhade alway.   5
      Depart a ſpace,
      And giue me place,
To wayle with griefe my reſtleſſe woe alone,
      For feare my cries,
      Conſtraine your eyes,   10
To ſhed forth teares, and help lament my mone.

And thou, my Muſe, that whilome wont to eaſe,
Thy Maiſters minde with layes of ſweete delight,
Now change thoſe tunes, no ioy my hart can pleaſe,
Gone is the day, come is the darkeſome night,   15
    Our Sunne cloſe hid in cloudes doth lie,
    We liue indeede, but liuing, die:
      No light we ſee,
      Yet wander wee,
We wander farre and neere without a guide: 20
      And all aſtray,
      We looſe our way,
For in this world n'is ſuch a Sunne beſide.

Ye Shepheards Boyes that leade your flocks a field,
The whilſt your ſheepe feede ſafely round about,   25
Breake me your Pipes that pleaſant ſound did yeeld,
Sing now no more the Songs of *Collin Clout:*
    Lament the end of all our ioy,
    Lament the ſource of all annoy:
      W I L L Y is dead,   30
      C 5   That

That wont to leade
Our flockes and vs in mirth and Shepheards glee:
Wel could he ſing,
Wel dance, and ſpring;   5
Of all the Shepheards was none ſuch as hee.

How often hath his skill in pleaſant Song
Drawn al the water-nimphs from out their bowers?
How haue they laine the tender graſſe along,
And made him Garlands gay of ſmelling flowers?   10
        Phœbus himſelfe that conquer'd *Pan*,
        Striuing with *Willy*, nothing wan.
                Ne thinkes I ſee,
                The time when hee
Pluckt from his golden lockes the Laurell crowne;   15
                And ſo to raiſe
                Our *Willies* praiſe,
Bedeckt his head, and ſoftly ſet him downe.

The learned Muſes flockt to heare his skill,
And quite forgot their water, wood, and mount;   20
They thought his Songs were done too quickly ſtil,
Of none but *Willies* Pipe they made account.
        Hee ſung; they ſeemd in ioy to flowe:
        He ceaſt; they ſeemd to weep for woe;
                The Rurall rout,   25
                All round about,
Like Bees came ſwarming thicke, to heare him ſing:
                Ne could they thinke,
                On meate or drinke,
While *Willies* muſicke in their eares did ring.   30
                                        But

But now (alas) ſuch pleaſant mirth is paſt,
Apollo weepes, the Muſes rend their haire.
No ioy on earth that any time can laſt,
See where his breathleſſe corps lies on the beare.   5
    That ſelfe ſame hand that reft his life,
    Hath turned Shepheards peace to ſtrife.
        Our ioy is fled,
        Our life is dead,
Our hope,our help,our glory all is gone: 10
        Our Poets praiſe,
        Our happy dayes,
And nothing left but griefe, to thinke thereon.

What *Thames*,what *Seuerne*,or what weſterne Seas,
Shall giue me floods of trickling teares to ſhed?   15
What comfort can my reſtleſſe griefe appeaſe?
O that mine eies were Fountaines in my head!
    Ah *Collin*! I lament thy caſe,
    For thee remaines no hope of grace.
        The beſt reliefe,   20
        Of Poets griefe,
Is dead,and wrapt full colde in filthy clay,
        And nought remaines,
        To eaſe our paines,
But hope of death,to ridde vs hence away.   25

Phillis, thine is the greateſt griefe aboue the reſt:
Where beene thy ſweeteſt Poſies feately dight,
Thy Girlonds with a true-loues Knot addreſt,
And all that erſt, thou *Willy*, didſt behight?
    Thy labour all is loſt in vaine,   30
                        The

The griefe whereof ſhall ay remaine.
　　　The Sunne ſo bright,
　　　That falles to night,
To morrow from the Eaſt againe ſhall riſe:　　5
　　　But we decay,
　　　And waſte away,
Without returne, alas, thy *Willy* dies.

See how the drooping Flockes refuſe to feede,
The Riuers ſtreame with teares aboue the bankes,　10
The Trees do ſhed their leaues, to waile agreede,
The beaſts vnfed, go mourning all in rankes.
　　　The Sunne denies the Earth his light,
　　　The Spring is kill'd with winters might:
　　　　　The flowers ſpill,　　　　　15
　　　　　The birds are ſtill:
No voyce of ioy is heard in any place.
　　　The Meddows greene,
　　　A change haue ſeene,
And *Flora* hides her pale disfigur'd face.　　20

Watch now, ye ſhepheards boyes, with waking eie,
And looſe your time of ſleepe, to learne to ſing.
Vnhappy skill, what good is got thereby,
But painted praiſe that can no profite bring?
　　　If Skill could moue the Siſters three,　　25
　　　Our *Willy* ſtill aliue ſhould be.
　　　　The woolfe ſo wood,
　　　　Amazed ſtood,
At ſound of *Willies* pipe, and left his pray:
　　　　Both Pipe and Skill,
　　　　　　　　　　The　　30

The Siſters ſpill,
So, worſe then any wicked Wolfe are they.

O flatt'ring hope of mortall mens delight,
So faire in outward ſhew,ſo foule within! 5
The deepeſt ſtreames do flow full calme to ſight,
The rau'ning Woolues do jet in Weathers skin;
 Wee deem'd our *Willy* ay ſhould liue,
 So ſweete a ſound his Pipe could giue:
  But cruel death 10
  Hath ſtopt his breath:
Dumbe lies his Pipe that wont ſo ſweete to ſound:
  Our flockes lament
  His life is ſpent,
And careleſſe wander all the woods around. 15

Come now,ye ſhepheards daughters,come no more
To heare the Songs that Cuddy wont to ſing:
Hoarſe is my Muſe, my throate with crying,ſore;
Theſe woods with Eccho of my griefe doe ring.
 Your *Willies* life was Cuddies ioy, 20
 Your *Willies* death hath kill'd the Boy:
  Broke lies my Pipe,
  Till Reedes be ripe
To make a new one,but a worſe,I feare:
  Saue yeere by yeere, 25
  To waile my Deere.
All Pipe and Song I vtterly forſweare.

Thenot.
Alacke and welladay may ſhepheards cry,

       Our

Our *Willy* dead, our *Collin* killd with care:
Who fhall not loathe to liue, and long to die?
And will not griefe our little Cuddy fpare,
But muft he too of forrow haue a fhare?   5
  Ay, how his ruefull Verfe hath prickt my hart!
  How feelingly hath hee expreft my fmart!

   Perin.

Ah *Thenot*, hadft thou feene his fory looke,
His wringed hands,his eies to heau'n vpkeft;   10
His teares,that ftream'd like water in the Brooke;
His fighes, that made his Rimes feeme rudely dreft,
To teares thou wouldft haue melted with the reft.
  But hie we homeward, night approcheth neere,
  And rainie cloudes in foutherne skies appeere.   15

     A. W.

       II.

[10] II. Eglogve.

Shepheard.   *Heard-man.*

COme gentle Heard-man, ſit by mee,
    And tune thy Pipe by mine   5
Heere vnderneath this Willow tree,
    To ſhield the hote Sunne-ſhine.
Where I haue made my Summer bower,
    For proofe of Summer beames,
And deckt it vp with many a flower,   10
    Sweete ſeated by the ſtreames.
Where gentle *Daphnee* once a day,
    Theſe flowry bankes doth walke,
And in her boſome beares away
    The pride of many a ſtalke.   15
But leaues the humble Heart behinde,
    That ſhould her Garland dight:
And ſhe, ſweete ſoule, the more vnkinde,
    To ſet true loue ſo light.
But, whereas others beare the Bell,   20
    As in her fauour bleſt;
Her ſhepheard loueth her as well,
    As thoſe whome ſhe loues beſt.

Heard-

Heard-man.

ALas, poore Paſtor, I finde,
    Thy loue is lodg'd ſo high,
That on thy flocke thou haſt no minde,   5
    But feedſt a wanton Eie.
If dainty *Daphnes* lookes beſot
    Thy doating hearts deſire,
Be ſure, that farre aboue thy lot,
    Thy liking doth aſpire.   10
To loue ſo ſweete a Nymph as ſhee,
    And looke for loue againe:
Is fortune fitting high degree,
    Not for a Shepheards ſwaine.
For ſhe of lordly lads becoyd,   15
    And ſought of great eſtates,
Her fauour ſcornes to be enioyde
    By vs poore lowly Mates.
Wherefore I warne thee to be wiſe,
    Go with me to my walke,
Where lowly Laſſes be not nice,   20
    There like and chuſe thy Make.
Where are no pearles nor Gold to view,
    No pride of ſilken ſight,
But Petticoates of ſcarlet hew,   25
    Which vaile the skin ſnow-white.
There trueſt Laſſes beene to get
    For loue and little coſt:
There ſweet deſire is payd his det,
    And labour ſeldome loſt.   30

Shep-

Shepheard.

NO Heardman, no, thou rau'ſt too lowde,
    Our trade ſo vile to hold.
My weede as great a Hart doth ſhrowde,   5
    As his that's clad in gold:
And take the truth that I thee tell,
    This Song faire *Daphnee* ſings,
That *Cupid* will be ſeru'd as well,
    Of Shepheards as of Kings.   10
For proofe whereof, old bookes recorde,
    That *Venus* Queene of Loue,
Would ſett aſide her warlike Lorde,
    And youthfull Paſtors proue.
How *Paris* was as well belou'de,   15
    A ſimple Shepheards Boy,
As after when that he was prou'de
    King *Priams* Son of Troy.
And therefore haue I better hope,
    As had thoſe Lads of yore,   20
My courage takes as large a ſcope,
    Although their haps were more.
And for thou ſhalt not deeme I ieſt,
    And beare a mind more baſe;
No meaner hope ſhall haunt my breſt,   25
    Then deereſt *Daphnees* grace.
My minde no other thought retaines,
    Mine Eye nought elſe admiers:
My hart no other paſſion ſtraines,
    Nor other hap deſiers.   30

                  My

My Mufe of nothing elfe entreates,
  My Pipe nought elfe doth found,
My Veines no other feauer heates,
  Such faith's in Shepheards found.   5

Heard-man.

AH Shepheard, then I fee, with griefe
  Thy care is paft all cure,
No remedy for thy reliefe,
  But patiently endure.   10
Thy wonted libertie is fled,
  Fond fancie breeds thy bane,
Thy fence of folly brought a bed,
  Thy wit is in the wane.
I can but forrow for thy fake,   15
  Since loue lulles thee afleepe.
And whilft out of thy dreame thou wake,
  God fhield thy ftraying fheepe.
Thy wretched Flocke may rue and curfe
  This proude defire of thine,   20
Whofe woefull ftate from bad to wurfe
  Thy careleffe eye will pine.
And e'en as they, thy felfe likewife
  With them fhalt weare and wafte,
To fee the fpring before thine eyes,   25
  Thou thirfty canft not tafte.
Content thee therefore with Conceit,
  Where others gaine the grace,
And thinke thy fortune at the height,
  To fee but *Daphnees* face.   30

Al-

Although thy truth deſerued well
    Reward aboue the reſt,
Thy haps ſhall be but meanes to tell
    How other men are bleſt.   5
So gentle Shepheard, farewel now,
    Bee warned by my reed,
For I ſee written in thy brow,
    Thy Hart for loue doth bleed.
Yet longer with thee would I ſtay,   10
    If ought would do thee good,
But nothing can the heate allay,
    Where Loue enflames the blood.

Shepheard.

THen Heardman,ſince it is my lot,   15
    and my good liking ſuch,
    Striue not to breake the faithfull knot
        That thinkes no paine too much.
For what contents my *Daphnee* beſt
    I neuer will deſpiſe;   20
So ſhe but wiſh my ſoule good reſt
    When death ſhall cloſe mine eyes.
Then Heard-man, farewel once againe,
    For now the day is fled:
So might thy cares,poore Shepheards Swaine,   25
    Flie from thy carefull head.

Ignoto.

IIII.

[11] IIII. Eglogve.

*Concerning olde Age. The beginning and end of
this Eglogue are wanting.*

Perin.   5

FOr when thou art not as thou wont of yore,
    No caufe why life fhould pleafe thee any more.
Whilome I was(in courfe of former yeeres,
Ere freezing Eld had coolde my youthly rage)
Of mickle worth among my Shepheards Peeres.   10
Now for I am fome-dele yftept in age,
For pleafance,ftrength,and beautie ginnes affwage.
    Ech litle Heard-groom laughs my wrinkled face,
    Ech bonny laffe for Cuddy fhunnes the place;
For all this woe none can wee iuftly twight,   15
But hatefull Eld, the foe to pleafant reft,
Which like a Theefe doth rob vs of delight.

Wrenock.

Perin,enough;few words beene alwayes beft,
Needs muft be borne that cannot be redreft.   20
    Selfe am I as thou feeft in thilke eftate,
    The griefe is eath to beare that haz a mate.
But ficker for to fpeake the truth indeed,
Thou feem'ft to blame that blamelelfe feems to me,
                                              And

And hurtleffe Eld to fneb:(ill mought he fpeed,
That flayes the Dog,for Wolues fo wicked bee)
The faults of men thou lay'ft on Age I fee,
    For which if Eld were in it felfe too blame,   5
    Then I and all my Peeres fhould tafte the fame.

Perin.

*Wreenock,*I weene thou doat'ft through rufty Eld,
And think'ft with fained words to bleare mine eie.
Thou for thy ftore art euer bliffefull held,   10
Thy heapes of gold nill let thee forrow fpie,
Thy Flocks full fafe here vnder fhade doe lie,
    Thy weanlings fat,thine ews with bladders blowne.
    A iollier Shepheard haue we feldome knowne.

Wrenock.   15

For thilke my ftore, great *Pan* yherried be;
But if for thy, mine age with ioy I beare,   .
How falles it that thy felfe vnlike to me,
Art vexed fo with griefe and bootleffe feare?
Thy ftore will let thee fleepe on either eare: 20
    But neither want makes Age to wifemen hard,
    Nor fools by welth from grieuous pains are bard.

                           Perin

Perin.

Seeſt not how free yond Lambkin skips and plaies;
And wrigs his tayle,and buts with tender head;
All for he feeles the heate of youngthly dayes,   5
Which ſecret law of kinde hath inly bred?
Thilke Ewe from whom all Ioy with youth is fled,
    See how it hangs the head, as it would weep,
    Whilome it skipt, vneathes now may it creep.

Wrenock.   10

No fellowſhip hath ſtate of Beaſts with man,
In them is nought but ſtrength of lim and bone,
Which endes with age as it with age began.
But man they ſaine (as other Creature none)
Hath vncouth fire conuayd from Heau'n by one,   15
    (His name I wiſt)that yeelds him inward light,
    Sike fire as Welkin ſhowes in winter night.

Which neither Age nor Time can weare away,
Which waxeth bett for vſe as Shepheards Crooke,
That euer ſhineth brighter day by day: 20
Al ſo though wrinkled ſeeme the aged looke,
Bright ſhines the fire that from the ſtars we tooke.
    And ſooth to ſay,thilke Ewe laments the paine,
    That thilke ſame wanton Lamb is like ſuſtaine.

Perin.

Perin.

Ah *Thenot*,be not all thy teeth on edge,
To ſee youngths folke to ſport in paſtimes gay?
To pitch the Barre, to throwe the weightie ſledge   5
To dance with *Phillis* all the holli-day,
To hunt by day,the Fox,by night,the Gray;
   Sike peereleſſe pleaſures wont vs for to queme,
   Now lig we laide,as drownd in heauy dreame.

Anomos.   10

Deeſt.

Sonnets, Odes, Elegies, and Madrigalls.

By

Francis Dauison
and } *Brethren.*
Walter Dauison

[12] SONET. I.

Dedication of these Rimes, to his first loue.

IF my harsh humble stile, and Rimes ill dressed,   5
   Arriue not to your worth and beautie glorious,
My Muses shoulders are with weight oppressed,
And heauenly beams are o're my sight victorious.
If these dimme colours haue your worth expressed,
   Laide by Loues hand, and not by Arte laborious;   10
Your Sun-like raies haue my wits haruest blessed,
Ennabling me to make your praise notorious.
But if alas! (alas the heauens defend it,)
   My lines your eies, my loue your hart displeasing,
Breed hate in you, and kill my hope of easing;   15
   Say with your self, how can the wretch amend it?
I wondrous faire, he wondrous deerely louing,
How can his thoughts but make his pen be mouing?

       D 2   SONNET.

[57]

---

[13] SONNET. II.

That he cannot hide or diſſemble his
affection.

I BEND my wits, and beate my wearie braine,   5
  To keep my inward griefe from outward ſhow.
  Alas I cannot: now tis vaine I know,
  To hide a fire, whoſe flame appeereth plaine.
I force my will, my ſences I conſtraine,
  T'impriſon in my heart my ſecret woe;   10
  But muſing thoghts, deep ſighs, or tears that flow,
  Diſcouer what my heart hides, al in vaine.
Yet blame not (Deere) this vndiſſembled paſſion;
  For wel may Loue, within ſmall limits bounded,
  Be wiſely maskte in a diſguized faſhion.   15
  But he, whoſe hart, like mine, is throghly woũded,
Can neuer faine, no though he were aſſured,
That Faining might haue greater grace procured.

SONET

[14] SONNET III.

Vpon his abfence from her.

THE faireft Eies,(O Eies in blackneffe faire!)
　That euer fhinde,and the moft heau'nly face,　　5
　The daintieft fmiling,the moft conquering grace,
　And fweeteft breath that e're perfumde the ayre.
The cherrieft lippes, whofe kiffe might well repaire
　A dead mans ftate;that fpeech which did difplace
　All meane defiers, and all affections bafe,　　10
　Clogging fwift Hope, & winging dead Difpaire.
That fnow-white breaft,& al thofe faultles features
　Which made her feeme a perfonage diuine,
　And farre excelling faireft humane creatures,
　Hath Abfence banifht from my curfed Eine.　　15
But in my Heart, as in a Mirrour cleere,
All thefe perfections to my thoughts appeere.

[15] SONNET. IIII.

*Vpon prefenting her with the fpeech of Grayes-Inne Maske
at the Court 1594. confifting of three partes, The Story
of Proteus Transformations, the wonders of the Ada-* 5
mantine Rocke, and a fpeech to her Maieftie.

WHo in thefe lines may better claime a parte,
    That fing the praifes of the *Britton* Queene,
    Then you, faire fweet, that only Soueraign beene,
    Of the poore Kingdome of my faithful Heart?   10
Or to whofe view fhould I this fpeech impart,
    Where th'adamātines rocks great powre is fhown:
    But to your cōq'ring eies, whofe force once known
    Makes euen Iron harts loath thence to parte?
Or who of Proteus fundry transformations,   15
    May better fend you the new-fayned Story,
    Then I, whofe loue vnfain'de felt no mutations,
    Since to be yours I firft receiu'de the glory?
Accept then of thefe lines, though meanely pend,
So fit for you to take , and me to fend.   20

Ele-

[16] Elegie. I.

He renounceth his food, and former delight in Muficke,
Poefie, and Painting.

SItting at board fometimes, preparde to eate,   5
  Ift hap my minde on thefe my woes to thinke,
Sighs fill my mouth in fteade of pleafant meate,
And teares do moift my lips in lieu of drinke:
    But yet, nor fighs, nor tears, that rū amain (paine.
    Can either ftarue my thoughts, or quench my   10

Another time with carefull thoughts o're-tane,
I thought thefe thoughts with muficks might to
But as I gan to fet my notes in frame,   (chace:
A fuddaine Paffion did my fong difplace.
    In ftead of Refts, fighes from my hart did rife,   15
    In ftead of Notes, deep fobs and mournful
                                                cries.
Then, when I faw, that thefe my thoughts increafde,
And that my thoughts vnto my woes gaue fire,
I hopte both thoughtes and woes might be releafde,
If to the Mufes I did me retire.   20
    Whofe fweet delights were wont to eafe my wo,
    But now (alas) they could do nothing fo.
                    D 4   For

For trying oft (alas) yet ftill in vaine,
To make fome pleafant numbers to arife,
And beating oft my dulled weary Braine,
In hope fome fweete Conceit for to deuife: (come,   5
    Out of my mouth no wordes but groanes would
    Out of my Pen no inke but teares would runne.

Of all my old Delights yet one was left,
Painting alone to eafe my minde remain'd;
By which, whenas I look't to be bereft   10
Of thefe heart-vexing woes that ftill me ftrain'd,
    From forth mine eies the blood for colours came,
    And teares withall to temper fo the fame.

Adieu my foode that wontft my tafte to pleafe,
Adieu my Songs that bred mine eares delight,   15
Adieu fweete Mufe that oft my minde didft eafe,
Painting, Adieu, that oft refrefht my fight,
    Since neither tafte, nor eares, nor fight, nor mind,
    In your Delights can aught faue forrow finde.

Son-

[17] SONNET. V.

To Pitty.

WAKE Pitty, wake, for thou haſt ſlept too long,
   Within the Tygriſh hart of that fierce faire,   5
  Who ruines moſt, where moſt ſhe ſhould repaire,
  And wher ſhe ows moſt right,doth greateſt wrōg.
Wake Pitty,wake, O do no more prolong
   Thy needeful help! but quickly heare my pray're,
  Quickly (alas) for otherwiſe Deſpaire,   10
  By guiltie death, will end my guiltleſſe wrong.
Sweet Pitty wake,and tell my cruell Sweete,
   That if my death her honour might encreaſe,
  I would lay downe my life at her prowd feete,
  And willing die,and dying,hold my peace.   15
Tell her I liue, and liuing, crie for grace,
Becauſe my death her glory would deface.

D 5   ODE

[18] ODE. I.

That only her beauty and voice pleaſe him.

I.

PAſſion may my Iudgement bleare,   5
Therfore ſure I will not ſweare,
     That others are not pleaſing:
But I ſpeake it to my paine,
And my life ſhall it maintaine,
     None elſe yeelds my hart eaſing.   10

II.

Ladies I doo thinke there bee,
Other ſome as faire as ſhee,
     (Though none haue fairer features:)
But my Turtle-like Affection,   15
Since of her I made Election,
     Scornes other faireſt creatures.

III.

Surely I wil not deny,
But ſome others reach as high   20
     With their ſweet warbling voices;
But ſince her Notes charmde mine Eare,
Euen the ſweeteſt Tunes I heare,
     To mee ſeeme rude harſh noyſes.

Ma-

[19] MADRIGAL I. *To Cupid.*

LOve, if a God thou art,
    Then euermore thou muſt,
    Be mercifull and iuſt.   5
If thou be iuſt; O wherefore doth thy Dart,
Wound mine alone, and not my Ladies Hart?

    If mercifull, then why
    Am I to paine reſeru'd,
    Who haue thee truely ſeru'd: 10
While ſhe that by thy powre ſets not a flie.
Laughs thee to ſcorne, and liues in libertie?

Then, if a God thou would'ſt accounted be,
Heale me like her, or elſe wound her like me.

[20] MADRIGAL II.   15

Vpon his Miſtreſſe ſickenes, and his owne health.

    IN health and eaſe am I,
Yet, as I ſenſleſſe were, it nought contents mee.
    You ſicke in paine do lie,
And (ah) your paine exceedingly torments mee: 20
Whereof, this only is the reaſon true,
That dead vnto my ſelfe, I liue in you.

                                              MA-

[21] MADRIGAL III.
He begs a Kiſſe.

SORROVV ſeldome killeth any,
  Sodaine Ioy hath murthered many.
    Then (Sweete) if you would end mee,
Tis a fond courſe with lingring griefe to ſpend mee.
    For, quickly to diſpatch me,
Your onely way is, in your armes to catch mee,
    And giue me a ſweete Kiſſe:
For ſuch exceſſiue and vnlookt for bliſſe,
  Would ſo much ouer-ioy mee,
  As it would ſtrait deſtroy mee.

5

10

[22] MADRIGAL IIII.
Vpon a Kiſſe receiued.

SINCE your ſweete cherry lippes I kiſt,
  No want of foode I once haue miſt.
My ſtomach now no meate requires:
My throate no drinke at all deſires.
For by your breath which then I gained,
Camelion-like my life's maintained.

Then grant me (Deere) thoſe cherries ſtill,
O let me feede on them my fill.
If by a ſurfet death I get,
Vpon my Tombe let this be ſet;
  Heere lieth hee whome Cherries two,
  Made both to liue, and life forgo.

15

20

25

ODE

[23] ODE II.

*Vpon her protesting, that now hauing tried his sin-
cere affection, she loued him.*

1
                                                                5
LADIE, you are with beauties so enriched
          Of body and of minde,
          As I can hardly finde,
Which of them all hath most my heart bewitched.

2
                                                                10
Whether your skin so white,so smoothe,so tender,
          Or Face so louely faire,
          Or long hart-binding haire,
Or dainty Hand,or Legge, and Foote so slender.

3
                                                                15
Or whether your sharpe wit and liuely spirit,
          Where Pride can finde no place;
          Or your most pleasing grace,
Or speech,which doth true eloquence inherit.

4
                                                                20
Most louely all, and each of them do moue mee,
          More then words can expresse;
          But yet I must confesse,
I loue you most,because you please to loue mee.

                                                ODE

[24] ODE II.

His reſtleſſe eſtate.

Your Preſence breedes my anguiſh,
Your abſence makes me languiſh: 5
Your ſight with woe doth fill mee,
And want of your ſweete ſight alas doth kill mee.

If thoſe deere Eyes that burne mee,
With milde aſpect you turne mee,
For life my weake hart panteth: 10
If frowningly, my Sprit and Life-blood fainteth.

If you ſpeake kindly to mee,
Alas, kind words vndoo mee:
Yet ſilence doth diſlike mee,
And one vnkind il word ſtark dead would ſtrike me. 15

Thus, Sunne nor ſhade doth eaſe mee,
Nor ſpeach, nor ſilence pleaſe mee:
Fauours and frownes annoy mee,
Both want and plentie equally deſtroy me.

ELEGIE

[25] ELEGIE II. *Or Letter in Verse.*

MY deereſt Sweete, if theſe ſad lines do happe
   The raging fury of the Sea to ſcape,
O be not you more cruell then the Seas;   5
Let Pitty now your angry Minde appeaſe,
So that your Hand may bee their bleſſed Port,
From whence they may vnto your Eyes reſort,
And at that Throane pleading my wretched caſe,
May moue your cruell Hart to yeeld mee grace.   10
So may no Cloudes of elder yeeres, obſcure
Your Sun-like Eyes, but ſtil as bright endure,
As then they ſhone when with one piercing Ray,
They made my ſelfe their ſlaue, my hart their pray:
So may no Sickneſſe nippe thoſe flowers ſweet,   15
Which euer flowring on your Cheekes doo meet:
Nor all-defacing Time haue power to raſe,
The goodly building of that heauenly Face.

Fountaine of Bliſſe, yet well-ſpring of my woe,
(O would I might not iuſtly terme you ſo!)   20
Alas,your cruell dealing, and my Fate,
Haue now reduc'de mee to that wretched ſtate,
That I know not how I my ſtyle may frame
To thanks, or grudging, or to praiſe, or blame;
And where to write, I al my powers do bend,   25
There wot I not how to beginne or ende.
And now my drifling teares trill downe apace,
As if the latter would the former chace,
Whereof ſome few on my pale Cheekes remaine,
Like wither'd flowers, bedewd with drops of raine: 30
                          The

The other falling, in my Paper finke,
Or dropping in my Pen, increafe my inke.
Which fuddaine Paffions Caufe if you would find,
A trembling feare doth now poffeffe my minde,   5
That you will not vouchfafe thefe lines to reede,
Left they fome pitty in your harte might breede:
But or with angry frownes refufe to take them,
Or taking them, the fires fewell make them,
Or with thofe hands (made to a milder end)   10
Thefe guiltleffe leaues all into peeces rend.
O Cruell Tyrant! (yet beloued ftill,)
Wherein haue I deferu'de of you fo ill,
That all my loue you fhould with hate requite,
And all my paines reward with fuch defpight?   15
Or if my faulte be great (which I proteft
Is only Loue, too great to be expreft,)
What, haue thefe Lines fo harmeleffe innocent
Deferu'd to feele their Mafters punifhment?
Thefe Leaues are not vnto my fault confenting: 20
And therefore ought not haue the fame tormenting,
When you haue read them, vfe them as you lift,
For by your fight they fhall be fully blift;
But till you reade them, let the woes I haue
This harmeleffe Paper from your fury faue.   25

Cleere vp mine eyes, & drie your felues, my Teares;
And thou my Harte bannifh thefe deadly feares;
Perfwade thy felfe, that though her harte difdaine,
Either to loue thy loue,   or rue thy paine,
Yet her faire Eyes will not a booke denie,   30
To this fad Story of thy Miferie.

O

O then, my Deere, behold the Portraiture
Of him that doth all kinde of woes endure,
Of him whofe Head is made a Hiue of woes,
Whofe fwarming number dayly greater growes: 5
Of him whofe Sences like a Racke are bent,
With diuerfe motions my poore foule to rent;
Whofe Minde a Mirrour is, which only fhowes,
The ougly Image of my prefent woes:
Whofe Memorie's a poyfon'd Knife to teare   10
The euer-bleeding wound my Breaft doth beare,
(The euer-bleeding wound not to be cured,
But by thofe Eyes that firft the fame procured.)
And that poore Harte, fo faithfull, conftant, true,
That only loues, and ferues, and honours you,   15
Is like a feeble Ship, which torne and rent,
The Maft of Hope being broke, and tackling fpent,
Reafon the Pilot dead, the Starres obfcured,
By which alone to faile it was enured,
No Porte, no Land, no Comfort once expected,   20
All hope of Safety vtterly neglected,
With dreadfull terror tumbling vp and downe,
Paffions vncertaine, waues with hideous found,
Doth daily, hourely, minutely expect,
When either it fhould runne, and fo be wreckt   25
Vpon Defpaires fharpe Rocke, or be o'rethrowne,
With Storme of your Difdaine fo fiercely blowne.

But yet, of al the woes that doe torment my hart,
Of all the Torments that do dayly rent my hart,
There's none fo great (although I am affured,   30
That euen the leaft can not bee long endured:)

As

As that ſo many weekes (nay months, nay yeares,
Nay tedious Ages, (for it ſo appeares)
My trembling Hart(beſides ſo many anguiſhes,)
Twixt hope & feare vncertaine howerly languiſhes: 5
Whether your hands,your Eyes, your Hart of ſtone
Did take my lines, and reade them,and bemone
With one kind word,one ſigh,one pittying teare,
Th'unfained griefe which for your loue I beare;
Whether y'accepted that laſt Monument   10
Of my deere Loue, the Booke (I meane) I ſent
To your deare ſelfe, when the reſpectleſſe winde
Bare me away, leauing my hart behinde.
And daigne ſometimes when you the ſame do view,
To thinke on him, who alwayes thinks on you.   15
Or whether you (as Oh I feare you doo)
Hate both my ſelfe, and Gifts, and Letters too.

I muſt confeſſe, that when I do conſither,
How ill, alas, how ill agree together,
So peereleſſe beautie, to ſo fierce a minde,   20
So hard an inſide to ſo faire a rinde,
A Hart ſo bloody to ſo white a breſt,
So proud diſdaine,with ſo milde lookes ſuppreſt;
And how my deere (Oh would it had beene neuer,
Accurſed word,nay would it might be euer;)   25
How once I ſay, till your Hart was eſtranged,
(Alas how ſoone my day to night was changed)
You did vouchſafe my poore Eyes ſo much grace,
Freely to viewe the Riches of your face,
And did ſo high exalte my lowly Hart,   30
To call it yours, and take it in good part.

                       And

And (which was greateſt bliſſe) did not diſdaine,
For boundleſſe loue to yeeld ſome loue againe.
When this, I ſay, I call vnto my minde,
And in my Harte and Soule no cauſe can finde,   5
No faƈt,no word,whereby my Hart hath merited,
Of your ſweete loue to be thus diſinherited,
Diſpaire it ſelfe cannot make mee diſpaire,
But that you'le prooue as kinde,as you are faire,
And that my lines,& booke, (O would twere true)   10
Are, though I know't not yet, receiu'de by you,
And often haue your cruelty repented,
Whereby my guiltleſſe Heart is ſo tormented,
And now at length in lieu of paſſed woe,
Will pitty, grace, and loue, and fauour ſhoe.   15

But when againe my curſed Memory,
To my ſad thoughts confounded diuerſly
Preſents the time,the teare-procuring time,
That wither'd my yong Ioyes before their prime ;
The time when I with tedious abſence tired,   20
With reſtleſſe loue, and rackt deſire inſpired,
Comming to finde my Earthly paradiſe,
To glaſſe my ſight in your two heauenly Eyes,
(On which alone my Earthly Ioyes depended:
And wanting which, my ioy and life were ended).   25
From your ſweete Roſie lippes, the ſprings of bliſſe,
To draw the Neƈtar of a ſweeteſt Kiſſe;
My greedy Eares on your ſweete wordes to feede,
Which canded in your ſweeteſt breath proceede,
In daintieſt accents through that Currall dore,   30
Guarded with pretious Pearle, and Rubies ſtore:
                                                      To

To touch your Hand ſo white,ſo moiſt, ſo ſoft,
And with a rauiſht kiſſe redoubled oft,
Reuenge with kindeſt ſpight the bloody theft,
Whereby it cloſely mee my Hart bereft: 5
And of all bliſſe to taſte the Conſummation,
In your ſweete, gracefull, heauenly Conuerſation,
By whoſe ſweet charms the ſoules you do inchaunt,
Of all that doo your louely preſence haunt;
In ſtead in all theſe Ioyes I did expect,   10
Found nought but frownes, vnkindnes,and neglect.
Neglect, vnkindnes, frownes? nay plaine contempt,
And open Hate, from no diſdaine exempt,
No bitter words, ſide lookes, nor aught that might
Engreeue, encreaſe ſo vndeſeru'd deſpight.   15
When this (I ſay) I thinke, and thinke withall,
How, nor thoſe ſhowers of Teares mine Eies let fall
Nor winde of bluſtring Sighes with all their force,
Could moue your rocky Heart once to remorce;
Can I expect that letters ſhould finde grace,   20
Or pitty euer in your harte haue place?
No no; I thinke, and ſad Diſpaire ſayes for mee,
You hate, diſdaine, and vtterly abhorre mee.

Alas, my deere, if this you doe deuiſe,
To try the virtue of your murthering Eyes,   25
And in the Glaſſe of bleeding harts, to vew
The glorious ſplendour of your Beauties hew,
Ah trie it, trie it on rebellious ſprights,
That doe withſtand the power of ſacred lights,
And make them feele (if any ſuch be found)   30
How deepe and cureleſly your Eyes can wound.
                                        But

But ſpare,O ſpare my yeelding Hart,and ſaue
Him,whoſe cheefe glory is to be your ſlaue:
Make mee,the matter of your Clemencie,
And not, the ſubieﬆ of your Tyrannie.   5

[26] ODE IIII.

*Being depriued of her ſweete lookes, wordes,and geſtures,
by his abſence in Italie, he deſires her to write
vnto him.*

I.   10

MY onely ﬆarre,
Why, why are your deere Eyes,
Where all my life's peace lies,
    With me at warre?
Why to my Ruine tending,   15
    Do they ﬆill lighten woe,
    On him that loues you ſo,
That all his thoughts,in you haue birth and ending?

II.
Hope of my Hart,   20
O wherefore do the wordes,

                                        Which

Which your fweet tongue affoordes,
　　　No hope impart?
But cruell without meafure,
　　　To my eternall paine,　　　　　　　　5
　　　Still thunder forth Difdaine,
On him whofe life depends vpon your pleafure.

III.

　　　Sunne-fhine of Ioy,
Why doe your Geftures,which　　　　　　10
All Eies and Hearts bewitch,
　　　My bliffe deftroy?
And Pities skie o're-clowding
　　　Of Hate an endleffe fhowre,
　　　On that poore heart ftill powre,　　　15
Which in your bofome feekes his onely fhrowding.

IIII.

　　　Balme of my wound,
Why are your lines, whofe fight
Should cure me with delight,
　　　My poyfon found?　　　　　　　　20
Which through my veines difperfing,
　　　Doth make my heart and minde,
　　　And all my fenfes finde,
A liuing death in torments paft reherfing.　　25

V.

　　　Alas, my Fate
Hath of your Eies depriu'd mee,
Which both kill'd and reuiu'd me,

　　　　　　　　　　　　　　　And

And fweetned Hate;
Your fweet Voice, and fweet Graces,
    Which cloathde in louely weedes,
    Your cruell wordes and deedes,   5
Are intercepted by farre diftant places.

VI.

    But O the Anguifh,
Which Prefence ftill pretended,
Abfence hath not abfented,   10
    Nor made to languifh.
No, no, t'encreafe my paining,
    The caufe being (ah) remoued,
    For which th'effect I loued,
Th'effect is ftill in greateft force remaining.   15

VII.

    O cruell Tyger,
If to your hard harts Center,
Teares, Vowes, and Prayers may enter,
    Defift your rigour: 20
And let kind lines affure mee,
    (Since to my deadly wound,
    No falue elfe can be found)
That you that kill me, yet at length will cure mee.

MADRI-

[27] MADRIGAL V.

Allusion to the Confusion of Babell.

THe wretched life I liue
In my weake Sences such confusion maketh,　　　　5
　　That like th'accursed Rabble
　　That built the Towre of Babble,
　　　　My wit mistaketh,
And vnto nothing a right name doth giue.

I terme her my deere loue, that deadly hates mee,　　10
My cheefest Good, her that's my cheefest euill;
Her Saint and Goddesse, who's a Witch, a Deuill;
Her my sole Hope, that with despaire amates mee,
　　My Balme I call her, that with poyson fills mee;
　　And her I terme my life, that daily kills mee.　　15

SONNET.

[28] SONNET. VI.

*Vpon her acknowledging his Deſarte, yet
reiecting his Affection.*

IF Loue conioyn'd with worth and great deſarte,   5
   Merit like loue in euery noble minde:
   Why then doo I you ſtill ſo cruell finde,
   To whom you do ſuch praiſe of worth imparte?
And if (my Deere) you ſpeake not from your harte,
   Two haynous wrongs you do together binde: 10
   To ſeeke with glozing words mine eies to blinde,
   And yet my Loue with hateful deedes to thwarte.
To want what one deſerues, engreeues his paine,
   Becauſe it takes away all ſelfe-accuſing,
   And vnder kindeſt words to maske diſdaine,   15
   Is to a vexed Soule too much abuſing.
Then ift bee falſe, ſuch gloſing words refraine,
If true, O then let worth his due obtaine!

E   SONNET.

[29] SONNET. VII.

Her Answere, in the same Rimes.

IF your fond Loue want worth and great desarte,
 Then blame your selfe, if you me cruell finde: 5
If worth alone moue euery noble minde,
 Why to no worth should I my loue imparte?
And if the lesse to greeue your wounded harte,
 I seeke your dazled eies with words to blinde,
 To iust disfauour I great fauor binde,   (thwarte.   10
With deeds, and not with words your loue to
The freeing of your minde from selfe-accusing,
 By granting your deserts should ease your paine;
 And since your fault's but loue, t'were some abu-
 With bitter words t'enuenom iust disdaine. (sing   15
Then ift bee true, all glozing I refraine;
If false, why should no worth,worths due obtaine?

ODE.

[30] ODE V.

His Farewell to his Vnkinde and Vnconstant
Mistresse.

SVVEETE, if you like and loue mee ſtill,   5
  And yeelde me loue for my good will.
And do not from your promiſe ſtart,
When your faire hand gaue me your hart.
    If deere to you I bee,
      As you are deere to mee.   10
Then yours I am, and will be euer,
Nor time,nor place my loue ſhall ſeuer,
But faithfull ſtill I will perſeuer,
    Like conſtant marble ſtone,
      Louing but you alone.   15

But if you fauour moe than mee,
(Who loue thee ſtill, and none but thee.)
If others doe the Harueſt gaine
That's due to me for all my paine.
    If that you loue to range,   20
      And oft to choppe and change:
Then get you ſome new-fangled Mate,
My doating Loue ſhall turne to Hate,
Eſteeming you(though too too late)
    Not worth a pebble ſtone,   25
      Louing not me alone.

[31] *A Prosopopœia: Wherein his Hart speakes to his second Ladies Breast.*

I Dare not in my masters bosome rest,
  That flaming *Etna* would to Ashes burne mee: 5
Nor dare I harbour in his Mistris brest,
The frosty Clymate into yce would turne mee:
  So, both from her and him I do retyre mee,
  Lest th'one should freeze me, & the other fire me.

Wing'd with true Loue, I flie to this sweet Brest,   10
Whose Snow, I hope, wil cool but t'yce not turn me:
Where fire and snow, I trust, so tempred rest,
As gentle heate will warme, and yet not burne mee:
  But (O deere Brest) from thee Ile ne're retire me,
  Whether thou cool, or warm, or freeze, or fire me. 15

[32] ODE VI.

Vpon her giuing him backe the Paper wherein the former Song was written, as though it had beene an answere thereunto.

LAdy of matchlesse beauty;   20
When into your sweet Bosome I deliuered
A paper, with wan lookes, and hand that quiuered
  Twixt hope, feare, loue, and duety;
                                    Thought

Thought you it nothing elfe contain'd,
But written words in Ryme reftraind?
   O then your thought abufed was,   (was.
My Hart clofe wrapt therein, into your Breft infufed   5

   When you that Scroule reftor'de me,
With grateful words, kind grace, & fmiling merrily,
My breft did fwell with ioy, fuppofing verily,
   You, anfwer did afford mee.
  But finding only that I writt,   10
  I hop't to finde my Hart in it:
   But you my hope abufed had,
And poifon of Difpaire in ftead thereof infufed had.

   Why, why did you torment mee,
With giuing back my humble Rymes fo hatefully?   15
You fhould haue kept both hart & paper gratefully;
   Or both you fhould haue fent mee.
  Hope you my Hart thence to remoue
  By fcorning mee, my Lines, my Loue?
   No, no; your hope abufed is,   20
Too deepe to be remou'd it in your Breft infufed is.

   O fhall I hide or tell it?
Deere with fo fpotleffe, zealous, firme Affection,
I loue your Beauty, Vertue, and perfection,
   As nothing can expell it.   25
  Scorne you my Rimes, my Loue defpight?
  Pull out my Hart, yea kill me quite
   Yet will your hate abufed bee,
For in my very foule, your loue & lookes infufed be.

      E 3   ODE

[33] ODE VII.

Commendation of her Beauty, Stature,
Behauiour and Witt.

SOme there are as faire to fee too;   5
  But by Art and not by Nature.
Some as tall and goodly bee too;
But want Beauty to their ftature.

Some haue gratious kinde behauour,
But are fowle,or fimple Creatures: 10
Some haue witt, but want fweet fauour,
Or are proud of their good features.
  Only you in Court or Citty,
    Are both fayre, Tall, Kinde, and Witty.

[34] MADRIGALL VI.   15

To her hand, vpon her giuing him her Gloue.

OHand of all handes liuing,
    The fofteft, moifteft, whiteft,
More skild then *Phœbus* on a Lute in running;
More then *Minerua*, with a Needle cunning;   20
  Then *Mercury* more wily,
  In ftealing Harts moft fliely.
                Since

Since thou,deere Hand, in theft ſo much delighteſt,
　　Why fall'ſt thou now a giuing?
Ay mee! thy gifts are thefts,and with ſtrange Art,
In giuing me thy Gloue,thou ſtealſt my Hart.　　　5

[35] MADRIGALL. VII.

Cupid proued a Fenſer.

AH *Cupid* I miſtooke thee;
I for an Archer, and no Fenſer tooke thee.
But as a Fenſer oft faines blowes and thruſts,　　　10
　　Where hee doth meane no harme;
　　Then turnes his balefull Arme,
And wounds his foe whereas hee leaſt miſtruſts:
　　So thou with fencing Art,
Fayning to wound mine Eyes,haſt hit my hart.　　　15

E 4　　　　　SONNET

[85]

[36] SONNET VIII.

*Vpon her commending (though moſt vndeſeruedly)
his Verſes to his firſt Loue.*

PRaiſe you thoſe barren Rimes long ſince cōpoſed?　　5
　　Which my great Loue, her greater Cruelty,
My conſtant faith, her falſe Inconſtancy,
　　My praiſeles ſtile, her o're-praiſd worth diſcloſed.
O if I lou'd a ſcornefull Dame ſo deerely;
　　If my wilde yeeres did yeeld ſo firme affection;　　10
　　If her Moon-beams, ſhort of your Suns perfectiō,
Taught my hoars Muſe to ſing (as you ſay) cleerly
How much, how much ſhould I loue & adore you,
　　(Diuineſt Creature) if you deign'd to loue me:
　　What beauty, fortune, time ſhould euer moue me　　15
In theſe ſtaid yeeres to like aught els before you?
And O! how ſhould my Muſe, by you inſpired,
Make Heauen & Earth reſound your praiſe admired.

MADRIGALL

[37] MADRIGAL VIII.

Hee compares himſelfe to a Candle-flie.

LIke to the feely flie,
   To the deere light I flie   5
Of your diſdainfull Eyes,
But in a diuerſe wiſe.
Shee with the flame doth play
By night alone; and I both night and day.
   Shee to a Candle runnes;   10
I to a light, far brighter then the Sunne's.
   Shee neere at hand is fyred;
I both neere hand, and far-away retyred.
She fondly thinkes, nor dead, nor burnt to bee,
But I my burning, and my death foreſee.   15

[38] MADRIGAL IX.

Anſwere to her queſtion, what loue was.

IF I behold your Eyes,
  Loue is a Paradize.
But if I veiw my Hart,   20
Ti's an infernall ſmart.

E 5   ODE

[39] ODE VIII.

*That all other Creatures haue their abiding in hea-
uen, hell, earth, ayre, water, or fire;
but he in all of them.*   5

IN Heau'n the bleſſed Angels haue their beeing;
  In hel the Fiends appointed to damnation.
To men and beaſts Earth yeelds firme habitation:
The wing'd Muſitians in the Aire are fleeing.
              With finnes the people gliding,   10
              Of Water haue th'enioying.
              In Fire (all elſe deſtroying.)
The Salamander findes a ſtrange abiding:
But I, poore wretch, ſince I did firſt aſpier,
To loue your beauty, Beauties all excelling,   15
              Haue my ſtrange diuerſe dwelling,
In heau'n, hell, earth, water, ayre, and Fier.

Mine Eare, while you do ſing, in Heau'n remaineth:
My mind in hell, through hope & feares contention.
Earth holds my droſſy wit and dull inuention.   20
Th'ill foode of airie ſighes my life ſuſtaineth.
              To ſtreames of teares ſtil flowing
              My weeping Eies are turned.
              My conſtant Heart is burned
In quenchleſſe fire within my boſome glowing.   25
O foole, no more, no more ſo high aſpier;
In Heau'n is no beauty more excelling,
              In Hell no ſuch pride dwelling,
Nor heart ſo hard in earth, ayre, water, fier.

                                        M A-

[40] MADRIGAL X.

Vpon his timerous silence in her presence.

ARE Louers full of fier?
How comes it then my Verses are so colde?   5
  And how,when I am nie her,
And fit occasion wills me to be bolde,
The more I burne, the more I do desier,
  The lesse I dare requier?
  Ah Loue! this is thy wondrous Art,   10
  To freeze the tongue, and fire the hart.

[41] MADRIGAL XI.

Vpon her long Absence.

IF this most wretched and infernall Anguish,
 Wherin so long your absence makes me languish,   15
  My vitall spirits spending,
  Do not worke out my ending.
Nor yet your long-expected safe returning,
To heau'nly ioy my hellish torments turning,
  With ioy so ouer-fill me,   20
  As presently it kill mee;
I wil conclude,hows'euer Schooles deceaue a man,
No Ioy, nor Sorrow, can of life bereaue a man.
        Vpon

[42] *Vpon seeing his Face in her Eie.*

FAireſt and kindeſt of all woman-kinde:
  Since you did me the vndeſerued grace,
In your faire Eye to ſhew me my bad face,   5
With loane Ile pay you in the ſelfe ſame kinde;
  Looke in mine Eie, and I will ſhew to you,
  The faireſt face that Heau'ns Eie doth view.

But the ſmall worthleſſe Glaſſe of my dimme Eie,
Scarce ſhewes the Picture of your heau'nly face,   10
Which yet each ſlighteſt turne doth ſtrait deface.
But could, O could you once my Heart eſpie,
  Your forme at large you there engrav'd ſhuld ſee,
  Which, nor by Time, nor Death can razed bee.

---

[43] MADRIGAL XII.   15

Vpon her hiding her face from him.

GOE wayling Accents, goe,
With my warm teares & ſcalding teares attended,
  To th' Author of my woe,
And humbly aske her, why ſhe is offended.   20
  Say, Deere, why hide you ſo,
  From him your bleſſed Eyes,
                   Where

Where he beholdes his earthly Paradife,
 Since he hides not from you
His heart, wherein Loues heau'n you may view?

Vpon her Beauty and Inconftancie.

Whofoeuer longs to trie,
 Both Loue and Iealoufie,
My faire vnconftant Ladie let him fee,
And he will foone a iealous Louer bee. 10

 Then he by proofe fhall know,
 As I doe to my woe,
How they make my poore heart at once to dwell,
In fire and froft, in heau'n and in hell.

[45] *A Dialogue betweene a Louers flaming Heart,*
and his Ladies frozen Breast.

Hart   Shut not (fweet Breaft) to fee me all of fire.
Breaft Flie not(deere Hart) to find me al of fnowe.   5
Hart   Thy fnow inflames thefe flames of my defire.
Breaft And I defire,Defiers fweet flames to know.
    Hart   Thy Snow n'ill hurt me.
    Breaft Nor thy Fire will harme me.
    Hart   This cold will coole me.   10
    Breaft And this heate wil warme me.

Hart   Take this chafte fire to that pure virgin fnow;
B.   Being now thus warm'd,Ile n'ere feek other fire;
H   Thou giu'ft more blis tha mortal harts may know;
Breaft More bliffe I take than Angells can defire.   15

Both together $\left\{\begin{array}{l}\text{Let one griefe harme vs;}\\\text{And let one ioy fill vs:}\\\text{Let one loue warme vs;}\\\text{And let one death kill vs.}\end{array}\right.$

[46] ELEGIE. III.

For what cause he obtaines not his Ladies fauour.

Deere,why hath my long loue, and faith vnfained,
At your faire hands no grace at all obtained?   5

Ift, that my Pocke-hol'd face doth beauty lacke?
  No: Your fweet Sex, fweet beauty praifeth;
  Ours,wit and valour chiefly raifeth.
Ift, that my musk-leffe cloaths are plaine & blacke?
  No: What wife Ladie loues fine noddies,   10
  With poore-clad mindes, and rich-clad bodies?
Ift, that no coftly gifts mine Agents are?
  No: My true Heart which I prefent you,
  Should more than golde or pearle content you.
Ift, That my Verfes want inuention rare?   15
  No: I was neuer skilfull Poet,
  I truely loue, and plainely fhow it.
Ift, That I vaunt, or am effeminate?
  O fcornefull vices! I abhorre you,
  Dwell ftill in Court, the place fit for you.   20
Ift, That you feare my loue foone turnes to hate?
  No: Though difdain'd, I can hate neuer,
  But lou'd,where once I loue, loue euer.
                         Ift;

Ift, That your fauours iealous Eies fuppreffe?
  No: onely Virtue neuer-fleeping,
  Hath your faire Mindes and Bodies keeping.
Ift, That to many moe I loue profeffe?   5
  Goddeffe, you haue my Hearts oblation,
  And no Saint elfe lippes inuocation.

No, none of thefe: The caufe I now difcouer;
No woman loues a faithfull worthy Louer.

[47] *A Quatrain.*   10

IF you reward my loue with loue againe,
  My bliffe, my life, my heau'n I will deeme you,
But if you prowdly quite it with difdaine,
My curfe, my death, my hell I muft efteeme you.

Son-

[48] SONNET IX.

To a worthy Lord (now dead) vpon presenting
him for a New-yeers-gift, with Cæsars
Commentaries and Corne- 5
lius Tacitus.

WOrthily, famous Lord, whose Virtues rare,
   Set in the golde of neuer-stain'd Nobilitie,
   And noble minde shining in true humilitie,
   Make you admir'de of all that vertuous are: 10
If as your Sword with enuy imitates
   Great *Cæsars* Sword in all his deedes victorious,
   So your learn'd Pen would striue to be glorious,
   And write your Acts perform'd in forrein States;
Or if some one with the deepe wit inspir'd, 15
   Of matchles *Tacitus* would them historifie,
   Thē *Cæsars* works so much we should not glorifie,
   And *Tacitus* would be much lesse desir'd.
But till your selfe, or some such put them forth,
Accept of these as Pictures of your worth. 20

To

[49] *To* SAMVEL DANIEL *Prince of
Engliſh Poets.*

Vpon his three ſeuerall ſortes of Poeſie,

Liricall, in his Sonnets.   5
Tragicall, in Roſamond and Cleopatra.
Heroicall, in his Ciuill Warres.

OLympiaes matchleſſe Son, whenas he knew
  How many crowns his fathers ſword had gaind,
With ſmoaking ſighs, and deep-fetcht ſobs did rew,   10
And his braue cheekes with ſcalding teares bedew,
  Becauſe that kingdomes now ſo few remain'd,
  By his victorious Arme to bee obtain'd.

So (Learned *Daniel*) when as thou didſt ſee,
  That *Spenſer* erſt ſo far had ſpred his fame,   15
That hee was Monark deem'd of Poeſie,
Thou didſt (I geſſe) eu'n burne with Iealouſie,
  Leſt Lawrell were not left enough to frame,
  A neaſt ſufficient for thine endleſſe Name.

But as that Pearle of *Greece,* ſoone after paſt   20
  In wondrous conqueſts his renowned ſire,
And others all, whoſe names by Fame are plac'te
In higheſt ſeate: So hath thy Muſe ſurpaſt
  Spenſer, and all that doe with hot deſire,
  To the Thunder-ſcorning Lawrel-crown aſpire,   25
                        And

And as his Empires linked force was knowne,
   When each of thofe that did his Kingdoms fhare,
The mighti'ft Kings in might did match alone:
So of thy skill the greatnes thus is fhowne,   5
   That each of thofe, great Poets deemed are,
   Who may in no one kinde with thee compare.

One fharde out *Greece*, another *Afia* held,
   And fertile *Egypt* to a third did fall,
But only *Alexander* all did wield.   10
So in foft pleafing Liricks fome are skild,
   In Tragicke fome, fome in Heroicall,
   But thou alone art matchleffe in them all.

Non equidem inuideo, miror magis.

Three

---

[50] *Three Epitaphs vpon the death of a rare Child*
of six yeares old.

1

WIts perfection, Beauties wonder,   5
    Natures pride, the Graces treasure,
Vertues hope, his friends sole pleasure,
This small Marble Stone lies vnder.
    Which is often moyst with teares,
    For such losse in such yong yeares.   10

2

Louely Boy, thou art not dead,
But from Earth to Heauen fled,
For base Earth was far vnfit,
For thy Beautie, Grace, and Wit.   15

3

Thou aliue on Earth sweete Boy,
Had'st an Angels wit, and face:
And now dead, thou dost enioy
In high Heauen an Angels place.   20

An

---

[51] *An Inscription for the Statue*
of DIDO.

O moſt vnhappy DIDO,
Vnhappy Wife, and more vnhappy Widow!   5
Vnhappy in thy Mate,
And in thy Louer moſt vnfortunate.
By treaſon th'one was reft thee,
By treaſon th'other left thee.
That left thee meanes to flie with,   10
This left thee meanes to die with.
The former being dead,
From Brothers ſword thou flieſt;
The latter being fled,
On Louers ſword thou dieſt.   15

Piu meritare, che conſeguire.

FRA. DAVISON.

[52] SONNET. I.

*Hee demaunds pardon, for looking, louing,
and writing.*

LEt not (fweet Saint) let not thefe lines offend you,   5
  Nor yet the Meffage that thefe lines imparte;
  The Meffage my vnfained Loue doth fend you,
  Loue, which your felfe hath planted in my harte.
For beeing charm'd by the bewitching arte
  Of thofe inveagling graces which attend you,   10
  Loues holy fire makes mee breathe out in parte,
  The neuer-dying flames my breft doth lend you.
Then if my Lines offend, let Loue be blamed.
  And if my Loue difpleafe, accufe mine Eies,
  If mine Eies finne, their finnes caufe onely lies   15
  On your brite eies, which haue my hart inflamed
Since eies, loue, lines, erre then by your direction;
Excufe mine Eies, my Lines, and my Affection.

SONNET.

[53] SONNET. II.

*Loue in Iuſtice punniſhable only with
like Loue.*

BVt if my Lines may not be held excuſed, 5
   Nor yet my Loue finde fauour in your Eyes,
  But that your Eyes as Iudges ſhall be vſed,
  Euen of the fault which frõ themſelues doth riſe,
Yet this my humble ſuite do not deſpiſe,
   Let mee bee iudged as I ſtand accuſed, 10
  If but my fault my doome doe equaliſe,
  What er'e it bee, it ſhal not be refuſed.
And ſince my Loue already is expreſſed,
   And that I cannot ſtand vpon deniall,
  I freely put my ſelfe vpon my triall, 15
  Let Iuſtice doome mee as I haue confeſſed.
For in my Doome if Iuſtice bee regarded,
My Loue with Loue againe ſhall bee rewarded.

SONNET

[54] SONET. III.

Hee calls his Eares, Eyes, and Hart as witnesses of her
sweet voyce, beauty, and inward vertuous
perfections.   5

FAyre is thy face, and great thy wits perfection,
　So fayre alas, so hard to bee exprest,
　That if my tyred pen should neuer rest,
　It should not blaze thy worth, but my affection.
Yet let me say, the Muses make election   10
　Of your pure minde, there to erect their neast,
　And that your face is such a flint-hard breast,
　By force thereof, without force feeles subiection.
Witnes mine Eare, rauisht when you it heares,
　Witnesse mine Eyes rauisht when you they see,   15
　Beauty and Vertue, witnesse Eyes and Eares,
　In you (sweet Saint) haue equall soueraingntie.
But if, nor Eyes, nor Eares, can prooue it true,
Witnesse my Hart, their's none that equalls you.

F   SONNET

[55] SONNET. V.

Prayſe of her Eyes, excelling all Compariſons.

I Bend my wit, but wit cannot deuiſe,
   Words fit to blaze the worth, your Eies, cōtains,   5
   Whoſe nameles woorth their worthles name dis-
For they in worth exceed the name of eies. (dains
Eyes they be not, but worldes in which theſe lies,
   More bliſſe then this wide world beſides cōtains;
   Worlds they be not, but ſtarres, whoſe influence   10
   Ouer my Life and Lifes felicities.   (raignes,
Stars they bee not, but Suns, whoſe preſence driues
   Darknes from night, and doth bright day impart;
   Suns they be not, which outward heate deriues,
   But theſe do inwardly inflame my hart.   15
Since then in Earth, nor Heau'n, they equal'd are,
I muſt confeſſe they be beyond compare.

ODE.

[104]

[56] ODE I.

His Lady to bee condemned of Ignorance
or Crueltie.

A S ſhee is faire, ſo faithfull I,   5
  My ſeruice ſhee, her grace I merit,
Her beautie doth my Loue inherit,
    But Grace ſhee doth deny.
O knowes ſhee not how much I loue?
    Or doth knowledge in her moue   10
        No ſmall Remorce?
    For the guilt thereof muſt lie
    Vpon one of theſe of force,
Her Ignorance, or Cruelty

As ſhee is faire, ſo cruell ſhee.   15
I ſowe true loue, but reape diſdaining;
Her pleaſure ſpringeth from my paining,
    Which Pitties ſource ſhould bee.
Too well ſhee knowes how much I loue,
    Yet doth knowledge in her moue,   20
        No ſmall remorce.
    Then the guilt thereof muſt lie
    Vpon this alone of force,
Her vndeſerued Cruelty.

As ſhee is faire, ſo were ſhee kinde: 25
Or beeing cruel, could I wauer,
Soone ſhould I, either win her fauer,
    Or a new Miſtreſſe finde.
        F 2   **But**

But neyther out alas may bee,
     Scorne in her, and loue in mee,
          So fixed are.
     Yet in whom moſt blame doth lie   5
     Iudge ſhee may, if ſhee compare
My loue vnto her Crueltie.

[57] Sonnet VI.

Contention of Loue and Reaſon for his Hart.

REaſon and Loue lately at ſtrife, contended,   10
     Whoſe Right it was to haue my minds protectiõ,
     Reaſon on his ſide, Natures wil pretended,
     Loues Title was, my Miſtreſſe rare perfection.
Of power to ende this ſtrife,each makes election,
     Reaſons pretence diſcourſiue thoughts defended;   15
     But loue ſoon broght thoſe thoghts into ſubiectiõ
     By Beauties troopes,which on my ſaint depended.
Yet,ſince to rule the minde was Reaſons dutie,
     On this Condition it by loue was rendred,
     That endles Praiſe by Reaſon ſhould be tendred,   20
     As a due Tribute to her conquering Beautie.
Reaſon was pleaſde withall,and to loues Royalty,
He pledg'de my Hart,as Hoſtage for his Loyalty.

Sonnet

[106]

[58] Sonnet IIII.

That ſhe hath greater poʷer ouer his happines
and life, then either Fortune, Fate,
or Starres. 5

LEt Fate, my Fortune, and my Starres conſpire,
 Ioyntly to poure on me their worſt diſgrace;
 So I be gracious in your heauenly Face,
 I wey not Fates,nor Starres,nor Fortunes yre.
T'is not the influence ofHeauens Fire,   10
 Hath power to make me bleſſed in my Race,
 Nor in my happineſſe hath Fortune place,
 Nor yet can Fate my poore lifes date expyre.
T'is your faire Eyes(my Starres) all bliſſe doo giue,
 Tis your diſdaine(my Fate)hath power to kill,   15
 T'is you (my Fortune)make me happy liue,
 Though Fortune,Fate,& Stars conſpyre mine ill.
Then(bleſſed Saint)into your fauour take mee,
Fortune,nor Fate, nor Stars can wretched make me.

      F 3   Sonnet

[59] SONNET. VII.

Of his Ladies weeping.

WHat need I fay, how it doth wound my breſt,
   By fate to bee thus baniſht from thine Eyes, 5
  Since your own Tears with me doo Sympathize,
  Pleading with ſlow departure there to reſt?
For when with floods of teares they were oppreſt,
  Ouer thoſe Iuory banks they did not riſe,
  Till others enuying their felicities, 10
  Did preſſe thē forth, that they might there be bleſt.
Some of which, Teares preſt forth by violence,
  Your lippes with greedy kiſſing ſtrait did drinke:
  And other ſome vnwilling to part thence,
  Inamourd on your cheekes in them did ſincke. 15
And ſome which from your Face were forc'd away,
In ſigne of Loue did on your Garments ſtay.

SONNET.

[108]

[60] SONNET. VIII.

Hee paints out his Torments.

SWeet,to my curfed life fome fauour fhowe,
 Or let me not (accurft) in life remaine,   5
 Let not my Senfes fence of life retaine,
 Since fence doth only yeeld mee fence of woe.
For now mine Eyes only your frownes doo know;
 Mine Eares heare nothing els but your difdaine,
 My lips tafte nought but teares: and fmel is paine,   10
 Banifht your lips,where *Indian* Odours grow.
And my deuoted Hart your Beauties flaue,
 Feeles nought but fcorne,oppreffion,& diftreffe,
 Made eu'n of wretchednes the wretched Caue,
 Nay,too too wretched for vilde wretchedneffe.   15
For euen fad fighes,as loathing there to reft,
Struggle for paffage from my Greefe-fwolne breft.

[61] ODE II.

A dialogue betweene him and his Hart.

AT her faire hands how haue I grace intreated,
   With prayers oft repeated,   5
   Yet ſtill my loue is thwarted:
Hart let her goe, for ſhee'le not be conuarted.
   Say, ſhal ſhee goe?
   Oh no,no,no,no,no.
Shee is moſt faire,though ſhee be marble harted.   10

How often haue my ſighs declar'de mine anguiſh?
   Wherein I dayly languiſh,
   Yet doth ſhee ſtill procure it:
Hart let her goe,for I can not endure it.
   Say, ſhal ſhee goe?   15
   Oh no,no,no,no,no.
Shee gaue the wound,and ſhee alone muſt cure it.

The trickling tears that down my cheeks haue flow-
   My loue haue often ſhowed; (ed,
   Yet ſtill vnkind I proue her: 20
Hart,let her goe,for nought I do can moue her.
   Say, ſhal ſhee goe?
   Oh no,no,no,no,no.
Though mee ſhee hate, I can not chuſe but loue her.

             But

But ſhall I ſtill a true affection owe her,
    Which prayers,ſighs,teares do ſhew her;
    And ſhall ſhee ſtill diſdaine mee?
Hart, let her goe,if they no grace can gaine mee.   5
    Say, ſhal ſhee goe?
    Oh no,no,no,no,no.
Shee made mee hers,and hers ſhee will retaine mee.

But if the Loue that hath,and ſtill doth burne mee,
    No loue at length returne mee,   10
    Out of my thoughts Ile ſet her:
Hart,let her goe, oh hart, I pray thee let her.
    Say,ſhal ſhee goe?
    Oh no,no,no,no,no.
Fixt in the hart,how can the hart forget her.   15

But if I weepe and ſigh,and often waile mee,
    Till teares,ſighes,prayers fayle mee,
    Shall yet my Loue perſeuer?
Hart,let her goe, if ſhee will right thee neuer.
    Say, ſhal ſhee goe?   20
    Oh no,nó,no,no,no.
Teares, ſighs,praiers faile,but true loue laſteth euer.

F 5   Sᴏɴɴᴇᴛ.

[62] SONNET. IX.

His Sighes and Teares are bootleſſe.

I Haue entreated, and I haue complained,
  I haue diſprays'd, and prayſe I like wiſe gaue,   5
  All meanes to win her Grace I tryed haue,
  And ſtill I loue, and ſtill I am diſdained.
So long I haue my Tongue and Pen conſtrained,
  To praiſe, diſpraiſe, complaine, and pitty craue,
  That now, nor Tongue, nor Pen, to me her ſlaue   10
  Remaines, whereby her Grace may be obtained.
Yet you (my Sighs) may purchace mee releeſe,
  And yee (my Teares) her rocky hart may moue;
  Therefore my ſighes ſigh in her eares my greeſe,
  And in her Hart my Teares imprint my Loue.   15
But ceaſe vaine ſighes, ceaſe ceaſe yee fruitles teares,
Teares cannot pierce her Hart, nor ſighes hir Eares.

SONNET.

[63] SONNET. X.

Her Beautie makes him loue, euen in
despaire.

WOunded with Greefe, I weepe, & sigh, & plaine,   5
   Yet neither plaints, nor sighs, nor tears do good;
But all in vaine I striue against the flood,
Gaining but greefe for greefe, & paine for paine.
Yet though in vaine my teares my cheekes distain;
   Leauing ingrauen Sorrow where they stood;   10
And though my sighs consuming vp my blood,
For Loue deseru'd, reape vndeseru'd Disdaine:
And though in vaine I know I beg remorce
   At your remorcelesse harte, more hard then steele;
Yet, such (alas) such is your Beauties force,   15
   Charming my Sence, that though this hell I feele,
Though neither plaints, nor sighs, nor tears cā moue
Yet must I still persist euer to loue you.   (you,

[64] SONNET XI.

Why her Lips yeeld him no words of Comfort.

OFt doo I plaine,and ſhee my plants doth reede
    Which in black colors do paint forth my, wo   5
So that of force ſhe muſt my ſorrow know;
    And know,for her diſdaine my hart doth bleede.
And knowledge muſt of Force ſome pitty breede,
    Which makes me hope,ſhe wil ſome fauour ſhow
    And from her ſugred lippes cauſe comfort flowe   10
Into mine Eares,my hart with ioy to feede.
Yet though ſhe reads,and reading knowes my griefe,
    And knowledge moues her pitie my diſtreſſe,
    Yet do her lips,ſweet lips,yeeld no releeſe.
    Much do I muſe, but find no cauſe but this,   15
That in her lips, her heauenly lips that bliſſe them,
Her words loth thence to part,ſtay there to kiſſe thē.

[65] SONNET. XII.

*Comparifon of his Hart to a Tempeſt-
beaten Ship.*

LIke a Sea-toſſed Barke with tackling ſpent,   5
   And Starres obſcur'd his watry iornies guide,
  By lowd tempeſtuous windes and raging tide,
  From waue to waue with dreadfull fury ſent,
Fares my poore Hart ; my Hart-ſtrings being rent,
   And quite diſabled your fierce wrath to bide,   10
  Since your faire eies my Stars thẽſelues do hide,
  Clouding their light in frownes and diſcontent.
For from your frowns do ſpring my ſighes & teares,
   Teares flow like ſeas,& ſighes like winds do bloe,
  Whoſe ioyned rage moſt violently beares   15
  My Tempeſt-beaten hart from woe to woe.
And if your Eyes ſhine not that I may ſhun it,
On Rocke,deſpaire,my ſighes,and teares wil run it.

SONNET.

[66] ELEGIE.
To his Lady, who had vowed Virginitie.

Ev'n as my hand my Pen on Paper laies,
My trembling hand my Pen from Paper ſtaies,   5
left that thine eies which ſhining made me loue you
Should frowning on my ſute, bid ceaſe to moue you,
So that I fare like one at his wits end,
Hoping to gaine, and fearing to offend.
What pleaſeth Hope, the ſame Diſpaire miſlikes,   10
What hope ſets down, thoſe lines deſpair outſtrikes,
So that my nurſing-murthering Pen affords,
A Graue and Cradle to my new-borne words.
But whil'ſt like clowds toſſt vp and downe the ayre,
I racked hang twixt Hope and ſadde Deſpaire,   15
Deſpaire is beaten vanquiſht from the field,
And vnto conq'ring Hope my Hart doth yeeld.

For when mine eies vnpartially are fixed,
On thy Roſe cheekes with Lillies intermixed,
And on thy forehead like a cloude of ſnow,   20
From vnder which thine eies like Sunnes do ſhow,
And all thoſe partes which curiouſly do meete,
Twixt thy large-ſpreading haire and pretty feete,
Yet looking on them all, diſcerne no one,
That owes not homage vnto *Cupids* Throne;   25
Then Chaſtitie (me thinkes) no claime ſhould lay
To this faire Realme, vnder Loues Scepters ſway.
For onely to the Queene of amorous pleaſure
Belongs thy Beauties tributary treaſure;
(Treaſure, which doth more than thoſe riches pleaſe   30
For

For which men plow long furrowes in the Seas.)
If you were wrinckled olde, or Natures fcorne,
Or time your beauties colours had out-worne;
Or were you mewed vp from gazing eies,   5
Like to a cloyftred Nunne, which liuing, dies:
Then might you waite on Chaftities pale Queene,
Not being faire, or being faire, not feene.
But you are faire, fo paffing paffing faire,
That loue I muft, though louing I defpaire,   10
For when I faw your eies (O curfed bliffe!)
Whofe light I would not laue, nor yet would miffe,
(For tis their light alone by which I liue,
And yet their fight alone my deaths wound giue.)
Looking vpon your heart-entangling looke,   15
I like a heedeleffe Bird was fnar'de and tooke.
It lies not in our will to hate or loue,
For Natures influence our will doth moue.
And loue of Beauty Nature hath innated,
In Harts of men when firft they were created.   20
For eu'n as Riuers to the Ocean runne,
Returning backe, from whence they firft begunne:
Or as the Skie about the Earth doth wheele,
Or giddy ayre like to a Drunkard reele,
So with the courfe of Nature doth agree,   25
That Eies which Beauties Adamant do fee,
Should on Affections line trembling remayne,
True-fubiect-like eying their Soueraigne.

If of mine Eies you alfo could bereaue me,
As you already of my hart deceiue me,   30
Or could fhut vp my rauifht eares, through which
                                You

You likewife did m'inchaunted Heart bewitch,
Or had in Abfence both thefe illes combinde;
(For by your Abfence I am deafe and blinde,
And, neither Eares, nor Eies in aught delight, 5
But in your charming fpeach,and gratious fight)
To roote out Loue all meanes you can inuent,
Were all but labour loft, and time ill fpent,
For as the fparkes being fpent,which fier procure,
The fire doth brightly-burning ftill endure: 10
Though Abfence fo your fparkling Eies remoue,
My Hart ftill burnes in endles flames of Loue.

Then ftriue not gainft the ftreame,to none effect,
But let due Loue yeeld Loue a due refpect.
Nor feeke to ruine what your felfe begunne, 15
Or loofe a Knot that cannot be vndone.
But vnto *Cupids* bent conforme your will,
For will you,nill you, I muft loue you ftill.
But if your Will did fwimme with Reafons tide,
Or followed Natures neuer-erring guide, 20
It cannot chufe but bring you vnto this,
To tender that which by you gotten is.
Why were you faire to be befought of many,
If you liue chafte, not to be wonne of any?
For if that Nature loue to Beautie offers, 25
And Beauty fhunne the loue that Nature proffers.
Then, either vniuft Beauty is too blame,
With fcorne to quench a lawfull kindled flame,
Or elfe vnlawfully if loue we muft,
And be vnlou'de, then Nature is vniuft. 30
Vniuftly then Nature hath heartes created,

There

There to loue moſt, where moſt their loue is hated,
And flattering them with a faire-ſeeming ill,
To poyſon them with Beauties ſugred Pill.

Thinke you that Beauties admirable worth   5
Was to no end, or idle end brought forth?
No, no; from Nature neuer deede did paſſe,
But it by wiſedomes hand ſubſcribed was.
But you in vaine are faire, if faire, not viewed,
Or being ſeene, mens hearts be not ſubdewed,   10
Or making each mans heart your Beauties thrall,
You be enioyed of no one at all.
For as the Lions ſtrength to ſeize his pray,
And fearefull Hares lightfoote to runne away,
Are as an idle Talent but abuſed,   15
And fruitleſſe had, if had, they be not vſed,
So you in vaine haue Beauties bonds to ſhow,
By which, mens Eies engaged Hearts do owe,
If Time ſhall cancell them before you gaine
Th'indebted Tribute to your Beauties raigne.   20

But if(theſe Reaſons being vainely ſpent)
You fight it out to the laſt Argument;
Tell me but how one Body can encloſe,
As louing friends two deadly hating foes.
But when as Contraries are mixt together,   25
The colour made,doth differ much from either.
Whil'ſt mutually at ſtrife they doe impeach
The gloſſe and luſtre proper vnto each.
So,where one body ioyntly doth inueſt
An Angells face,and cruell Tygres breſt,   30

                                        There

There dieth both Allegeance and Command,
For felf-deuided kingdomes cannot ftand.
But as a Child that knowes not what is what,
Now craueth this, and now affecteth that,   5
And hauing, weyes not that which he requires,
But is vnpleafde,euen in his pleafde defires:
Chafte Beauty fo,both will, and will not haue,
The felf-fame thing it childifhly doth craue:
And wanton-like,now Loue,now Hate affecteth,   10
And Loue,or Hate obtain'd as faft neglecteth.
So (like the Webb *Penelope* did weaue,
Which made by day,fhee did at night vnreaue)
Fruitleffe Affections endleffe threede is fpunne,
At one felfe inftant twifted, and vndone.   15
Nor yet is this chafte Beauties greateft ill,
For where it fpeaketh faire,it there doth kill.
A Marble hart vnder an amorous looke,
Is of a flattering baite the murthering hooke:
For from a Ladies fhining-frowning Eyes,   20
Deaths fable Darte,and *Cupids* Arrow flies.

Since then,from Chaftity and Beauty fpring,
Such muddy ftreames,where each doth raign as king;
Let Tyrant Chaftities vfurped Throane,
Bee made the feate of Beauties grace alone;   25
And let your Beauty bee with this fuffiz'd,
That my harts Cittie is by it furpriz'd:
Raze not my Hart,nor to your Beauty raife,
Blood-guilded Trophees of your Beauties praife;
For wifeft Conquerors doo Townes defire,   30
On honourable termes and not with fyre.

SON-

[120]

[67] SONNET. XIII.

That he cannot leaue to loue,though commanded.

HOw can my Loue in equitie bee blamed,
    Still to importune though it ne'r obtayne;   5
  Since though her face and voice will me refraine,
  Yet by her Voyce and Face I am inflamed?
For when(alas)her face with frownes is framed,
    To kill my Loue,but to reuiue my payne;
  And when her voice commands, but all in vayne,   10
  That loue both leaue to be, and to bee named.
Her *Syren* voyce doth such enchantment moue,
    And thogh she frown,eu'n frowns so louely make
  That I of force am forced still to loue;   (her.
Since then I must,and yet can not forsake her,   15
My fruitles praiers shall ceafe in vaine to moue her,
But my deuoted Hart ne're ceafe to moue her.

SON-

[68] SONNET. XIIII.

He defires leaue to write of his Loue.

MVſt my deuoted Heart defiſt to loue her?
 No, loue I may, but I may not confeſſe it.   5
 What harder thing than loue, and yet depreſſe it?
 Loue moſt conceal'd, doth moſt it ſelfe diſcouer.
Had I no pen to ſhew that I approue her,
 Were I tongue-tide that I might not addreſſe it,
 In Plaints and Prayr'es vnfained to expreſſe it,   10
 Yet could I not my deepe affection couer.
Had I no pen, my very teares would ſhow it,
Which write my true affection in my face.
 Were I tong-tide, my ſighs wold make her know
 Which witnes that I grieue at my diſgrace.   (it,   15
Since then, though ſilent, I my loue diſcouer,
O let my pen haue leaue to ſay, I loue her!

Quid

[69] *Quid pluma leuius? Puluis. Quid puluere? Ventus.*
     Quid vento? Mulier. Quid muliere? Nihil.

Tranſlated thus;

DVſt is lighter than a Feather,   5
   And the Winde more light than eather.
But a Womans fickle minde,
More than Feather, Duſt, or Winde.

W. D.

SONETS, ODES, ELEGIES
and other POESIES.

Splendidis longum valedico nugis.

ANOMOS.

III. Sonnets for a Proeme to the Poems following.

That Loue onely made him a Poet, and that all
sortes of Verses, both in Rime and Mea-   5
sure, agree with his Lady.

[70] SONNET I.

SOme men, they say, are Poets borne by kinde,
   And suck that science from their mothers brest:
   An easie Arte that comes with so great rest,   10
   And happy men to so good hap assignde.
In some, desire of praise enflames the minde,
   To clime with paine *Parnassus* double crest:
   Some, hope of rich Rewardes hath so possest,
   That Gold, in Castall Sands they seeke to finde.   15
Me, neither Nature hath a Poet made,
Nor loue of Glory mou'de to learne the trade,
   Nor thirst of Golde perswaded for to write;
For Natures graces are too fine for mee,
Praise like the Peacockes pride her selfe to see,   20
   Desire of Gaine the basest mindes delight.

                       G   SON-

[71] SONNET. II.

WHat mou'd me then? fay Loue, for thou cāft tel;
    Of thee I learn'd this skill, if skill I haue:
      Thou knowft the Mufe, whofe help I alwais craue   5
      Is none of thofe that on *Parnaffus* dwell.
My Mufe is fuch as doth them all excell,
    They all to her alone their cunning gaue,
      To fing, to dance, to play, to make fo braue;
      Thrice threefold Graces her alone befell.   10
From her do flow the ftreames that water mee,
Hers is the praife, if I a Poet bee;
      Her only looke both will and skill doth giue.
What maruaile then if I thofe lawes refufe,
Which other Poets in their making vfe,   15
      Since by her lookes I write, by which I liue?

SONNET.

[72] SONNET. III.

THus am I free from lawes that other binde,
  Who diuerse verse to diuerse matter frame;
  All kinde of Stiles doo serue my Ladies name,   5
  What they in all the world, in her I finde.
The lofty Verse doth shew her noble minde,
  By which shee quencheth Loues enraged flame,
  Sweet Liricks sing her heauenly beauties fame,
  The tender Elege speakes her pitty kinde.   10
In mournefull Tragicke Verse for her I die,
In Comicke shee reuiues me with her eye,
  All serue my Goddesse both for mirth and mone,
Each looke she casts doth breede both peace & strife,
Ech word she speakes doth cause both death & life,   15
  Out of my selfe I liue in her alone.

G 2   ODE

[129]

[73] ODE I.

Where his Lady keepes his hart.

SWeete Loue, mine only treasure
 For seruice long vnfained,   5
Wherein I nought haue gained,
Vouchsafe this little pleasure,
  To tell mee in what parte,
  My Lady keepes my Harte.

If in her haire so slender,   10
Like golden nets vntwined,
Which fire and art haue fined,
Her thrall my hart I render,
  For euer to abide
  With locks so dainty tide.   15

If in her Eyes shee binde it,
Wherein that fire was framed,
By which it is inflamed,
I dare not looke to finde it;
  I only wish it sight,   20
  To see that pleasant light.

But if her Breast haue dained
With kindnes to receiue it,
I am content to leaue it,
Though death thereby were gained; 25
  Then Lady take your owne,
  That liues for you alone.

             To

[74] *To her Eyes.*

FAine would I learne of thee thou murth'ring Eie,
  Whether thy glance bee fire, or elſe a dart:
For with thy looke in flames thou mak'ſt mee frie,   5
And with the ſame thou ſtrik'ſt mee to the hart.
   Pierſt with thy lookes I burne in fire,
   And yet thoſe lookes I ſtill deſire.

The flie that buzzeth round about the flame
Knows not(poore Soule)ſhe gets her death therby,   10
I ſee my death, and ſeeing, ſeeke the ſame,
And ſeeking, finde, and finding, chuſe to die.
   That when thy lookes my life haue ſlaine,
   Thy lookes may giue mee life againe.

Turne then to mee thoſe ſparkling Eyes of thine,   15
And with their firy glances pierce my hart.
Quench not my light, leſt I in darknes pine,
Strike deepe and ſpare not, pleaſant is the ſmart.
   So by thy lookes my life bee ſpilt,
   Kill mee as often as thou wilt.   20

G 3   As

[75] ODE. II.

*The more fauour he obtaines, the more
he defires.*

A S foone may water wipe me drie,   5
    And fire my heate allay,
As you with fauour of your eye,
    Make hotte defire decay:
        The more I haue,
        The more I craue;   10
The more I craue, the more defire,
As piles of wood encreafe the fire.

The fenceleffe ftone that from on hie
    Defcends to Earth below,
With greater hafte it felfe doth plie,   15
    The leffe it hath to goe:
        So feeles defire
        Encreafe of fire,
That ftill with greater force doth burne,
Till all into it felfe it turne.   20

The greater fauour you beftow,
    The fweeter my delight;
And by delight Defire doth grow,
    And growing gathers might.
        The leffe remaines,
        The more my paines,   25
To fee my felfe fo neere the brinke,
And yet my fill I cannot drinke.

Loue

[76] *Loue the onely price of Loue.*

THe faireſt Pearles that Northerne Seas do breed,
  For pretious ſtones from Eaſterne coaſts are ſold.
Nought yeelds the earth that frõ exchange is freed,   5
Gold valews all, and all things valew Gold.
    Where goodnes wants an equall change to make,
    There greatnes ſerues,or number place doth take.

No mortall thing can beare ſo hie a price,
But that with mortall thing it may be bought.   10
The corne of *Sicill* buies the weſterne ſpice,
French wine of vs, of them our cloth is ſought.
    No pearles, no gold,no ſtones,no corne,no ſpice,
    No cloth,no wine,for loue can pay the price.

What thing is loue,which nought can counteruaile?   15
Nought ſaue it ſelfe, eu'n ſuch a thing is Loue.
All worldly wealth in worth as far doth faile,
As loweſt earth doth yeeld to heau'n aboue.
    Diuine is Loue, and ſcorneth worldly pelfe,
    And can be bought with nothing, but with ſelfe.   20

Such is the price my louing heart would pay,
Such is the pay thy Loue doth claime as due.
Thy due is Loue, which I (poore I) aſſay,
In vaine aſſay to quite with friendſhip true:
    True is my loue,and true ſhall euer bee,   25
    And trueſt loue is farre too baſe for thee.

G 4   Loue

Loue but thy felfe, and loue thy felfe alone,
For faue thy felfe, none can thy loue requite:
All mine thou haft, but all as good as none,
My fmall defart muft take a lower flight.   5
    Yet if thou wilt vouchfafe my hart fuch blis,
    Accept it for thy Prifner as it is.

[77] *His Hart arraigned of Theft, and acquitted.*

MY Hart was found within my Ladies Breft,
    Clofe coucht for feare that no mã might him fee,   10
On whom fufpect did ferue a ftraight Arreft,
And Felon-like hee muft arraigned bee.
    What could he meane fo clofely there to ftay,
    But by deceit to fteale her hart away?

The Bench was fet, the Prifoner forth was brought,   15
My Miftreffe felfe cheefe Iudge to heare the caufe;
Th'Enditemẽt read, by which his blood was fought,
That he (poore hart) by ftealth had broke the lawes:
    His Plea was fuch as each man might defcry,
    For grace and ruth were read in either Eye.   20

Yet forc'd to fpeake, his farther Plea was this,
That fore purfude by mee that fought his blood,
Becaufe fo oft his prefence I did mis,
                    Whil'ft

Whil'ſt, as he ſaid, he labour'd for my good:
   He, voyd of helpe to haue his harmes redreſt,
   Tooke Sanctuary within her ſacred breſt.

The gentle Iudge that ſaw his true intent,   5
And that his cauſe did touch her honor neere,
Since he from me to her for ſuccour went;
That ruth may raigne, where rigour did appeere,
   Gaue ſentence thus; that if he there would bide,
   That place was made the guiltles hart to hide.   10

[78] MADRIGAL. I.

    THine Eyes ſo bright
      Bereft my ſight,
When firſt I viewed thy face.
    So now my light   15
    Is turn'd to night,
I ſtray from place to place.
   Then guide me of thy kindeneſſe,
   So ſhall I bleſſe my blindeneſſe.

G 5   PHA-

[79] Phalevciaks. I.

TIme nor place did I want,what held me tongtide?
  What Charmes, what magicall abufed Altars?
Wherefore wifht I fo oft that hower vnhappy,   5
When with freedome I might recount my tormēts,
And pleade for remedy by true lamenting?
Dumbe,nay dead in a trance I ftood amazed,
When thofe looks I beheld that late I long'd for;
No fpeech, no memory, no life remained,   10
Now fpeech prateth apace, my griefe bewraying,
Now bootleffe memory my plaints remembreth,
Now life moueth againe, but al auailes not.
Speech,life, and memory die altogether,
With fpeech, life,memory, Loue onely dies not.   15

[80] *Deadly Sweetnes.*

SWeet thoghts,the food on which I feeding fterue,
  Sweet tears,the drink that more augmēts my thirft
Sweet eies,the ftars by which my courf doth fwerue
Sweet hope,my death,which waft my life at firft.   20
  Sweet thoughts,fweet teares,fweet hope, fweet
  How chance that death in fweetnes lies?   (eies,

M A-

[81] MADRIGAL II.

Verball Loue.

IF Loue be made of words, as woods of Trees,
    Who more belou'd then I?   5
If loue be hotte where true defire doth freeze,
    Who more then fhe doth frie?
Are droanes that make no hony counted Bees?
    Is running water drie?
Is that a gainefull trade that has no fees,   10
    Hee liue that dead doth lie?
What elfe but blinde is he that nothing fees,
    But deafe that heares no crie?
    Such is her vowed loue to mee,
    Yet muft I thinke it true to bee.   15

[82] *Ladies eyes, ferue Cupid both for Darts
and Fire.*

OFt haue I mus'd the caufe to finde,
    Why Loue in Ladies eies doth dwell:
I thought, becaufe himfelfe was blinde,   20
Hee lookt that they fhould guide him well.
    And fure his hope but feldome failes,
    For Loue by Ladies eyes preuailes.

                                                                        But

But Time,at laft,hath taught me wit,
Although I bought my wit full deere,
For by her Eies my heart is hit,
Deepe is the wound though none appeere,   5
   Their glauncing beames as darts he throwes,
   And fure he hath no fhaftes but thofe.

I mufde to fee their eies fo bright,
And little thought they had beene fire;
I gazde vpon them with delight,   10
But that delight hath bred defire;
   What better place can Loue require,
   Than that where grow both fhafts and fire?

[83] *Loues Contrarieties.*

I Smile fometimes amids my greateft griefe,   15
   Not for Delight,for that long fince is fled,
Defpaire did fhut the Gate againft Releefe,
When Loue, at firft, of death the fentence read.
But yet I fmile fometimes in midft of paine,
To thinke what toyes do toffe my troubled head.   20
How moft I wifh, that moft I fhould refraine,
And feeke the thing that leaft I long to finde,
And finde the wound by which my heart is flaine,
Yet want both skill and will to eafe my minde.

Againft

Againſt my will I burne with free conſent,
I liue in paine, and in my paine delight,
I cry for death, yet am to liue content,
I hate the day, yet neuer wiſh for night;   5
I freeze for colde, and yet refraine the fire;
I long to ſee, and yet I ſhunne her ſight,
I ſcalde in Sunne, and yet no ſhade deſire,
I liue by death, and yet I wiſh to die,
I feele no hurte, and yet for help enquire,   10
I die by life, and yet my life deſie.

Heu, cogor voti neſcius eſſe mei.

[84] ODE III.

DEſire and Hope haue mou'd my minde,
    To ſeeke for that I cannot finde,   15
Aſſured faith in woman-kinde,
    And loue with loue rewarded;
Selfe-loue, all but himſelfe diſdaines,
Suſpeꞔt as chiefeſt virtue raignes,
Deſire of change vnchang'd remaines,   20
    So light is Loue regarded.

True friendſhip is a naked name,
That idle braines in paſtime frame,
Extreames are alwayes worthy blame,
    Enough is common kindnes.   25

                                        What

[139]

What floods of teares do Louers fpend?
What fighes from out their hearts they fend?
How many, may, and will not mend?
    Loue is a wilfull blindneffe.   5
What is the Loue they fo defire?
Like loue for loue, and equall fire;
Good louing wormes, which loue require,
    And know not when they haue it.
Is Loue in wordes? faire wordes may faine.   10
Is Loue in lookes? fweet lookes are vaine;
Both thefe in common kindnes raigne,
    Yet few or none fo craue it.

Thou wouldft be lou'de, and that of one,
For vice? thou maift feeke loue of none: 15
For virtue? why of her alone?
    I fay fo more, fpeake you that know the truth,
    If fo great loue be aught but heate of youth?

---

[85] MADRIGAL III.

SHe onely is the pride of Natures skill: 20
  In none, but her, al Graces friendly meete.
In all, faue her, may *Cupid* haue his will,
By none, but her, is Fancy vnder feete.
    Moft ftrange of all, her praife is in her want,
    Her Heart that fhould be flefh, is Adamant.   25
                Laudo quod lugeo.

                            Smoothe

[86] SMoothe are thy lookes, fo is the deepeft ftreame:
Soft are thy lippes, fo is the fwallowing Sand.
Faire is thy fight, but like vnto a dreame;
Sweet is thy promife, but it wil not ftand.   5
   Smooth, foft, faire, fweet, to thē that lightly tuch,
   Rough, hard, foule, fowre to them that take too
                            (much.
Thy looks fo fmoothe haue drawne away my fight.
Who would haue thoght that hooks could fo be hid?
Thy lips fo foft haue fretted my delight,   10
Before I once fufpe&ted what they did.
   Thy face fo faire hath burnt mee with defire,
   Thy wordes fo fweete were bellowes for the fire.

And yet I loue the lookes that made me blinde,
And like to kiffe the lippes that fret my life,   15
In heate of fire an eafe of heate I finde,
And greateft peace in midft of greateft ftrife.
   That if my choice were now to make againe,
   I would not haue this ioy without this paine.

P H A-

[87] PHALEVCIACKS II.

HOw,or where haue I loft my felfe? vnhappy!
 Dead,nor liue am I neither,and yet am both.
Through defpayre am I dead,by hope reuiued,   5
Weeping wake I the night from eue to morning,
Sighing wafte I the day from morne to euening.
Teares are drink to my thirft,by teares I thirft more,
Sighes are meate that I eate, I hunger eating,
Might I,O that I might refraine my feeding,   10
Soone would eafe to my hart by death be purchaft.
Life and light do I lacke, when I behold not
Thofe bright beams of her Eies,*Apollo* darkning :
Life and light do I loofe when I behold them,
All as Snow by the Sun refolu'd to water.   15
Death and life I receiue her Eyes beholding;
Death and life I refuze not in beholding,
So that,dead or alive I may behold them.

[88] L'ENVOY *in ryming Phaleuciacks.*

MVfe not,Lady,to reade fo ftrange a Meeter;   20
 Strange griefe,ftrange remedy for eafe requireth.
When fweet Ioy did abound, I writt the fweeter,
Now that weareth away,my Mufe retireth:
 In you lyes it alone to cure my fadneffe,
 And therewith to reuiue my hart with gladneffe.   25

SON-

[89] SONNET. IIII.

WRongde by Defire I yeelded to difdaine,
    Who call'd reuenge to worke my fpite therby.
  Rafh was Reuenge and fware defire fhould die.   5
  No price nor prayer his pardon might obtaine.
Downe to my Hart in rage hee haftes amaine,
    And ftops each paffage left Defire fhould flie:
  Within my Eares difdainfull words did lie,
  Proud lookes did keepe mine Eyes with fcornfull   10
Defire that earft but flickred in my breft,   (traine.
And wanton-like now prickt,now gaue me reft,
    For feare of death funke deeper in my hart.
There raignes he now,and there will raigne alone,
Defire is iealous,and giues part to none,   15
    Nor hee from mee,nor I from him can ftart.

---

[90] *That he is vnchangeable.*

The loue of chāge hath chāg'd the world throwout
  And nought is counted good,but what is ftrang;
New things waxe olde,olde new,all turne about,   20
And all things change except the loue of change.
  Yet feele I not this loue of change in mee,
  But as I am, fo will I alwayes bee.

For

For who can change that likes his former choice,
Who better wiſh,that knowes he hath the beſt?
How can the heart in things vnknowne reioyce,
If ioy well tride can bring no certaine reſt?   5
  My choyce is made,change he that liſt for mee,
  Such as I am,ſuch will I alwaies bee.

Who euer chang'd,and not confeſt his want?
And who confeſt his want,and not his woe?
Then change who liſt, thy woe ſhall not be ſcant,   10
Within thy ſelfe thou feedſt thy mortall foe.
  Change calls for change,no end,no eaſe for thee,
  Then,as I am,ſo will I alwaies bee.

Mine eies confeſſe they haue their wiſhed ſight,
My heart affirmes it feeles the loue it ſought.   15
Mine inward thoughts are fed with true delight,
Which full conſent of conſtant ioy hath wrought.
  And full Content deſiers no Change to ſee,
  Then,as I am,ſo will I always bee.

Reſt then(my Hart)and keep thine olde delight,   20
Which like the Phœnix waxeth yong each day:
Each houre preſents new pleaſure to my ſight,
More cauſe of ioy increaſeth eu'ry way.
  True loue with age doth daily cleerer ſee,
  Then,as I am, ſo wil I always bee.   25

What gain'd faire *Creſſide* by her faithleſſe change,
But loſſe of fame,of beauty,health,and life?

Marke

[144]

Marke *Iasons* hap, that euer lou'de to range,
That loſt his children, and his princely wife.
    Then Change farewell, thou art no Mate for me,
    But, as I am, ſo will I alwayes be.   5

Iamais aultre.

[91] *To his Eies.*

VNhappy Eies, the cauſers of my paine,
    That to my foe betray'd my ſtrongeſt hold,
Wherein, he like a Tyrant now doth raigne,   10
And boaſts of winning that which treaſon ſolde.
Too late you call for help of me in vaine,
Whom Loue hath bound in chaines of maſſie gold;
The teares you ſhed increaſe my hote deſire,
As water on the Smithie kindles fire.   15
    The ſighs that from my Heart aſcend,
Like winde diſperſe the flame throughout my breſt,
No part is left to harbour quiet reſt,
    I burne in fire, and do not ſpend;
        Like him, whoſe growing maw,   20
        The vulture ſtill doth gnaw.

Vpon

[92] Ode IIII.

Vpon visiting his Lady by Moon-light.

THe night say all, was made for rest,
   And so say I, but not for all:
To them the darkest nights are best,
Which giue them leaue asleepe to fall:
    But I that seeke my rest by light,
    Hate sleepe, and praise the cleerest night.

Bright was the Moone, as bright as day,
And *Venus* glistred in the West,
Whose light did leade the ready way,
That brought mee to my wished rest:
    Then each of them encreast their light,
    While I inioy'd her heauenly sight.

Say, gentle Dames, what mou'd your minde
To shine so bright aboue your wont?
Would *Phœbe* fayre *Endimion* finde?
Would *Venus* see *Adonis* hunt?
    No no, you feared by her sight,
    To loose the prayse of Beauty bright.

At last, for shame you shrunke away,
And thought to reaue the world of light:
Then shone my Dame with brighter ray,
Then that which comes from *Phœbus* sight:
    None other light but hers I prayse,
    Whose nights are cleerer then the dayes.

                               Vpon

5

10

15

20

25

[93] *Vpon her Absence.*

The summer Sun that scalds the groūd with heate,
  And burns the Grasse,& dries the Riuers source,
With milder beames,the fartheft earth doth beate,   5
When through the frozen Gote he runs his courfe.
   The fire that burnes what euer comes to hand,
   Doth hardly heate that fartheft off doth ftand.

Not fo, the heate that fets my heart on fire,
By diftance, flakes, and lets me coole againe: 10
But ftill, the farther off, the more defire,
The abfent fire doth burne with hotter paine.
   My Ladies prefence burnt me with defire,
   Her abfence turnes me into flaming fire.

Whofo hath feene the flame that burneth bright,   15
By outward colde in narrow roome fuppreft,
Encreafe in heate and rage with greater might,
May gheffe what force of fire torments my breft:
   So run the fwelling ftreames with double force,
   Where locks or piles are fet to ftay their courfe.   20

For when my heart perceiu'd her parting neere,
By whofe fweete fight he liues that elfe fhould die,
It cloafde it felfe,to keepe thofe beames fo cleere,
Which from her looke had pierft it through the Eie.
   The firy beams which would breake out fo faine,   25
   By feeking vent,encreafe my burning paine.
                         But

But if my Deere returne aliue, and found,
That thefe mine eyes may fee her beautie bright,
My Hart fhall fpread with ioy that fhall abound,
And open wide, receiuing cleerer light.   5
   Shee fhall recouer that which I poffeffe,
   And I thereby enioy no whit the leffe.

[94] ODE V.

Petition to haue her leaue to die.

WHen will the fountaine of my Teares be drie?   10
     When will my fighes be fpent?
When will Defire agree to let me die?
     When will thy hart relent?
   It is not for my life I pleade,
   Since death the way to reft doth leade,   15
     But ftay for thy confent,
     Left thou be difcontent.

For if my felfe without thy leaue I kill,
     My Ghoft will neuer reft:
So hath it fworne to worke thine only will,   20
     And holds that euer beft.
   For fince it only liues by thee,
   Good reafon thou the ruler bee:
     Then giue me leaue to die,
     And fhew thy powre thereby.   25

The

[95] THe frozen Snake oppreſt with heaped ſnowe,
   By ſtrugling hard gets out her tender head:
And ſpies far off from where ſhee lies belowe,
The winter Sun that from the North is fled: 5
   But all in vaine ſhee lookes vpon the light,
   Where heate is wanting to reſtore her might.

What doth it helpe a wretch in priſon pent,
Long time with biting hunger ouer-preſt;
To ſee without or ſmell within the ſent,   10
Of daintie fare for others tables dreſt?
   Yet Snake and priſ'ner both behold the thing,
   The which(but not with ſight)might cōfort bring.

Such is my ſtate,or worſe,if worſe may bee,
My heart oppreſt with heauy froſt of care,   15
Debar'd of that which is moſt deere to mee,
Kild vp with colde,and pinde with euill fare:
   And yet I ſee the thing might yeeld reliefe,
   And yet the ſight doth breed my greater griefe.

So *Thisbe* ſaw her louer through the wall,   20
And ſaw thereby,ſhee wanted that ſhee ſaw:
And ſo I ſee, and ſeeing want withall,
And wanting ſo,vnto my death I draw:
   And ſo my death were twenty times my frend,
   If with this Verſe my hated life might end.   25
                                           If

[96] Ode VI.

IF my decay be your encreafe,
  If my diftreffe bee your delight,
If warre in me procure your peace,   5
If wrong to me, to you be right,
    I would decay, diftreffe, warre, wrong,
    Might end the life that ends fo long.

Yet, if by my decay you grow,
When I am fpent your growth is paft: 10
If from my griefe your Ioy do flow,
When my griefe ends, your Ioy flies faft:
    Then for your fake, though to my paine,
    I ftriue to liue, to die full faine.

For if I die, my warre muft ceafe;   15
Then can I fuffer wrong no more:
My warre once done, farewel your peace,
My wrong, your right doth ftill reftore:
    Thus, for your right I fuffer wrong,
    And for your peace, my warre prolong.   20

But fince no thing can long indure,
That fometime hath not needefull reft,
What can my life your ioy affure,
If ftill I waile with griefe oppreft?
    The ftrongeft ftomacke faints at laft,   25
    For want of eafe and due repaft.

                                    My

My restlesse sighes breake out so fast,
That time to breathe they quite deny:
Mine Eyes so many teares haue cast,
That now the springs themselues are dry: 5
 Then grant some little ease from paine,
 Vntill the springs bee full againe.

The Gyant whom the Vulture gnawes,
Vntill his heart be growne, hath peace:
And *Sisyphus* by hellish lawes,   10
Whilste that the stone rowles downe, doth cease:
 But all in vaine I striue for rest,
 Which breedes more sorrow in my brest.

Let my Decay bee your encrease,
Let my distresse bee your delight: 15
Let warre in mee procure your peace,
Let wrong in mee to you bee right;
 That by my Griefe your Ioy may liue,
 Vouchsafe some little rest to giue.

[97] ODE VII.   20

CLose your lids, vnhappy Eyes,
 From the sight of such a change:
Loue hath learned to despise,
Selfe-conceit hath made him strange:
 Inward now his sight he turneth,   25
 With himselfe in loue hee burneth.

H   If

If abroad he beautie fpie,
As by chance he lookes abroad,
Or it is wrought by his eye,
Or forc'de out by Painters fraude: 5
   Saue himfelfe none faire he deemeth,
   That himfelfe too much efteemeth.

Coy difdaine hath kindnes place,
Kindnes forc'de to hide his head:
True Defire is counted bafe,   10
Hope with hope is hardly fed:
   Loue is thought a fury needleffe,
   Hee that hath it, fhal die fpeedleffe.

Then mine eies, why gaze you fo?
Beautie fcornes the Teares you fhed;   15
Death you feeke to end my woe,
O that you of death were fped!
   But with Loue hath death confpired,
   To kill none whom Loue haue fired.

---

[98] C*Vpid* at length I fpie thy crafty wile,   20
   Though for a time thou didft me fore beguile,
When firft thy fhaft did wound my tender hart,
It toucht mee light, mee thought I felt fome paine;
Some litle prick at firft did make mee fmart,
But yet that griefe was quickly gone againe.   25
Full fmall account I made of fuch a fore,
As now doth ranckle inward more and more.

                             So

So poyſon firſt the ſinewes lightly ſtraines,
Then ſtraies,and after ſpreads through al the vaines,
No otherwiſe,then he, that prickt with thorne,
Starts at the firſt,and feeles no other griefe,   5
As one whoſe hart ſo litle hurt did ſcorne,
And deigned not to ſeek deſpis'd reliefe:
At laſt, when reſt doth after trauaile come,
That litle pricke the joynt with paine doth numme.

What may I thinke the cauſe of this thy craft,   10
That at the firſt thou ſtick'ſt not deepe thy ſhaft?
If at the firſt I had thy ſtroke eſpi'de,
(Alas I thought thou wouldſt not dally ſo)
To keepe my ſelfe all wayes I would haue tride,
At leaſt, I thinke I might haue cur'd my woe: 15
Yet,truth to ſay,I did ſuſpect no leſſe,
And knew it too,at leaſt,I ſo did gheſſe.

I ſaw,and yet would willingly be blinde.
I felt the ſting, yet flatt'red ſtill my minde,
And now too late I know my former guilt,   20
And ſeeke in vaine to heale my cureleſſe ſore;
My life, I doubt, my health I know is ſpilt,
A iuſt reward for dallying ſo before:
For I that would not when I might haue eaſe,
No maruell though I cannot when I pleaſe.   25

Clipeum poſt vulnera.

H 2   *A*

[99] A Paraphrasticall tranflation of Petrarkes
Sonnet, beginning,

S'Amor non è, che dunque è quel ch'io fento.

IF Loue bee nothing but an idle name,   5
A vaine deuife of foolifh Poets skill:
A fained fire, deuoyd of fmoke and flame;
Then what is that which mee tormenteth ftill?
 If fuch a thing as Loue indeede there bee,
 What kind of thing,or which,or where is hee?   10

If it be good, how caufeth it fuch paine?
How doth it breed fuch greefe within my breft?
If naught,how chance the greefe that I fuftaine,
Doth feeme fo fweet amidft my great vnreft?
 For fure mee thinkes it is a wondrous thing,   15
 That fo great paine fhould fo great pleafure bring.

If with my will amidft thefe flames I fry,
Whence come thee teares?how chance I thus com-
Ifforce perforce I beare this mifery, (plaine?
What help thefe Teares that cannot eafe my paine?   20
 How can this fancy beare fuch fway in mee,
 But if my felfe confent, that fo it bee?

And if my felfe confent,that fo it bee,
Vniuft I am thus to complaine and cry;
To looke that other men fhould fuccour mee,   25
Since by my fault I feele fuch mifery:
 Who will not helpe himfelfe when well hee can,
 Deferues fmall helpe of any other man.
         Thus

Thus am I toſt vpon the troublous Seas,
By ſundry winds,whoſe blaſtes blow ſundry waies:
And eu'ry blaſt ſtill driuing where it pleaſe,
Brings hope and feare to end my lingring dayes: 5
    The Steers-man gone, faile, helme, & tackle loſt,
    How can I hope to gayne the wiſhed Coaſt?

Wiſedome and folly is the luckleſſe fraight,
My ſhip therewith ballaſt vnequally:
Wiſedome too light, folly of too great waight,   10
My Barke and I, through them, in ieopardie:
    Thus, in the midſt of this perplexity,
    I wiſh for death, and yet am loath to die.

[100] FAyre is thy face,and that thou knoweſt too well,
    Hard is thy Hart,and that thou wilt not knowe: 15
Thou hear'ſt and ſmil'ſt,when I thy prayſes tell,
But ſtopſt thine Eares when I my greef would ſhow:
    Yet though in vaine,needs muſt I ſpeake,
    Or elſe my ſwelling Hart would breake.

And when I ſpeake,my breath doth blow the fire,   20
With which my burning Hart conſumes away:
I call vpon thy name and helpe require,
Thy deereſt Name which doth mee ſtill betray:
    For grace,ſweet Grace thy name doth ſound,
    Yet ah!in thee no grace is found.   25

H 3   Alas

Alas, to what parte fhal I then appeale?
Thy face fo faire difdaines to looke on mee:
Thy tongue commands my hart his griefe conceale,
Thy nimble feete from me do alwayes flee: 5
   Thine Eyes caft fire to burne my hart,
   And thou reioyceft in my fmart.

Then,fince thou feeft the life I leade in paine,
And that for thee I fuffer all this griefe,
O let my Heart this fmall requeft obtaine,   10
That thou agree it pine without reliefe!
   I aske not Loue for my good will,
   But leaue,that I may loue thee ftill.

Quid minus optari per mea vota poteſt.

[101] ODE. VIII.   15

DIfdaine that fo doth fill mee,
   Hath furely fworne to kill mee,
      And I muft die.
Defire that ftill doth burne mee,
To life againe will turne mee   20
      And liue muft I.
O kill mee then difdaine!
That I may liue againe.

Thy lookes are life vnto mee,
And yet thofe lookes vndoo mee,   25
      O death and life!

Thy

[156]

Thy ſmile ſome reſt doth ſhow mee,
Thy frowne with warre o'rethrow mee,
　　　O peace and ſtrife!
Nor, life nor death is either,　　　　　　　5
Then giue mee both, or neither.

Life only cannot pleaſe mee,
Death only cannot eaſe mee,
　　　Change is delight.
I liue that death may kill mee,　　　　　　10
I die that life may fill mee,
　　　Both day and night.
If once Deſpaire decay,
Deſire will weare away.

───────────────────────

　　[102] *An Inuectiue againſt Loue.*　　15
ALL is not Gold that ſhineth bright in ſhow,
　Nor eu'ry flower ſo good, as faire, to ſight,
The deepeſt ſtreames, aboue do calmeſt flow,
And ſtrongeſt Poyſons oft the taſte delight,
　The pleaſant baite doth hide the harmeful hooke,　20
　And falſe deceit can lend a friendly looke.

Loue is the gold whoſe outward hew doth paſſe,
Whoſe firſt beginnings goodly promiſe make,
Of pleaſures faire and freſh as Summers graſſe,
Which neither Sun can parch, nor winde can ſhake;　25
　But when the Mould ſhould in the fire be tride,
　The Gold is gone, the droſſe doth ſtill abide.
　　　　　　H 4　　　　　　Beau-

───────────────────────

Beautie,the flower ſo freſh, ſo faire, ſo gay,
So ſweet to ſmell,ſo ſoft to touch and taſte,
As ſeemes it ſhould endure,by right,for ay,
And neuer be with any ſtorme defaſte: 5
   But when the baleful Southerne wind doth blow,
   Gone is the glory which it erſt did ſhow.

Loue is the ſtreame, whoſe waues ſo calmely flow,
As might intice mens mindes to wade therein:
Loue is the poyſon mixt with ſugar ſo,   10
As might by outward ſweetnes liking win.
   But as the deepe o'reflowing ſtops thy breath,
   So poyſon once receiu'd brings certaine death.

Loue is the baite,whoſe taſte the fiſh deceaues,
And makes them ſwallow down the choking hooke: 15
Loue is the face whoſe fairenes iudgement reaues,
And makes thee truſt a falſe and fained looke:
   But as the hooke,the fooliſh fiſh doth kill,
   So flatt'ring lookes, the Louers life do ſpill.

Vſque adeo dulce puella malum eſt.   20

Vpon

[103] *Vpon an Heroicall Poeme which hee had begunne*
(in Imitation of Virgil,) of the first Inha-
biting this famous Ile by Brute, and
the Troyans.   5

MY wanton Muse that whilome wont to sing,
 Faire *Beauties* praise and *Venus* sweet delight,
Of late had chang'd the tenor of her string,
To higher tunes then serue for *Cupids* fight: (strong,
 Shril Trumpets sound, sharpe Swords & Lances 10
 Warre, bloud, and death, were matter of her song.

The God of Loue by chance had heard thereof,
That I was prou'd a Rebell to his Crowne,
Fit words for Warre, quoth he, with angry skoff,
A likely man to write of *Marses* frowne: 15
 Well are they sped whose praises he shall write,
 Whose wanton Pen can nought but Loue indite.

This said, he whiskt his parti-coulor'd wings,
And down to earth he comes more swift thē thoght
Then to my hart in angry haste he flings,   20
To see what chāge these news of wars had wroght:
 He pries, and lookes, he ransacks eu'ry vaine,
 Yet findes he nought, saue loue, and Louers paine.

H 5   Then

Then I that now perceiu'd his needles feare,
With heauy ſmile began to pleade my cauſe:
In vayne (quoth I) this endleſſe greefe I beare,
In vaine I ſtriue to keepe thy greeuous Lawes,　　　　5
　　If after proofe ſo often truſty found,
　　Vniuſt Suſpect condemne mee as vnſound.

Is this the guerdon of my faithfull hart?
Is this the hope on which my life is ſtaide?
Is this the eaſe of neuer-ceaſing ſmart?　　　　10
Is this the price that for my paines is paid?
　　Yet better ſerue fierce *Mars* in bloody field,
　　Where death,or conqueſt,end or ioy doth yeeld.

Long haue I ſeru'd: what is my pay but payne?
Oft haue I ſude : what gaine I but delay?　　　　15
My faithfull loue is quited with diſdaine,
My greefe a game, my pen is made a play:
　　Yea,Loue that doth in other fauour find,
　　In mee is counted madnes out of kind.

And laſt of all,but greeuous moſt of all,　　　　20
Thy ſelfe,ſweet Loue,hath kild me with ſuſpect ;
Could Loue beleeue, that I from Loue would fall?
Is warre of force to make mee Loue neglect?
　　No, *Cupid* knowes,my mind is faſter ſet,
　　Then that by war I ſhould my Loue forget.　　　　25

My

My Mufe indeed to War enclines her minde,
The famous Actes of worthy *Brute* to write:
To whom the Gods this Ilands rule affignde,
Which long he fought by feas throgh *Neptunes* fpight   5
   With fuch conceits my bufie head doth fwel,
    But in my hart nought els but Loue doth dwell.

And in this warre thy part is not the leaft,
Heere fhall my Mufe *Brutes* noble Loue declare:
Heere fhalt thou fee the double Loue increaft,   10
Of fayreft Twins that euer Lady bare:
   Let *Mars* triumph in Armour fhining bright,
    His conquerd Armes fhall be thy triumphs light.

As hee the world, fo thou fhalt him fubdue,
And I thy glory through the world will ring: 15
So bee my paines, thou wilt vouchfafe to rue,
And kill defpayre: With that he whisk't his wing, ·
   And bade me write, and promift wifhed reft,
    But fore I hope falfe hope will bee the beft.

Vpon

[161]

[104] *Vpon his Ladies buying ſtrings for her Lute.*

IN happy time the wiſhed Fayre is come,
  To fitt thy Lute with ſtrings of eu'ry kinde:
Great pitty ti's, ſo ſweete a Lute be dumme,   5
That ſo can pleaſe the Eare, and eaſe the minde:
    Go take thy choice, and chuſe the very beſt,
    And vſe them ſo, that head and hart find reſt.

Reſt thou in ioy, and let me waile alone,
My pleaſant dayes haue tane their laſt farewell: 10
My Hart-ſtrings Sorrow ſtrook ſo long with mone,
That at the laſt they all in pieces fell:
    And now they lie in pieces brooke ſo ſmall,
    That ſcarce they ſerue to make mee frets withall.

And yet they ſerue and binde my hart ſo ſtrait,   15
That frets indeed they ſerue to fret it out:
No force for that, in hope thereof I waite,
That death may rid mee both of hope and doubt:
    But death, alas, drawes backward all too long,
    And I each day feele now encreaſe of wrong.   20

Care

[105] *Care will not let him liue, nor Hope let him die.*

MY heauy Hart which Greefe and hope torment,
Beates all in vaine againſt my weary breſt:
As if it thought with force to make a vent,   5
That Death might enter to procure my reſt:
  But, fooliſh hart, thy paynes are loſt, I ſee,
  For death and life both flie and follow thee.

When weight of care would preſſe mee downe with
That I might ſinck to depth of death below: (paine,   10
Hope lends me wings, and lifts me vp againe,
To ſtriue for life, and liue in greater woe:
  So fares the bote, which winds driue to the ſhore,
  And Tide driues backward where it was before.

Thus neyther Hope will let me die with Care,   15
Nor Care conſent that Hope aſſure my life:
I ſeeke for life, death dooth his ſtroke prepare,
I come to death, and life renewes my ſtrife:
  All as the ſhadow follow them that flie,
  And flies from them that after it do hie.   20

What is my hope? that hope will faile at laſt,
And greefe gett ſtrength to worke his will on mee:
Eyther the Waxe with which hopes wings are faſt,
By ſcalding ſighes mine Eyes ſhall melted ſee:
  Or els my Teares ſhall wett the feathers ſo,   25
  That I ſhall fall and drowne in waues of woe.

                                                          A

[106] *Cupids Mariage with Diſſimulation.*

A New-found match is made of late,
   Blinde *Cupid* needs will change his wife;
New-fangled Loue doth *Pſyche* hate,   5
With whom ſo long he led his life.
       Deſſembling, ſhee
       The Bride muſt bee,
  To pleaſe his wanton eye.
       Pſyche laments   10
       That Loue repents,
  His choyce without cauſe why.

Cytheron ſounds with muſicke ſtrange,
Vnknowne vnto the Virgins nine:
From flat to ſharpe the Tune doth range,   15
Too baſe, becauſe it is too fine.
       See how the Bride
       Puft vp with pride,
  Can mince it paſſing well,
       Shee trips on toe,   20
       Full faire to ſhow,
  Within doth poyſon dwell.

Now wanton Loue at laſt is ſped,
Diſſembling is his only Ioy,
Bare Truth from *Venus* Courte is fled,   25
Diſſembling pleaſures hides annoy.
       It were in vaine
       To talke of paine,

                         The

The wedding yet doth laſt,
  But paine is neere,
  And will appeere,
With a diſſembling caſt.   5

Diſpaire and hope are ioyn'd in one,
And paine with pleaſure linked ſure:
Not one of theſe can come alone,
No certaine hope, no pleaſure pure.
   Thus ſowre and ſweete   10
   In loue do meete,
Diſſembling likes it ſo,
  Of ſweete ſmall ſtore,
  Of ſowre the more,
Loue is a pleaſant woe.   15

    Amor & mellis & fellis,

   [107] ODE. X.

Diſpraiſe of Loue, and Louers follies.

IF Loue be life, I long to die,
  Liue they that liſt for mee: 20
And he that gaines the moſt thereby,
  A foole, at leaſt, ſhall bee.

        But

But he that feeles the foreſt fits,
Scapes with no leſſe than loſſe of wits;
    An happy life they gaine,
    Which Loue doo entertaine.   5

In day by fained lookes they liue,
    By lying dreames in night.
Each frowne a deadly wound doth giue,
    Each ſmile a falſe delight.
Ift hap their Lady pleaſant ſeeme,   10
It is for others loue they deeme,
    If voyde ſhe ſeeme of ioy,
    Diſdaine doth make her coy.

Such is the peace that Louers finde,
    Such is the life they leade.   15
Blowne here and there with eu'ry winde,
    Like flowers in the Meade.
Now warre, now peace, then warre againe,
Deſire, Diſpaire, Delight, Diſdaine,
    Though dead in midſt of life,   20
    In peace, and yet at ſtrife.

In amore hæc inſunt mala.

The

[108] THe golden Sunne that brings the day,
       And lends men light to see withall,
In vaine doth cast his beames away,
Where they are blinde on whom they fall.   5
       There is no force in all his light,
       To giue the Mole a perfect sight.

But thou, my Sunne, more bright then hee,
That shines at noone in Summer tide,
Hast giuen me light and power to see,   10
With perfect skill my sight to guide.
       Till now I liu'de as blinde as Mole,
       That hides her head in earthly hole.

I heard the praise of beauties grace,
Yet deem'd it nought but Poets skill.   15
I gaz'de on many a louely face,
Yet found I none to binde my will.
       Which made me thinke, that beauty bright,
       Was nothing elfe but red and white.

But now thy beames haue cleer'd my sight,   20
I blush to thinke I was so blinde.
Thy flaming Eies affoord mee light,
That Beauties blaze each where I finde:
       And yet thefe Dames that shine so bright,
       Are but the shadow of thy light.   25

                                        ODE

[109] ODE XI.
To his Muse.

REst, good my Mufe, and giue me leaue to reft,
     We ftriue in vaine.   5
Conceale thy skill within thy facred breft,
     Though to thy paine.
The honor great which Poets wont to haue,
With worthy deedes is buried deepe in graue,
      Each man will hide his name,   10
      Thereby to hide his fhame,
And filence is the praife their virtues craue.

To praife, is flattery, malice to difpraife,
     Hard is the choice.
What caufe is left for thee, my Mufe, to raife   15
     Thy heau'nly voice?
Delight thy felfe on fweet *Parnaffus* hill,
And for a better time referue thy skill,
      There let thy filuer found,
      From *Cyrrha* wood rebound,   20
And all the vale with learned Muficke fill.

Then fhall thofe fooles that now preferre ech Rime
     Before thy skill,
With hand and foote in vaine affay to clime
     Thy facred hill.   25
There fhalt thou fit and skorne them with difdaine,
To fee their fruitles labour all in vaine;
      But they fhall fret with fpight,
      To fee thy glory bright,
And know themfelues thereto cannot attaine.   30
                   Mine

[110] MIne eies haue spent their teares, & now are drie,
My weary hand will guide my pen no more.
My voice is hoarse, and can no longer cry,
My head hath left no new complaints in store.   5
    My heart is ouerburdned so with paine,
    That sence of griefe doth none therein remaine.

The teares you see distilling from mine eies,
My gentle Muse doth shed for this my griefe.
The plaints you heare are her incessant cries,   10
By which she calles in vaine for some reliefe.
    She neuer parted since my griefe begunne,
    In her I liue, she dead, my life were done.

Then (louing Muse) departe, and let me die,
Some brauer Youth will sue to thee for grace,   15
That may aduance thy glory to the skie,
And make thee scorn blind Fortunes frowning face.
    My heart and head that did thee entertaine,
    Desire and Fortune with despite haue slaine.

My Lady dares not lodge thee in her brest,   20
For feare, vnwares she let in Loue with thee.
For well she thinkes some part in thee must rest,
Of that which so possest each part of mee.
    Then (good my Muse) flie back to heau'n againe,
    And let me die, to end this endlesse paine.   25

Breake

[111] BReake heauy hart, and rid mee of this paine,
    This paine that ftill encreafeth day by day:
By day with fighes I fpend my felfe in vaine,
In vayne by night with teares I wafte away: 5
    Away I wafte with teares by night in vaine,
    Teares, fighs, by night, by day encreafe this paine.

Mine Eyes no Eies, but fountaines of my teares,
My teares no teares, but floods to moyft my hart:
My hart no hart, but harbour of my feares,   10
My feares no feares, but feelings of my fmart:
    My fmart, my feares, my hart, my teares, mine eies
    Are blind, dryde, fpent, paft, wafted with my cries.

And yet mine Eyes, thogh blind, fee caufe of greefe:
And yet my teares, thogh dride, run down amaine: 15
And yet my hart, though fpent, attends releefe,
And yet my feares, though paft, encreafe my paine:
    And yet I liue, and liuing, feele more fmart,
    And fmarting, cry in vaine, breake heauy hart.

[112] WHere witt is ouer-rulde by will,   20
    And will is led by fond defire:
There Reafon were as good bee ftill,
As fpeaking, kindle greater fire:
    For where defire doth beare the fway,
    The hart muft rule, the head obay.   25

                              What

What bootes the cunning Pilots skill,
To tell which way to fhape their courfe:
When hee that fteers will haue his will,
And driue them where he lift perforce: 5
  So Reafon fhewes the truth in vaine,
  Where fond defire as King doth raigne.

[113] TWixt heate and colde, twixt death and life,
 I freeze and burne, I liue and die:
Which ioyntly worke in me fuch ftrife,   10
I liue in death, in cold I fry,
  Nor hot, nor cold, nor liue, nor dead,
  Neither, and both, this life I lead.

First, burning heate fets all one fire,
Whereby I feeme in flames to fry: 15
Then colde defpayre kills hotte defire,
That drenched deepe, in death I lie:
  Heate driues out cold, and keepes my life,
  Cold quencheth heate, no end of ftrife.

The leffe I hope to haue my will,   20
The more I feele defire encreafe.
And as defire encreafeth ftill,
Defpayre to quench it doth not ceafe:
  So liue I as the Lampe, whofe light,
  Oft comes, oft goes, now dim, now bright.   25

A

Sonnets, Odes, Elegies,

[114] *A liuing death.*

IF meanes be none to end my reftleffe care,
  If needes I muft orewhelm'd with forrow lie.
What better way this forrow to declare,   5
Then, that I dying liue, and cannot die.

If nought but loffe I reape in fteade of gaine,
If lafting paine doe euery day encreafe;
To thee(good Death) alas, I muft complaine,
Thou art of force to make my forrow ceafe.   10

If thou, becaufe I thee refufde fometime,
Now fhut thine eares, and my requeft deny,
Still muft I loue, and waile in woefull Rime,
That dying ftill I am, and cannot die.
              Spiro, non viuo.   15

[115] YE walles that fhut me vp from fight of men,
  Inclofde wherein, aliue I buried lie.
And thou, fometime my bed, but now my den,
Where, fmothred vp the light of Sunne, I flie.
    O fhut your felues, ech chinke and creuis ftraine,   20
    That none but you may heare me thus complain

My hollow cries that beate thy ftony fide,
Vouchfafe to beate, but beate them backe againe,
That when my griefe hath fpeech to me denide,
Mine eares may heare the witnes of my paine.   25
    As for my Teares, whofe ftreames muft euer last
    My filent cowch fhall drinke them vp as faft.
              Hopeleffe

THough naked Trees seeme dead to sight,
  When winter winde doth keenely blow,
Yet if the roote maintaine her right,   5
The Spring their hidden life will show.
    But if the roote be dead and drie,
    No maruell though the branches die.

While Hope did liue within my brest,
No winter storme could kill desire.   10
But now disdaine hath hope opprest,
Dead is the roote, dead is the spire.
    Hope was the roote, the spire was Loue,
    No sap beneath, no life aboue.

And as we see the rootelesse stocke   15
Retaine some sap, and spring a while,
Yet quickely prooue a lifelesse blocke,
Because the roote doth life beguile;
    So liues Desire which Hope hath left,
    As twylight shines when Sunne is reft.   20

ODE.

[117] ODE XII.

To his Heart.

NAy, nay, thou ſtriu'ſt in vaine, my Hart,
  To mend thy miſſe.   5
Thou haſt deſeru'd to beare this ſmart,
  And worſe then this.
   That wouldſt thy ſelfe debaſe,
   To ſerue in ſuch a place.

Thou thoughtſt thy ſelfe too long at reſt, 10
  Such was thy Pride.
Needes muſt thou ſeeke a nobler breſt,
  Wherein to bide.
   Say now, what haſt thou found?
   In fetters thou art bound.   15

What hath thy faithfull ſeruice wonne,
  But high diſdaine?
Broke is the threede thy fancie ſpunne,
  Thy labour vaine.
   Falne art thou now with paine,
   And canſt not riſe againe.   20

        And

And canſt thou looke for helpe of mee
      In this diſtreſſe?
I muſt confeſſe I pittie thee,
      And can no leſſe.   5
    But beare a while thy paine,
    For feare thou fall againe.

Learne by thy hurt to ſhunne the fire,
      Play not with all:
When clyming thoughts high things aſpyre,   10
      They ſeeke their fall.
    Thou ween'ſt nought ſhone but golde,
    So waſt thou blind and bolde.

Yet lie not ſtill for this diſgrace,
      But mount againe: 15
So that thou know the wiſhed place
      Bee worth thy paine.
    Then, though thou fall and die,
    Yet neuer feare to flie.

I   PHA-

[118] PHALEVCIACKS. II.

WIſdome warns me to ſhun that once I ſought for,
    And in time to retire my haſty footſteps:
Wiſdome ſent from aboue, not earthly wiſdome,   5
No ſuch thoughts can ariſe from earthly wiſdome.
Long, too long haue I ſlept in eaſe vneaſie,
On falce worldly releeſe my truſt repoſing;
Health and wealth in a bote, no ſterne nor ankor,
(Bold and blinde that I was) to Sea be taking: 10
Scarce from ſhore had I lancht, when all about mee,
Waues like hilles did ariſe, till help from heauen,
Brought my Ship to the Porte of late repentance.

> *O nauis, referent in mare te noui*
> *Fluctus.*————————   15

ODE.

[119] ODE XIII.

NOw haue I learn'd with much a doo at laſt,
    By true diſdaine to kill deſire:
This was the marke at which I ſhot ſo faſt,   5
    Vnto this height I did aſpire:
Proud Loue,now do thy worſt,and ſpare not,
For thee and all thy ſhafts I care not.

What haſt thou left wherewith to moue my minde,
    What life to quicken dead Deſire?   10
I count thy words and oathes as light as winde,
    I feele no heate in all thy fire.
Go change thy bow and get a ſtronger,
Go breake thy ſhafts and buy thee longer.

In vaine thou bait'ſt thy hooke with beauties blaze,   15
    In vaine thy wanton Eyes allure.
Theſe are but toyes for them that loue to gaze,
    I know what harme thy lookes procure:
Some ſtrange conceit muſt be deuiſed,
Or thou and all thy skill deſpiſed.   20

Scilicet aſſerui iam me, fugique catenas.

I 2   *Be-*

[120] *Being scorned, and disdained, hee inueighs against*
his Lady.

SInce iust disdaine began to rise,
 And cry reuenge for spitefull wrong: 5
What erst I praisde, I now despise,
And thinke my Loue was all too long.
  I tread in durt that scornefull pride,
  Which in thy lookes I haue descride:
  Thy beautie is a painted skin,   10
  For fooles to see their faces in.

Thine Eyes that some as Starres esteeme,
From whence themselues, they say, take light,
Like to thee foolish fire I deeme,
That leades men to their death by night.   15
  Thy words and othes are light as winde,
  And yet farre lighter is thy minde:
  Thy friendship is a broken reede,
  That failes thy friends in greatest neede.
    Vitijs patientia victa est.   20

[121] ODE XIIII.
The Tombe of dead Desire.

WHen *Venus* saw Desire must die,
   Whom high disdayne
   Had iustly slaine   25
  For killing Truth with scornefull Eye;

           The

The Earth fhee leaues, and gets her to the fkie,
  Her golden hayre fhee teares,
  Blacke weedes of woe fhee weares;
For helpe vnto her father doth fhee cry,   5
  Who biddes her ftay a fpace,
  And hope for better grace.

To faue his life fhee hath no skill,
  Whom fhould fhee pray,
  What doo or fay,   10
But weepe for wanting of her will?
Meane time, Defire hath tane his laft farewell;
  And in a Meddow faire,
  To which the Nymphs repayre,
His breathles Corps is laid with wormes to dwell; 15
  So Glory doth decay,
  When Death takes life away.

When Morning Starre had chafde the night,
  The Queene of Loue
  Lookt from aboue,   20
To fee the Graue of her delight:
And as with heedfull Eye fhee viewd the place,
  Shee fpide a flower vnknowne,
  That on his graue was growne,
Inftead of learned Verfe his Tombe to grace. 25
  If you the Name require,
  Hearts-eafe from dead Defire.

I 3   *An*

*My Mufe by thee reftor'd to life,
To thee Difdaine, this Altare reares,
Whereon fhe offers caufleffe ftrife,
Self-fpending fighs, and bootleffe teares*

5

*Long Sutes in vaine,
Hate for Good will:
Still-dying paine,
Yet liuing ftill.
Selfe-louing pride,
Lookes coyly ftrange,
Will Reafons guide,
Defire of change.
And laft of all,
Blinde Fancies fire;
Falfe Beauties thrall,
That bindes defire.*

10

15

*All thefe I offer to Difdaine,
By whome I liue from fancie free.
With vow, that if I loue againe,
My life the facrifice fhall bee.*

20

Vicimus & domitum pedibus calcamus amorem.
ANOMOS.

Certaine other Poems vpon diuerſe Subiects,
by the ſame Author.

Three Odes tranſlated out of Anacreon, *the Greeke
Lyrick Poet.*   5

[123] ODE I.

OF *Atreus* Sonnes faine would I write,
    And faine of *Cadmus* would I ſing:
My Lute is ſet on Loues delight,
And onely Loue ſounds eu'ry ſtring.   10

Of late my Lute I alt'red quite,
Both frets and ſtrings for tunes aboue,
I ſung of fierce *Alcides* might,
My Lute would ſound no tune but Loue,
    Wherefore yee worthies all farewell,   15
    No tune but Loue my Lute can tell.

I 4   ODE

[124] ODE II.

THe Bull by nature hath his hornes,
  The Horſe his hooues to daunt their foes,
The light-foot Hare the hunter ſcornes,   5
The Lions teeth his ſtrength diſcloſe.

The Fiſh, by ſwimming, ſcapes the weele,
The Bird, by flight, the fowlers net,
With wiſedome Man is arm'd as ſteele,
Poore women none of theſe can get.   10

What haue they then? faire Beauties grace,
A two-edg'd Sworde, a truſty Shielde,
No force reſiſts a louely face,
Both fire and ſworde to Beautie yielde.

[125] ODE. III.   15

OF late, what time the Beare turnd round
  At midnight in her woonted way,
And men of all ſorts ſlept full ſound,
O'recome with labour of the day.

The God of Loue came to my dore,   20
And tooke the ring and knockt it hard.
Who's there, quoth I, that knocks ſo ſore,
You breake my ſleepe, my dreames are marde?

A

A little boy forſooth, quoth hee,
Dung-wet with raine this Mooneleſſe night;
With that mee thought it pittied mee,
I ope the dore, and candle light.   5

And ſtraight a little boy I ſpide,
A winged Boy with ſhaftes and bow,
I tooke him to the fire ſide,
And ſet him downe to warme him ſo.

His little hands in mine I ſtraine,   10
To rub and warme them therewithall:
Out of his locks I cruſh the raine,
From which the drops apace downe fall.

At laſt, when he was waxen warme,
Now let me try my bow, quoth hee,   15
I feare my ſtring hath caught ſome harme,
And wet, will proue too ſlacke for mee.

Hee ſaid, and bent his bow, and ſhot,
And wightly hit me in the hart;
The wound was ſore and raging hot,   20
The heate like fury rekes my ſmart.

Mine hoſt, quoth he, my ſtring is well,
And laugh't, ſo that he leapt againe:
Looke to your wound for feare it ſwell,
Your heart may hap to feele the paine.   25

I 5   Ana-

[126] *Anacreons second Ode, otherwise.*

" **N**Ature in her worke doth giue,
" To each thing that by her doth liue:
" A proper gift whereby fhee may,   5
" Preuent in time her owne decay.
  The Bull a horne, the horfe a hoofe,
  The light-foote hare to run aloofe:
  The Lyons ftrength who may refift,
  The birds aloft, flie where they lift.   10
  The fifh fwimmes fafe in waters deepe,
" The filly worme at leaft can creepe:
  What is to come, men can forecaft,
" And learne more witt, by that is paft:
  The womans gift what might it bee,   15
" The fame for which the Ladies three,
" *Pallas, Iuno, Venus* ftraue,
" When each defired it to haue.

T. S.

Ana-

[184]

[127] *Anacreons third Ode, otherwise.*

CVpid abroad, was lated in the night,
 His Wings were wett, with ranging in the raine,
Harbour hee ſought, to mee hee tooke his flight,   5
To dry his plumes, I heard the Boy complayne.
  I opte the doore, and granted his deſire,
  I roſe my ſelfe, and made the Wag a fire.

Prying more narrow by the fiers flame,
I ſpide his Quiuer hanging at his backe: 10
Doubting the Boy might my misfortune frame,
I would haue gone for feare of further wracke.
  But what I feard, did mee poore wretch betide,
  For forth hee drew an Arrow from his ſide.

Hee pierſt the quicke, and I began to ſtart,   15
A pleaſing wound, but that it was too high:
His ſhaft procurde a ſharpe, yet ſugred ſmart,
Away hee flew, for now his wings were dry;
  But left the Arrow ſticking in my Breſt,
  That ſore I greeue, I welcom'd ſuch a Gueſt.   20

R. G.

The

[128] THe loweſt Trees haue tops, the Ante her gall,
  The flie her ſplene, the little ſparkes their heate:
The ſlender haires caſt ſhadowes, though but ſmall,
And Bees haue ſtings, although they be not great: 5
  Seas haue their ſourſe, & ſo haue ſhallow ſprings,
  And loue is loue, in Beggars, as in Kings.

Where riuers ſmootheſt run, deepe are the foords,
The Diall ſtirres, yet none perceiues it mooue:
The firmeſt faith is in the feweſt wordes,   10
The Turtles cannot ſing, and yet they loue:
  True Harts haue eyes, & eares, no tongs to ſpeake,
  They heare, & ſee, and ſigh, and then they breake.

       Incerto.

[129] *An Anſwere to the firſt Staffe, that Loue is vnlike* 15
   in Beggers and in Kings.

COmpare the Bramble with the Cedar tree,
  The Piſmyres anger which the Lyons rage:
What is the Buzzing flie where Eagles bee?
A drop the ſparke, no ſeas can *Aetna* ſwage.   20
  Small is the heat in Beggers breſts that ſprings,
  But flaming fire conſumes the hearts of Kings.

          Who

who fhrouds himfelf where flender hairs caft fhade?
But mighty Oakes may fcorne the Summer Sun:
Smal cure wil ferue,wher Bees the woũd haue made
But Dragons poyfon through each part doth run:　　5
　　Light is the loue that Beggers bofome ftings,
　　Deepe is the wound that *Cupid* makes in Kings.

Smal channels ferue,where fhallow fprings do flide,
And little helpe will turne or ftay their courfe:
The higheft banks fcarce holde the fwelling tide,　　10
Which ouer-throwes all ftops with raging force:
　　The bafer fort fcarce wett them in the fprings,
　　Which ouer-whelme the heads of mighty kings.

What though in both the hart bee fet of Loue?
The felf fame ground both corne and cockle breeds　　15
Faft by the Bryer,the Pine-tree mounts aboue,
One kinde of graffe,the Iade,and Iennet feedes:
　　So from the hart, by fecret virtue fprings,
　　Vnlike defire in Beggers and in Kings.

ANOMOS　　　　　　　　　　　20

A fong

[130] *A Song, in praife of a Beggers life.*

BRight fhines the Sun, play Beggers play,
   Here's fcraps enough to ferue to day.
What noyfe of Vials is fo fweete,   5
As when our merry clappers ring?
What mirth doth want where Beggers meete?
A Beggers life is for a King.
    Eate, drinke, and play, fleepe when wee lift,
    Go where wee will, fo ftocks be mift.   10
    Bright fhines, &c.

The world is ours, and ours alone,
For wee alone haue world at will,
Wee purchafe not, all is our owne,
Both fields and ftreetes wee Beggers fill.   15
    Nor care to get, nor feare to keepe,
    Did euer breake a Beggers fleepe.
    Bright fhines, &c.

A hundred head of blacke and white,
Vpon our downes fecurely feede,   20
If any dare his mafter bite,
He dies therefore as fure as Creede.
    Thus Beggers Lord it as they pleafe,
    And none but Beggers liue at eafe.
    Bright fhines the Sun, &c.   25

Vpon

[131] *Vpon beginning without making an end.*

Begin, and halfe is done, yet halfe vndone remaines,
Begin that half, & al is done, & thou art easd of pains
The second halfe is all, when halfe thereof is dun,   5
The other halfe is al again, new work must be begun
Thus he that stil begins, doth nothing but by halues,
And things half done, as good vndone, half oxen are
        (but calues.

[132] *An Epigram to Sir Phillip Sydney in Elegicall Verse,
 Tranflated out of Iodelle, the French Poet.*   10

         (Altar,
Cambridge, worthy *Philip*, by this verfe builds thee an
 Gainst time & tempeft, ftrong to abide for euer,
That praife of verfes no length of time can abollifh,
 Which *Greece* & *Italy* purchafed endles honor.
I then purfuing their fteps like glory to purchafe,   15
 Wil make thy memory famous in after ages,
And in thefe meafured verfes thy glory be founded,
 So be thy holy fauor, help to my holy fury.

        H ex-

[133] HEXAMETERS, *Vpon the neuer-enough praiſed
Sir Phillip Sidney.*

WHat can I now ſuſpect? or, what can I feare any longer?
Oft did I feare, oft hope, whil'ſt life in *Sidney* remained.
Of nothing can I now deſpaire, for nought can I hope for;
This good is in miſery, when great extreamitie grieues vs,
That neither hope of good, nor feare of worſe can affright vs.
And can I then complaine, when no complaint can auaile me?
How can I ſeeme to be diſcontent, or what can I weepe for?
He liues eternall, with endleſſe Glorie bedecked:
Yea ſtill on earth hee liues, and ſtill ſhall liue by the Muſes.

5

10

An-

[134] *An other vpon the ſame.*

WHat ſtrange aduenture? what now vnlook't for arriuall,
 Hath drawne the Muſes from ſweete *Boœtia* mountaines,
To chuſe our country, to ſeeke in *London* abiding?
Are faire *Caſtalian* ſtreames dride? ſtands *Cyrrha* no longer?
Or loue the Muſes, like wantons, oft to be changing?   5
Scarſe can I that ſuppoſe, ſcarſe thinke I thoſe to be Muſes.
No ſound of melody, no voyce but drery lamenting.
Yet well I wot too well, Muſes moſt dolefully weeping.
See where *Melpomene* ſits hidde for a ſhame in a corner.
Heare ye the carefull ſighes, fetcht from the depth of her entrailes? 10
There weepes *Calliope*, there ſometimes luſty *Thaleia.*
Ay me! alas, now know I the cauſe, now ſeeke I no further,
Heere lies their glory, their hope, their onely reioycing.
Dead lies worthy *Philip*, the care and praiſe of *Apollo*,
Dead lies his carcaſe, but fame ſhall liue to the worldes end. 15

Others

Sonnets, Odes, Elegies,

[135] *Others vpon the fame.*

WHom can I firſt accuſe? whoſe fault account I the greateſt?
  Where kept the Muſes,what countries haunted *Apollo*?
Where loytred bloody *Mars*? where lingred worthy *Minerua*?
What could three Siſters doe more then nine in a combat?
Was force of no force? was fayre entreatie refuſed?   5
Where is the Muſicke, that ſometimes mooued *Alecto*?
That gaind *Eurydice*, that left *Proferpina* weeping;
Chooſe whether of the twoo you liſt,your skill to be nothing,
Or your moſt faithfull feruants vnkindly rewarded.
And thou that braggeſt of skilfull furgery knowledge,   10
That canſt of Simples diſcerne the qualitie ſecret,
And giue fitt plaſters,for wounds that ſeeme to be cureleſſe,
Whereto auailes thy skill? that can not *Sidney* recouer,
And couldſt thou whilome preuaile with deſtinie fatall: 15

For

For King *Admetus* gainſt courſe of naturall order,
And canſt doe nothing to faue ſo faithfull a feruant?
As for *Mars* well I wot, cold froſt of *Thracia* kingdome,
Hath kild all kindnes, no ruth of him can be lookt for:
And daintie *Pallas* diſdain'd for-footh to be preſent,
Enuie perhaps: nay greefe as I geſſe, was cauſe of her abſence.
Only wee poore wretches, whom gods and Muſes abandon,
Lament thy timeleſſe decay with ſorrowfull outcries,
But yet if hap ſome Muſe, would adde new grace to my verſes,
Germany, France, Italy, Spaine, Denmark, Perſia, Turkey,
India where *Phœbus* climes from the ſea to the ſkie-ward,
India where *Phœbus* declines from ſkie to the Sea-ward,
Tartary, Pole, Lettow, Muſcouy, Bohemia, Norway,
All coaſts where riſing or falling *Phœbus* appeereth,
Should heare, and wonder to heare thy glory refounded:
Armenian Tigres enrag'd for theft of a youngling,

Princely

Sonnets, Odes, Elegies,

Princely Lions roaring, for want of prey to be ſtarued,
Fierce Beares, and grunting wild Boares,vpon *Arcady* mountaines,
Should ſtand aſtoniſht, forgetting naturall of-ſpring,
Forgetting hunger, forgetting ſlaughter appoynted.   5
As when *Calliopes* deere ſonne, ſweete harmony ſinging,
Vnto the true conſent of his Harpe-ſtrings tuned in order,
Drew from their places wilde beaſts and trees by the muſicke.
Swift-flowing *Hebrus* ſtai'd all his ſtreames in a wonder,
As if chill coldenes frorne had them downe to the bottome,   10
But for I wote too well my ſlender ſkill to be nothing,
Heere will I quite forſweare both Verſe and Muſe in an anger,
Leſt hap my rudeneſſe diſgrace thy glory by praiſing.

Dignum laude virum Muſa vetat mori.

To

[136] *To Time.*

ETernall time, that wasteſt without waſte,
That art, and art not, dieſt, and liueſt ſtill:
Moſt ſlowe of al, and yet of greateſt haſte,   5
Both ill, and good, and neither good, nor ill.
    How can I iuſtly praiſe thee, or diſpraiſe?
    Darke are thy nights, but bright & cleer thy daies.

Both free and ſcarce, thou giu'ſt and tak'ſt againe,
Thy wombe that all doth breed, is Tombe to all: 10
Whatſo by thee hath life, by thee is ſlaine,
From thee do all things riſe, by thee they fall.
    Conſtant, inconſtant, moouing, ſtanding ſtill,
    Was, is, ſhall bee, do thee both breed and kill.

I looſe thee, while I ſeeke to finde thee out,   15
The farther off, the more I follow thee;
The faſter hold, the greater cauſe of doubt,
Was, is, I know, but ſhall, I cannot ſee.
    All things by thee are meaſur'de, thou by none,
    All are in thee, thou in thy ſelfe alone.   20

A

[137] *A Meditation* ᴠpon *the frailty of this Life.*

O Trifling toyes that toſſe the braines,
  While loathſome life doth laſt!
O wiſhed wealth, O ſugred ioyes,   5
  O life when death is paſt:
Who loaths exchange of loſſe with gaine?
  Yet loath we deathe as hel.
What woefull wight would wiſh his woe?
  Yet wiſh we here to dwell.   10
O fancy fraile that feedes on earth,
  And ſtayes on ſlipp'ry ioyes:
O noble minde, O happy man,
  That can contemne ſuch toyes.

Such toyes as neither perfect are,   15
  And can not long endure,
Our greateſt skill, our ſweeteſt ioy,
  Vncertaine and vnſure:
For life is ſhort and learning long,
  All pleaſure mixt with woe;   20
Sicknes and ſleepe ſteale time vnſeene,
  And ioyes doe come and goe.
Thus learning is but learn'd by halfes,
  And ioy enioy'd no while,
That ſerues to ſhew thee what thou want'ſt.   25
  This helpes thee to beguile.
                                         But

But after death is perfect skill,
    And ioy without decay,
Whēn sinne is gone that blindes our eyes,
    And steales our ioyes away: 5
No crowing cocke shall raise vs vp,
    To spend the day in vaine,
No weary labour shall vs driue
    To goe to bed againe.
But for wee feele not wee want,   10
    Nor know not what we haue,
Wee loue to keepe the bodies life,
    We loathe the Soule to saue.

---

[138] *A Dialogue betweene the Soule and the Body.*
                  Soule.   15

A Y me, poore Soule, whom bound in sinful chains
    This wretched body keepes against my will!
Body Aye mee poore Body, whom for all my paines,
    This froward soule causlesse condemneth stil.
Soule Causles? whenas thou striu'st to sin each day? 20
    Causles: whenas I striue thee to obay.

Soule Thou art the meanes, by which I fall to sin,
Body Thou art the cause that set'st this means awork
Soule No part of thee that hath not faultie bin:
Body I shew the poyson that in thee doth lurke. 25
Soule I shall be pure when so I part from thee:
    So were I now, but that thou stainest mee.
                              Sap-

---

[139] *Sapphicks. Vpon the Paſſion of Chriſt.*

HAtred eternall, furious reuenging,
Mercileſſe raging, bloody perſecuting,
Slanderous ſpeeches, odious reuilings,
    Cauſeleſſe abhorring;   5
Impious ſcoffings by the very Abiects,
Dangerous threatning by the Prieſts annointed,
Death full of torment in a ſhamefull order,
    Chriſt did abide here.   10
Hee that in glory was aboue the Angels,
Changed his glory for an earthly Carkaſſe,
Yeelded his glory to a ſinfull out-caſt,
    Glory refuſing.
Mee that in bondage many ſinnes retained,   15
Hee for his goodnes, for his only goodnes,
Brought from hell-torments to the ioyes of heauen,
    Not to bee numbred.
Dead in offences, by his ayde reuiued,
Quickned in ſpirit, by the grace hee yeeldeth,   20
Sound then his prayſes, to the worlds amaſement,
    Thankfully ſinging.

ANOMOS

DIVERSE POEMS OF SVNDRY AVTHORS

K

[140] *A Hymne in prayse of Musicke.*

PRayse, Pleasure, Profit,is that three-fold band,
  Which ties mēs minds more fast thē Gardiōs knot
Each one some drawes,al three none can withstand,   5
Of force conioyn'd, Conquest is hardly got.
    Then Musicke may of harts a Monarke bee,
    Wherein Praise,Pleasure,Profit, so agree.

Praise-worthy Musicke is, for God it prayseth,
And pleasant, for brute beasts therein delight: 10
Great profit from it flowes, for why it raiseth
The minde ouerwhelmed with rude passions might.
    When against reason passions fond rebell,
    Musicke doth that confirme, and these expell.

If Musicke did not merit endlesse prayse,   15
Would heau'nly Spheres delight in siluer round?
If ioyous pleasure were not in sweet layes,
Would they in Court and Country so abound?
    And profitable needs wee must that call,
    Which pleasure linkt with praise doth bring to al.   20

Heroicke minds with praises most incited,
Seeke praise in Musicke, and therein excell:
God,man,beasts,birds,with Musicke are delighted;
And pleasant t'is, which pleaseth all so well.
    No greater profit is then selfe content,   25
    And this doth Musick bring,and care preuent.

K 2   When

When Antique Poets Muficks praifes tell,
They fay it beafts did pleafe,and ftones did moue:
To proue more dul then ftones,then beafts more fel,
Thofe men,which pleafing Mufick did not Loue.   5
  They fain'd, it Cities built, and States defended,
  To fhew the profit great on it depended.

Sweet birds (poore mens Mufitians) neuer flake
To fing fweet Muficks prayfes day and night:
The dying Swans in Muficke pleafure take,   10
To fhew, that it the dying can delight;
  In ficknes,health,peace,war,wee do it need,
  Which proues, fweet Muficks profit doth exceed.

But I, by niggard prayfing, do difprayfe
Prayfe-worthy Muficke in my worthles Ryme: 15
Ne can the pleafing profit of fweet layes,
Any faue learned Mufes well define.
  Yet all by thefe rude lines may clearly fee,
  Prayfe,Pleafure,Profit,in fweet Muficke bee.

I. D.   20

Ten

Ten Sonnets, to Philomel.

[141] SONNET I.

Vpon Loues entring by his Eares.

OFt did I heare, our Eyes the paſſage were,   5
    By which Loue entred to auaile our hearts;
    Therefore I guarded them, and voyd of feare
    Neglected the defence of other parts.
Loue knowing this, the vſuall way forſooke;
    And ſeeking,found a by-way by mine Eare: 10
    At which hee entring,my Hart pris'ner tooke,
    And vnto thee ſweet *Philomel* did beare.
Yet let my hart, thy hart to pittie moue,
    Whoſe paine is great,although ſmal fault appeare:
    Firſt it lies bound in fettering chaines of Loue,   15
    Then each day it is rackt with hope and feare.
And with loues flames t'is euermore conſumed,
Only,becauſe to loue thee it preſumed.

K 3   SON-

[142] SONNET. II.

O Why did Fame my Hart to Loue betray,
   By telling my Deares vertue and perfection?
Why did my Traytor Eares to it conuay,   5
   That Syren-song cause of my Harts infection?
Had I bene deafe,or Fame her gifts concealed,
   Then had my Hart been free from hopeles Loue:
Or were my state likewise by it reuealed,
   Well might it *Philomel* to pitty moue.   10
Thē shold she kno how loue doth make me lāguish,
   Distracting mee twixt hope and dreadfull feare:
Then shold she kno my care,my plants,& anguish
   All which for her deere sake I meekely beare.
Yea I could quietly deaths paynes abide,   15
So that shee knew that for her sake I dide.

SON-

[143] SONNET III.

Of his owne, and his Miſtris ſicknes at one time.

SIckenes entending my Loue to betray,
   Before I ſhould ſight of my Deare obtaine: 5
  Did his pale collours in my face diſplay,
   Leſt that my Fauour might her fauour gaine.
Yet not content herewith, like meanes it wrought,
   My *Philomels* bright beauty to deface:
  And Natures glory to diſgrace it ſought,   10
   That my conceiued Loue it might diſplace.
But my firme Loue could this aſſault well beare,
   Which Vertue had, not beauty for his ground:
  And yet bright beames of beauty did appeare,
   Throgh ſicknes vail, which made my loue aboūd.   15
If ſicke (thought I) her beauty ſo excell,
How matchleſſe would it bee if ſhee were well?

K 4   SON-

[144] Sonnet IIII.

Another of her Sicknes,and Recouery.

PAle Death himſelfe did Loue my *Philomel*,
　　When hee her Vertues and rare beutie ſaw:　　5
　　Therefore hee ſickneſſe ſent,which ſhould expell,
　　His Riuall life,　and my Deere to him draw.
But her bright beauty dazeled ſo his Eyes,
　　That his dart life did miſſe,　though her it hitt:
　　Yet not therewith content,new meanes hee tries,　　10
　　To bring her vnto Death, and make life flitt.
But Nature ſoone perceiuing, that hee meant
　　To ſpoyle her only Phœnix,her chiefe pride:
　　Aſſembled all her force, and did preuent
　　The greateſt miſchiefe that could her betide.　　15
So both our liues and loues Nature defended,
For had ſhee dide, my loue and life had ended.

SON-

[145] SONNET V.

*Allusion to Theseus voyage to Crete, against
the Minotaure.*

MY Loue is sayl'd, against dislike to fight,   5
   Which, like vild monster, threatens his decay:
   The ship is Hope, which by Desires great might,
   Is swiftly borne towards the wished Bay:
The company which with my Loue doth fare,
   (Though met in one) is a dissenting crew;   10
   They are Ioy, Greefe, and neuer sleeping Care,
And doubt, which ne'r beleeues good news for true
Black feare the Flag is, which my ship doth beare,
   Which (Deere) take downe, if my Loue victor be:
   And let white Comfort in his place appeare,   15
   When Loue victoriously returnes to mee,
Lest I from rocke Despayre come tumbling downe,
And in a Sea of Teares bee forc't to drowne.

            K 5   SON-

[146] SONNET. VI.

Vpon her looking secretly out of a window as hee passed by.

ONce did my *Philomel* reflect on mee 5
   Her Chriftall pointed Eyes as I paſſt by,
Thinking not to be ſeene, yet would mee ſee;
But ſoone my hungry Eyes their foode did ſpie.
Alas, my Deere, couldſt thou ſuppoſe, that face
   Which needs not enuy *Phœbus* cheefeſt pride, 10
   Could ſecret bee, although in ſecret place,
   And that tranſparāt glas ſuch beams could hide?
But if I had beene blinde, yet Loues hot flame
   Kindled in my poore heart by thy bright Eye,
   Did plainely ſhew when it ſo neere thee came, 15
   By more then vſuall heate, the cauſe was nie:
So though thou hidden wert, my hart and eye
Did turne to thee by mutuall *Sympathy*.

SON-

[147] SONNET. VII.

WHen time nor place would let me often view
    Natures chiefe Mirror, and my sole delight;
  Her liuely Picture in my hart I drew,   5
  That I might it behold both day and night,
But shee, like *Phillips* Son, scorning that I
  Should portray her wanting *Apelles* Art,
  Commaunded Loue (who nought dare hir deny)
  To burne the Picture which was in my Hart.   10
The more Loue burn'd the more her picture shin'd;
  The more it shin'de, the more my hart did burne:
  So what to hurt her picture was assign'd,
  To my Harts ruine and decay did turne.
Loue could not burne the Saint, it was diuine,   15
And therefore fir'd my hart, the Saints poore shrine.

SON-

[148] SONNET. VIII.

WHenas the Sun eclipſed is, ſome ſay,
   It thunder,lightning,raine,& wind portendeth:
   And not vnlike but ſuch things happen may, 5
   Sith like effects my Sun eclipſed ſendeth.
Witnes my throat made hoars with thundring cries,
   And hart with loues hot flaſhing lightnings fired,
   Witnes the ſhowers which ſtil fal from mine eies,
   And breſt with ſighs like ſtormy winds neare riued 10
Shine then once againe, ſweete Sun on mee,
   And with thy beames diſſolue clouds of diſpaire,
   Whereof theſe raging Meteors framed bee,
   In my poore hart by abſence of my faire,
So ſhalt thou proue thy Beames, thy heate, thy light, 15
To match the Sun in glory, grace, and might.

SON-

[149] SONNET. IX.

Vpon sending her a Gold Ring, with this Posie
Pure, and Endlesse.

IF you would know the Loue which you I beare,   5
  Compare it with the Ring, which your faire hand
  Shal make more pretious, when you shal it weare;
  So my Loues Nature you shall vnderstand
Is it of mettall pure? so you shall proue
  My Loue, which ne're disloyal thought did stain,   10
  Hath it no end? so endles is my Loue,
  Vnlesse you it destroy with your disdaine.
Doth it the purer waxe the more tis tride?
  So doth my Loue: yet herein they dissent,
  That whereas Gold the more tis purifi'd,   15
  By waxing lesse, doth shew some part is spent,
My Loue doth wax more pure by you more trying,
And yet encreaseth in the purifying.

SON-

[211]

[150] SONNET X.

MY Cruell Deere hauing captiu'de my hart,
   And bound it faſt in Chaynes of reſtles Loue:
  Requires it out of bondage to depart,
  Yet is ſhee ſure from her it cannot moue.   5
Draw back(ſayd ſhee) your hopeleſſe loue from me,
   Your worth requireth a more worthy place:
  Vnto your ſute though I cannot agree,
  Full many will it louingly embrace.   10
It may bee ſo(my Deere) but as the Sun
   When it appeares doth make the ſtars to vaniſh:
  So when your ſelfe into my thoughts do run,
  All others quite out of my Hart you banniſh.
The beames of your Perfections ſhine ſo bright,   15
That ſtraightway they diſpell all others light.

Melophilus.

A

[151] *A Hymne in praise of Neptune.*

OF Neptunes Empyre let vs sing,
  At whose command the waues obay:
To whom the Riuers tribute pay,   5
  Downe the high mountaines sliding.
To whom the skaly Nation yeelds
Homage for the Cristall fields
       Wherein they dwell;
And euery Sea-god paies a Iem,   10
Yeerely out of his watry Cell,
To decke great *Neptunes* Diadem.

The *Trytons* dauncing in a ring,
Before his Pallace gates, doo make
The water with their Ecchoes quake,   15
  Like the great Thunder sounding:
The Sea-Nymphes chaunt their Accents shrill,
  And the *Syrens* taught to kill
       With their sweet voyce;
Make eu'ry ecchoing Rocke reply,   20
Vnto their gentle murmuring noyse,
The prayse of *Neptunes* Empery.

             Th. Campion.

*This Hymne was sung by Amphitryte Thamesis , and
  other Sea-Nimphes in Grayes-Inne Maske, at the 25
  Court.* 1594.

                          Of

[152] *Of his Miſtreſſes Face.*

ANd would you ſee my Miſtres face?
  It is a flowry garden-place:
Where knots of beauty haue ſuch grace,   5
That al is worke, and no where ſpace.

It is a ſweet delicious Morne,
Where day is breeding,neuer borne:
It is a Meadow yet vnſhorne,
Which thouſand flowers do adorne.   10

It is the Heauens bright reflexe,
Weake eyes to dazle and to vexe:
It is th'Idæa of her ſex,
Enuie of whom doth world perplex.

It is a face of death that ſmiles,   15
Pleaſing, though it kill the whiles:
Where death and loue in pretty wiles,
Each other mutually beguiles.

It is fayre Beauties freſheſt youth,
It is the fain'd *Eliziums* truth: 20
The ſpring that wintred Harts renu'th,
And this is that my Soule purſu'th.

              Th. Campion.

                    Vpon

[153] *Vpon his Palenesse.*

(bee,
BLame not my Cheeks, though pale with loue they
  The kindly heate into my hart is flowne:
To cheerifh it that is difmaid by thee,   5
Who art fo cruell and vnftedfaft growne.
  For Nature cald for by diftreffed hartes,
  Neglects,and quite forfakes the outward partes.

But they whofe cheeks with careles blood are ftaind,
Nurfe not one fparke of Loue with their harts: 10
And when they woo,they fpeake with paffion faind,
For their fat loue lies in their outward partes.
  But in their brefts wher loue his court fhuld hold,
  Poore *Cupid* fits,and blowes his nayles for cold.

Th. Campion.   15

Of

[154] *Of Corinnaes finging.*

WHen to her Lute *Corinna* fings,
   Her voyce reuiues the leaden ftrings,
And doth in higheft notes appeere,   5
As any challeng'd Eccho cleere.
But when fhee doth of mourning fpeake,
Eu'n with her fighes the ftrings do breake.

And as her Lute doth liue or die,
Led by her paffions, fo muft I: 10
For when of pleafure fhee doth fing,
My thoughts enioy a fodaine fpring:
But if fhe doe of forrow fpeake,
Eu'n from my heart the ftrings doe breake.

                           Th: Campion.   15

[155] *A Dialogue betwixt the Louer and his Lady.*

LAdy, my flame ſtill burning,
  And my conſuming anguiſh,
Doth grow ſo great, that life I feele to languiſh,   5
Then let your Heart be moued,
To end my griefe and yours, ſo long time proued.
And quench the heate that my chiefe part ſo fireth,
Yeelding the fruit that faithfull loue requireth.

[156] *Her Anſwere.*   10

SWeet Lord, your flame ſtill burning,
  And your conſuming anguiſh,
Cannot be more than mine, in which I languiſh,
Nor more your Heart is moued,
To end my griefe and yours ſo long time proued.   15
But if I yeelde, and ſo your loue decreaſeth,
Then I my Louer looſe, and your loue ceaſeth.

Ignoto.

An

[157] *An Elegie.*

O Faithles World, and thy moſt faithles part,
 A Womans Harte:
The true Shop of varietie, where ſittes,   5
 Nothing but fittes,
And feauers of Deſire, and pangs of Loue,
 Which toyes remoue.
Why was ſhee borne to pleaſe, or I to truſt
 Words writ in duſt?   10
Suffring her eyes to gouerne my Deſpaire,
 My paine for Aire,
And fruit of time rewarded with vntruth,
 The food of youth.
Vntrue ſhee was, yet I belieue'd her eyes,   15
 Inſtructed ſpies,
Till I was taught; that Loue was but a Schoole
 To breed a foole.
Or ſought ſhe more then Triumphs of deniall,
 To ſee a tryall.   20
How farre her Smiles commanded my weakenes?
 Yeeld and confeſſe:
Excuſe not now thy folly, nor her Nature;
 Bluſh and endure
Aſwell thy ſhame, as paſſions that were vaine,   25
 And thinke thy gaine,
To know that Loue, lodg'd in a Womans Breſt
 Is but a Gheſt.

H. W.

Con-

[158] COnceipt begotten by the eyes,
    Is quickly borne, and quickly dies:
For while it seekes our harts to haue,
Meane while there Reason makes his graue: 5
For many things the eyes approue,
Which yet the hart doth seldome loue.

For as the seedes in spring time sowne,
Die in the ground ere they be growne,
Such is conceipt, whose rooting failes,   10
As childe that in the cradle quailes,
Or else within the Mothers wombe,
Hath his beginning,and his tombe.

Affection followes Fortunes wheeles;
And soone is shaken from her heeles;   15
For following beautie or estate,
Hir liking still is turn'd to hate.
For all affections haue their change,
And fancie onely loues to range.

Desire himselfe runnes out of breath,   20
And getting,doth but gaine his death:
Desire, nor reason hath, nor rest.
And blinde doth sildome chuse the best,
Desire attain'd is not desire,
But as the sinders of the fire.   25

As

As fhippes in ports defir'd are drownd,
As fruit once ripe, then falles to ground,
As flies that feeke for flames, are brought
To cinders by the flames they fought: 5
So fond Defire when it attaines,
The life expires, the woe remaines.

And yet fome Poets faine would proue,
Affection to be perfit loue,
And that Defire is of that kinde,   10
No leffe a paffion of the minde.
As if wilde beafts and men did feeke,
To like, to loue, to chufe alike.

                  W. R.

[159] MADRIGAL.   15

FAuftina hath the fairer face,
  And *Phillida* the feater grace,
    Both haue mine eie enritched.
This fings full fweetely with her voyce,
Her fingers make as fweete a noyfe,   20
    Both haue mine eare bewitched.
Ay me! fith Fates haue fo prouided,
My heart (alas) muft be diuided.

                        To

[160] *To his Ladies Garden, being abſent*
far from her.

GArden more then *Eden* bleſſed
  Art thou, thus to haue thy bowers,   5
Free'd from Winter,and ſtill dreſſed
With her faces Heau'n-ſet flowers.

Happy too are theſe thy Allies,
Where her faire feete deigne to tred,
Which departing Earths low Vallies,   10
Shall the Milky way be led.

Thy Trees whoſe Armes her embraced,
And whoſe fruit her lips did kis,
In whoſe vertuous minde well placed
The rare Tree of knowledge is.   15

Happy are: So thy Birds bee,
Whom ſhee learnes to ſing by Art,
Who in heauenly harmonie
With the Angels beares a part.

Happy, bleſt,and fortunate,   20
Bowers, Allies Trees,and Burds,
But my moſt vnhappy ſtate,
Far ſurmounts all reach of words.

T. Sp.

Vpon

[161] *Vpon his Ladies Sickneſſe of the Small Pockes.*

CRuel and vnpartiall Sickneſſe,
  Sword of that Arch-Monarke Death,
That ſubdues all ſtrength by weakeneſſe,   5
Whom all Kings pay tribute breath.

Are not theſe thy ſteps I tracke,
In the pure ſnow of her face,
When thou didſt attempt to ſacke
Her liues fortreſſe and it raſe?   10

Th'Heauenly Honny thou didſt ſucke,
From her Roſe Cheekes might ſuffize;
Why then didſt thou mar and plucke
Thoſe deere flowers of rareſt prize?

Mean'ſt thou thy Lord to preſent   15
With thoſe ritch ſpoyles and adorne,
Leauing mee them to lament,
And in Inkes blacke teares thus mourne?

No: Ile in my Boſome weare them,
And cloſe locke them in my hart: 20
Thence, nor time, nor death, ſhall beare them
Till I from my ſelfe do part.

Th. Sp.

[162] *A Reporting Sonnet.*

Her Face, her Tongue, her Witt, ſo fayre, ſo ſweet, ſo ſharpe,
   Firſt bent, then drew, now hitt, mine Eye, mine Eare, my Hart:
Mine Eye, mine Eare, my Hart, to like, to learne, to loue,
Her face, her tongue, her witt, doth leade, doth teach, doth moue.
Her face, her tongue, her witt, with beames, with ſound, with Art,   5
Doth blinde, doth charme, doth rule, mine Eye, mine Eare, my Hart:
Mine Eye, mine eare, my hart, with life, with hope, with skill,
Her face, her tongue, her witt, doth feede, doth feaſt, doth fill.
O face, O tongue, O witt, with frownes, with checks, with ſmart,
Wring not, vexe not, wound not, mine Eye, mine eare, my hart,   10
This Eye, this eare, this Hart, ſhall ioy, ſhall binde, ſhall ſweare,
Your face, your tongue, your witt, to ſerue, to loue, to feare.

[163] SONNET.

ONly (sweet loue) afforde mee but thy hart,
　　Then close thine eies within their iuory couers
　　That they to mee no beame of light impart,　　　5
　　Although they shine on all thy other louers.
As for thy lip of ruby, cheeks of rose,
　　Though I haue kist them oft with sweet Content
　　I am content that sweet content to lose,
　　If thy sweet will will bar me, I assent.　　　10
Let me not touch thy hand, but through thy gloue,
　　Nor let it bee the pledge of kindnes more;
　　Keepe all thy beauties to thy selfe, sweet loue,
　　I aske not such bold fauours as before.
I beg but this, afforde mee but thy hart,　　　15
For then I know thou wilt the rest impart.

L 2　　　　　　　ODE.

[164] ODE.

ABfence,heare thou my Proteftation,
   Againft thy ftrength,
   Diftance,and length;   5
Do what thou canft for alteration.
  For hearts of trueft mettle,
Abfence doth ioyne, and Time doth fettle.

Who loues a Miftris of fuch qualitie,
   Hee foone hath found   10
   Affections ground
Beyond time,place,and all mortality.
  To harts that cannot vary,
Abfence is prefent, Time doth tarry.

My Sences want their outward motions,   15
   Which now within
   Reafon doth win,
Redoubled in her fecret notions:
  Like rich men that take pleafure,
In hiding,more then handling Treafure.   20

By Abfence, this good meanes I gaine,
   That I can catch her,
   Where none can watch her,
In fome clofe corner of my braine,
  There I embrace and kiffe her,   25
And fo I both enioy and miffe her.
     L 2   Loue

[165] LOue is the linke, the knot, the bande of vnitie,
    And al that loue, do loue with their belou'd to be:
        Loue only did decree,
        To change his kind in mee.   5
For though I lou'd with all the powers of my mind,
And though my reftles thoughts, their reft in her did
        Yet are my hopes declinde, (find:
        Sith fhee is moft vnkinde.
For fince her beuties fun my fruitles hope did breede 10
By abfence from that fun, I hop't to fterue that weed
        Though abfence did indeede
        My hopes not fterue, but feede.
For when I fhift my place, like to the ftricken deere,
I cannot fhift the fhaft, which in my fide I beare: 15
        Ay mee it refteth there
        The caufe is not elfewhere.
So haue I feene the fick to turne & turne againe,
As if that outward chāge, could eafe his inward pain
        But ftill alas in vaine,   20
        The fitt doth ftil remaine. (grow,
Yet goodnes is the fpring from whence this ill doth
For goodnes caufde the loue, which great refpect did
        Refpect true loue did fhow, (owe:
        True loue thus wrought my woe.   25

Ignoto.

ODE

[166] SONNET.

BEft pleas'd fhee is, when Loue is moft expreft,
    And fomtime faies that loue fhold be requited;
      Yet is fhe grieu'd my loue fhould now be righted   5
      When that my faith hath prou'd what I proteft.
Am I belou'd whofe hart is thus oppreft?
    Or deere to her, and not in her delighted:
      I liue to fee the Sun, yet ftill benighted,
      By her defpayre is blam'de,and hope fuppreft.   10
Shee ftill denies, yet ftill her hart confenteth,
    Shee grants mee all, but that which I defire;
      Shee fuell fends, but bids mee leaue the fire,
      Shee lets me die, and yet my death lamenteth.
O foolifh Loue, by reafon of thy blindnes,   15
I die for want of Loue,yet kild with kindnes.

L 3

A MA-

---

[167] SONNET.

WHen a weake Child is ficke,and out of quiet,
    And for his tendernes can not fuftaine
    Phificke of equall ftrength vnto his payne,   5
    Phifitions to the Nurfe prefcribe a Diet.
Oh I am ficke,and in my fickneffe weake,
    And through my weakenes dead; if I but take
    The pleafanteft receipt that Art can make,
    Or if I heare but my Phifition fpeake.   10
But ah (fayre God of Phifick) it may bee,
    But Phifick to my Nurfe would mee recouer;
    Shee whom I loue with beautie nurfeth mee,
    But with a bitter mixture kils her Louer.
Yet I affure my felfe, I fhould not die,   15
If fhee were purged of her crueltie.

Son-

[168] SONNET.

WEre I as baſe as is the lowly playne,
   And you (my Loue,)as high as heau'n aboue,
Yet ſhould the thoughts of me your humble ſwaine,   5
Aſcend to Heauen, in honour of my Loue.
Were I as hight as Heau'n aboue the playne,
And you (my Loue) as humble and as low
As are the deepeſt bottoms of the Mayne,
Wherſo'ere you were,with you my Loue ſhould go.   10
Were you the Earth(deere Loue) and I the skies,
My loue ſhould ſhine on you like to the Sun,
And looke vpon you with ten thouſand Eyes,
Till heau'n wax't blind, and til the world were dun.
   Wherefo'ere I am,below,or els aboue you,   15
   Wherefo'ere you are,my hart ſhal truly loue you.

I. S.

L 4   *A*

[169] A MADRIGAL.

MY Loue in her Attyre doth ſhew her witt,
    It doth ſo well become her:
For eu'ry ſeaſon ſhe hath dreſſings fitt,   5
      For Winter, Spring,and Summer.
     No Beautie ſhee doth miſſe,
     When all her Robes are on:
     But Beauties ſelfe ſhee is,
     When all her Robes are gone.   10

[170] A MADRIGAL.

WHen I to you complayne,
    Of all the woe and payne,
Which you make mee endure without releaſe:
    You anſwere nought againe,   15
    But, Beare and hold your peace.
Deer I will beare,and hold my peace,if you,
Will hold your peace,and beare what I ſhall doo.

Son-

[171] SONNET.

THe Poets fayne that when the world beganne,
    Both ſexes in one body did remaine;
    Till *Ioue*(offended with this double man)   5
    Cauſd *Vulcan* to diuide him into twaine.
In this deuiſion, he the hart did ſeuer,
    But cunningly he did indent the hart,
    That if there were a reuniting euer,
    Ech part might know which was his counterpart.   10
See then(deere loue)th'Indenture of my hart,
    And reade the Cou'nants writ with holy fire:
    See(if your hart be not the counterpart,
    Of my true harts indented chaſt deſire.)
And,if it bee, ſo may it euer bee,   15
Twoo harts in one,twixt you my Loue and mee.

I. S.

L 5   SON-

[172] *An Inuectiue against Women.*

ARe women faire? I wondrous faire to see to,
  Are women sweete? Yea passing sweet they be to;
Most faire and sweete to them that inlie loue them,   5
Chaste & discreet to all, saue those that proue them.

Are women wise? Not wise, but they be witty,
Are women witty? Yea, the more the pitty:
They are so witty, and in witte so wily,
That, be you ne're so wise, they will beguile yee.   10

Are women fooles? Not fooles, but fondlings many,
Can women fond be faithfull vnto any?
When snow-white swans do turne to colour sable,
Then women fond will be both firme and stable.

Are women Saints? No Saints, nor yet no Deuills,   15
Are women good? Not good, but needefull euills.
So Angel-like, that Deuills I do not doubt them;
So needefull ills, that few can liue without them.

Are women prowd? I passing prowd, & praise them,
Are women kind? I wondrous kind, and please them: 20
Or so imperious, no man can indure them;
Or so kinde-hearted, any may procure them.

                              Ignoto.

                                   An

[173] *An Elegie in Trimeter Iambickes.*

Vnhappy Verſe! the witnes of my vnhappy ſtate,
Make thy ſelf fluttring wings of thy faſt flying thoght
And fly forth vnto my Loue, whereſoeuer ſhe be.   5

Whether lying reſtleſſe in heauy bed, or elſe
Sitting ſo cheereleſſe at the cheerefull boord, or elſe
Playing alone careleſſe on hir heau'nly Virginalls.

If in Bed, tel her that mine eies can take no reſt:
If at Board, tel her that my mouth can taſte no food: 10
If at her Virginalls, tell her I can heare no mirth.

Asked why, ſay waking Loue ſuffreth no ſleepe:
Say that raging Loue doth appall the weake ſtomak:
Say that lamenting Loue marreth the muſicall.

Tel hir, that hir pleſures were wont to lul me aſleep 15
Tel hir, that hir beautie was wont to feed mine eies:
Tel hir, that her ſweet tongue was wont to make me
            (mirth
Now do I nightly waſte, wanting my kindely reſt:
Now do I daily ſtarue, wanting my liuely foode:
Now do I alwayes die, wanting my timely mirth. 20

And if I waſte, who will bewaile my heauy chance?
And if I ſtarue, who will record my curſed end?
And if I die, who will ſay, this was *Immerito?*
        Edmund Spencer.
          Son-

[174] SONNET

MIne eie with all the deadly finnes is fraught,
  1. First *prowd*, fith it prefum'd to looke fo hie:
a watchman being made, ftoode gazing by,   5
  2. and *idle*,tooke no heede till I was caught:
And *enuious*,beares enuy that by thought
fhould in his abfence be to her fo nie:
to kill my heart, mine eye let in her eie,
  4. and fo confent gaue to a *murther* wrought: 10
5. And *couetous*, it neuer would remoue
from her faire haire, gold fo doth pleafe his fight:
  6. *vnchafte*,a bawde betweene my heart and loue:
  7. a *glutton* eye,with teares drunke euery night.
Thefe finnes procured haue a Goddeffe ire: 15
Wherefore my heart is damnd in Loues fweete fire.
                         H. C.

                             SON-

[175] SONNET.

*To t'wo most Honorable and Virtuous
Ladies, sisters.*

YEe Sister-Muses, doe not yee repine,   5
   That I *two* Sisters doe with *nine* compare,
   Since each of these is farre more truely rare,
   Then the whole Troope of all the heau'nly nine.
But if yee aske me which is more diuine,
   I answer, Like to their twinne-eies they are,   10
   Of which, ech is more bright than brightest starre
   Yet neither doth more bright than other shine.
Sisters of spotlesse fame, of whom alone
   Malitious tongues take pleasure to speake well,
   How should I you commend, sith eyther one   15
   All things in heau'n and earth so farre excell?
The onely praise I can you giue, is this,
That One of you like to the Other is.

                H. C.

                       Of

[176] ODE.

Of Cynthia.

TH' Ancient Readers of Heauens Booke,
  Which with curious eye did looke
      Into Natures ſtory;   5
All things vnder *Cynthia* tooke
      To bee tranſitory.

This the learned only knew,
But now all men finde it true,   10
      Cynthia is deſcended;
With bright beames,and heauenly hew,
      And leſſer ſtarres attended.

Landes and Seas ſhee rules below,
Where things change,and ebbe,and flowe,   15
      Spring,waxe olde,and periſh;
Only Time which all doth mowe,
      Her alone doth cheriſh.

Times yong howres attend her ſtill,
And her Eyes and Cheekes do fill,   20
      With freſh youth and beautie:
All her louers olde do grow,
But their hartes, they do not ſo
      In their Loue and duty.

This Song was ſung before her ſacred Maieſtie at a   25
  ſhew on horſebacke, wherwith the right Honorable
  the Earle of Cumberland preſented her Highneſſe
  on Maie day laſt.

Finis.

[236]

Additional Poems
in the Edition of 1608 (*B*)

Yet other 12. wonders of the world
neuer yet publiſhed.

1. *The Courtier.*

LOng haue I liu'd in Court,yet learn'd not all this while.
 To ſell poore ſutors, ſmoke: nor where I hate to ſmile;5
 Superiors to adore, inferiors to deſpiſe,
To flie from ſuch as fall,to follow ſuch as riſe,
To cloake a poore deſire vnder a rich array,
Nor to aſpire by vice,though t'were the quicker way.

2. *The Diuine.* 10

My calling is diuine,and I from God am ſent,
I will no chop-church be, nor pay my patron rent,
Nor yeeld to ſacriledge; but like the kind true mother
Rather will looſe all the child, then part it with another.
Much wealth I will not ſeeke;nor worldly maiſters ſerue,15
So to grow rich and fat,while my poore flocke doth ſterue.

3. *The Souldier.*

My occupation is the noble trade of kings,
The triall that decides the higheſt right of things:
Though *Mars* my maiſter be, I do not *Venus* loue,20
Nor honour *Bacchus* oft, nor often ſweare by *Ioue.*
Of ſpeaking of my ſelfe I all occaſion ſhunne,
And rather loue to do, then boaſt what *I* haue done.

4. *The Lawyer.*

The Law my calling is, my robe,my tongue,my pen,25
Wealth and opinion gaine, and make me Iudge of men.
The knowne diſhoneſt cauſe I neuer did defend,
Nor ſpun out ſutes in length,but wiſht and ſought an end.

Nor counſaile did bewray,nor of both parties take,
Nor euer tooke *I* fee for which *I* neuer ſpake.

5 *The Phiſitian.*

I ſtudy to vphould the ſlipperie ſtate of man,
Who dies, when we haue done the beſt, and all we can.
From praᶜtiſe and from bookes I draw my learned skill,
Not from the knowne receipt or *Pothecaries* bill.
The earth my faults doth hide,the world my cures doth ſee,
What youth and time affeᶜts, is oft aſcrib'de to me.   10

6 *The Merchant.*

My trade doth euery thing, to euery land ſupply,
Diſcouers vnknowne coſts, ſtrange Countries doth allye
I neuer did foreſtall, I neuer did engroſſe,
Nor cuſtome did withdraw, though I return'd with loſſe.   15
I thriue by faire exchange,by ſelling and by buying,
And not by *Ieʼwiſh* vſe, repriſall fraud, or lying.

7 *The Country-Gentleman.*

Though ſtrange outlādiſh ſpirits praiſe,ᴛownes & Country
The country is my home I dwel where I was borne. (ſcorne   20
There profite and command, with pleaſure *I* pertake,
Yet doe not Haukes and dogs,my ſole companions make.
I rule but not oppreſſe,end quarrels,not maintain,
See townes but dwell not there t'abridge my charge or train.

8 *The Bacheler.*   25

How many things as yet are deere alike to me,
The field,the Horſe,the Dog,Loue armes or libertie.
I haue noe wife as yet, whom I may call mine owne,
I haue no children yet,that by my name are knowne.
Yet if I married were, I would not wiſh to thriue,   30
If that *I* could not tame the verieſt ſhrew aliue.

9 *The Married man.*

I only am the man among all married men
That do not wifh the prieft to be vnlink'd agen,
And though my fhoo did wring,*I* would not make my mone   5
Nor think my neighbors chaunce, more happy then mine
Yet court *I* not my wife,but yeeld obferuãce due,   (owne.
Being neither fond, nor croffe, nor iealous,nor vntrue.

10 *The Wife.*

The firft of all our Sex came from the fide of man,   10
I thither am returnd, from whence our fex began.
I do not vifit oft,nor many, when *I* doo,
I tell my minde to few, and that in counfaile too.
I feeme not fick in health, nor fullen but in forrow,
I care for fomewhat elfe,then what to weare to morrow.   15

11 *The Widowe.*

My dying husbãd knew,how much his death wold grieue me
And therfore left me wealth to comfort and releeue me.
Though I no more will haue, I muft not loue difdaine,
Penelope her felfe did Sutors entertaine.   20
And yet to draw on fuch, as are of beft efteeme,
Nor yonger then *I* am, nor richer will *I* feeme.

12. *The Maide.*

I Marriage would forfweare,but that *I* heare men tell,
That fhe that dies a maide, muft lead an Ape in hell.   25
Therefore if fortune come,I will not mock and play,
Nor drive the bargain on, till it be driuen away.
Titles and lands *I* like, yet rather fancy can,
A man that wanteth gould, then gould that want's a man.

                          IOHN DAVYS.   30

A Lotterie preſented before the
late Queenes Maieſtie at the Lord
Chancellors houſe.1601.

A Marriner with a Box vnder his arme, containing all the ſeue-
rall things following, ſuppoſed to come from the Carrick, came
into the preſence ſinging this Song.

CYnthia Queene of ſeas and lands,
That fortune euery where commands,
Sent forth Fortune to the ſea
To try her fortune euery way.
There did I Fortune meet, which makes me now to ſing,
There is no fiſhing to the ſea, nor ſeruice to the king.

All the Nymphes of *Thetis* traine,
Did *Cynthiaes* fortune entertaine.
Many a iewell, many a iem,
Was to her fortune brought by them.
Her fortune ſped ſo well, as makes me now to ſing,
There is no fiſhing to the ſea, nor ſeruice to the king.

Fortune that it might be ſeene,
That ſhe did ſerue a royall Queene,
A franke and royall hand did beare,
And caſt her fauors euery where.
Some toyes fell to my ſhare, which makes me now to ſing,
There is no fiſhing to the ſea, nor ſeruice to the king.

And the ſong ended, he vttered this ſhort ſpeech.

GOd ſaue you faire Ladies all: and for my part, if euer I be
brought to anſwer for my ſinnes, God forgiue me my ſharking
and lay Vſurie to my charge. I am a Marriner, and am now
come from the ſea, where I had the fortune to light vpon theſe few

The Lottery.

Trifles. I muſt confeſſe I came but lightly by them, but I noe ſoo-
ner had them, but I made a vow, that as they came to my hands
by fortune, ſo I would not part with them but by fortune. To
that end I haue euer ſince caried theſe lots about me, that if 5
I met with fit company I might deuide my booty among them. And
now (I thanke my good fortune) I am lighted into the beſt compa-
ny of the world, a company of the faireſt Ladies that euer I ſaw.
Come Ladies try your fortunes, and if any light vpon an vn-
fortunate blank, let her thinke that fortune doth but mock her in 10
theſe trifles, and meanes to pleaſure her in greater matters.

The lots.

1 *Fortunes wheeles.*

Fortune muſt now no more on triumph ride,
The wheeles are yours that did her chariot guide.　　　　　15

2 *A Purſe.*

You thriue, or would, or may, your lot's a purſe,
Fill it with gould and you are ne're the worſe.

3 *A Mask.*

Want you a mask, heere fortune giues you one,　　　　　20
Yet nature giues the roſe, and lylly none.

4 *A Looking Glaſſe.*

Blinde fortune doth not ſee how faire you be,
But giues a glaſſe that you your ſelfe may ſee.

5 *A Hand-cherchef.*　　　　　25

whether you ſeeme to weepe, or weep indeed,
This hand-cherchefe will ſtand you well in ſteed.

6 *A Plaine Ring.*

Fortune doth ſend you, hap it well or ill,
This plaine gold ring to wed you to your will.　　　　　30

[243]

7 *a Ring with this Posy,*
   As faithfull as I finde.

Your hand by fortune on this ring doth light,
And yet the words doth hit your humor right.

8 *A Paire of gloues.*

Fortune thefe gloues to you in challenge fends
For that you loue not fooles that are her frends.

9 *A Dozen of points.*

You are in euery point a louer true,
And therefore Fortune giues the points to you.

10 *A Lace.*

Giue her the lace that loues to bee ftraight lac'd
So Fortunes litle gift, is aptly plac'd.

11 *A paire of Kniues.*

Fortune doth giue thefe paire of Kniues to you,
To cut the thrid of loue if't be not true.

12 *A Girdle.*

By Fortunes girdle you may happy be,
But they that are leffe happy are more free.

13 *A Paire of writing-tables.*

Thefe tables may containe your thoughts in part,
But write not all that's written in your hart.

14 *A Paire of garters.*

Though you haue Fortunes garters, you muft be
More ftaid and conftant in fteps then fhe.

15 *A Coyfe and Croffe-cloath.*

Frowne in good earneft, or be ficke in Ieft,
This coyfe and croffe-cloath will become you beft.

16 *A Scarfe.*

Take you this fcarfe, bind *Cupid* hand and foot
So loue muft aske you leaue before fhe fhoot.

17 *A falling band.*

Fortune would haue you rife, yet guides your hand,
From other lots to take the falling band.

18 *A ftomacher.*

This ftomacher is full of windowes wrought,
Yet none through them can fee into your thought.

19 *A paire of Sizzers*

Thefe fizzers doe your hufwifrie bewray,
You loue to worke though you were borne to play.

20 *A Chaine.*

Becaufe you fcorne loues Captiue to remaine,
Fortune hath fworne to lead you in a chaine.

21 *A Prayer-booke.*

Your fortune may prooue good another day,
Till fortune come, take you a booke to pray.

22 *A Snuftkin.*

Tis Summer yet a Snufkin is your lot,
But t'will be winter one day, doubt you not.

23 *A Fanne.*

You loue to fee, and yet to be vnfeene,
Take you this fan to be your beauties skreene.

24 *A Paire of bracelets.*

Lady your hands are fallen into a fnare
For Cupids manacles thefe bracelets are.

25 *A bodkin*.

Euen with this bodkin you may liue vnharmed,
Your beautie is with vertue ſo well armed.

26 *A Necklace*.

Fortune giues your faire neck this lace to weare,
God graunt a heauier yoke it neuer beare.

27 *A Cuſhinet*.

To her that litle cares what lot ſhe winnes,
Chaunce giues a litle cuſhinet to ſtick pinnes.

28 *A Dyall*.

The dyal's yours watch time left it be loſt,
Yet they moſt looſe it that do watch it moſt.

29 *A Nutmeg with a blanck parchment in it*.

This Nutmeg houlds a blanck but chaunce doth hide it,
Write your owne wiſh and Fortune wil prouide it.

30 B*lanke*.

Wot you not why fortune giues you to no prize
Good faith ſhee ſaw you not, ſhe wants her eyes.

31 *Blank*.

You are ſo daintie to be pleaſ'd God wot
Chance knowes not what to giue you for a lot.

32 B*lank*.

Tis pittie ſuch a hand ſhould draw in vaine
Though it gaine nought yet ſhall it pittie gaine.

33 *Blank*

Nothing's your lot, that's more then can be tould,
For nothing is more pretious then gould.

34 *Blank*.

You faine would haue but what, you cannot tell:
In giuing nothing fortune ſerues you well.

FINIS.   I. D.

A Contention betwixt a WIFE,
a WIDDOVVE and a MAIDE.

Wife.   WIDDOVV well met; whither goe you to day,
Will you not to this solemne offring goe?
You know it is ASTREAS holy day,   5
The Saint to whom all hearts deuotion owe.

Widow   Mary what else: I purpos'd so to doe;
Doe you not mark how all the wiues are fine,
And how they haue sent presents ready too
To make their offring at ASTREAS shrine.   10

See then the shrine and tapers burning bright.
Come friend, and let vs first our selues aduance
Wee know our place and if we haue our right
To all the parish we must lead the daunce.

But soft what means this bould presumpteous maid   15
To goe before without respect of vs?
Your forwardnes (proud girle) must now, bestaid
Where learnd you to neglect your betters thus?

Maide. Elder you are, but not my betters here,
This place to Maides a priuiledge must giue,   20
The Goddesse being a maid holds maidens deare,
And graunts to them her owne prerogatiue.

Besides on all true virgins at their birth
Nature hath set a crowne of excellence,
That all the wiues and widowes of the earth   25
Should giue them place and doe them reuerence.

Wife.   If to be borne a maid be such a grace,
So was I borne and grac't by nature to,
But seeking more perfection to embrace
I did become a Wife as others doe.   30

Widow.   And if the maide and wife such honour haue,
          I haue beene both, and hould a third degree:
          Most maides are Wardes, and euery wife a slaue,
          I haue my liuery sued and I am free.

Maide.   That is the fault that you haue maidens binne
          And were not constant to continue so:
          The fall of Angels did encrease their sinne,
          In that they did so pure a state forgoe.

          But Wife and Widowe if your wits can make
          Your state and persons of more worth then mine
          Aduantage to this place I will not take,
          I will both place and priuiledge resigne.

Wife.   Why marriage is an honourable state,
Widow   And widowhood is a reuerend degree,
ᴍ*aide*.   But maidenhead that will admit no mate
          Like maiestie it selfe must sacred be.

Wife.   The wife is mistresse of her family,
Widow   Much more the widow for she rules alone:
Maide.   But mistresse of mine owne desires am I,
          When you rule others wills and not your owne.

Wife.   Only the wife enioyes the vertuous pleasure,
Widow   The widow can abstaine from pleasures knowne.
Maide.   But th'uncorrupted maide obserues such measure
          As being by pleasures wooed she cares for none.

Wife   The wife is like a faire supported vine,
Widow. So was the widow but now stands alone,
          For being growne strong, she needs not to encline.
Maide.   Maides like the Earth, supported are of none.

a wife, a widow, and a maide.

Wife.   The wife is as a Diamond richly set,
Maide. The maide vnſet doth yet more rich appeare,
Wid.   The widow a Iewell in the cabinet
        which though not worne is ſtill eſteem'd as deare.   5

Wife.   The wife doth loue,and is belou'd againe,
Wid.   The widow is awak'te out of that dreame,
Maide. The maides white minde had neuer ſuch a ſtaine.
        No paſſion troubles her cleare vertues ſtreame.

        Yet if I would be lou'd, lou'd would I be,   10
        Like her,whoſe vertue in the bay is ſeene:
        Loue to wife fades with ſatietie,
        Where loue neuer enioyed, is euer greene.

Wid.   Then what's a virgin but a fruitleſſe bay?
Maide. And whats a widow but a roſe-leſſe bryer?   15
        And what are wiues but woodbindes which decay,
        The ſtately oakes by which themſelues aſpire,

        And what is mariage but a tedious yoake?
Widow. And what virginitie, but ſweet ſelfe loue?
Wife.   And what's a widow but an axell broke?   20
        Whoſe one part failing neyther part can moue?

Widow. Wiues are as birds in goulden cages kept:
Wife.   Yet in thoſe cages chearefully they ſing.
Widow. Widowes are birds out of thoſe cages lept,
        Whoſe ioyfull notes make all the forreſt ring   25

Maide. But maides are birdes amidſt the woodes ſecure,
        Which neuer hand could touch,nor net could take
        Nor whiſtle could deceiue nor bait alure,
        But free vnto themſelues do muſicke make.

Wife.	The vvife is as the turtle with her mate,
Widow.	The widow as the widow doue alone;
	Whofe truth fhines moft in her forfaken ftate,
Maide.	The maide a Phœnix, and is ftill but one.

Wife.	The wif's a foule vnto her body tied:
Widow.	The widow a foule departed into bliffe,
Maide	The maide an Angell which vvas ftellified,
	And now t'as faire a houfe defcended is.

Wife.	Wiues are faire houfes kept and furnifht well,
Widow.	widowes ould caftles void, but full of ftate,
Maide.	But maides are temples vvhere the gods do dvvell,
	To vvhom alone, themfelues they dedicate.

10

	But mariage is a prifon during life,
	vvhere one vvay out but many entries bee,
Wife.	The Nun is kept in cloyfter, not the wife:
	Wedlock alone doth make the virgin free.

1

Maide.	The maid is euer frefh-like morne in May.
Wife.	The wife with all her beames is beautifide,
	Like to high noone the glorie of the day.
Widow	The widow like a mild fweet euentide.

20

Wife.	An office well fupplide is like the wife.
Widow.	The widow like a gainfull office voide.
Maide	But maides are like contentment in this life,
	Which all the world haue fought, but none enioyd.

2

	Go wife to Dunmow, & demand your flitch.
Widow	Go gentle maid, go leade the Apes in hel.
Wife.	Go widow make fome yonger brother rich,
	And then take thought and die, and all is well.

<table>
<tr><td></td><td>Alas poore maid, that haſt no helpe nor ſtay.</td></tr>
</table>

	Alas poore maid, that haſt no helpe nor ſtay.	
Wid.	Alas poore wife, that nothing doſt poſſeſſe:	
Maide.	Alas poore widow, charity doth ſay,	
	Pitie the widow and the fatherleſſe.	5
Wid.	But happie widowes haue the world at will.	
Wife.	But happier wiues, whoſe ioyes are euer double.	
Maide.	But happieſt maides whoſe hearts are calme & ſtil,	
	Whō fear, nor hope, nor loue, nor hate doth troble.	
Wife.	Euery true wife hath an indented hart,	10
	Wherein the couenants of loue are writ,	
	Whereof her husband keepes the counterpart,	
	And reads his comforts and his ioyes in it.	
Wid.	But euery widowes hart is like a booke,	
	Where her ioyes paſt imprinted do remaine;	15
	But when her iudgements eye therein doth looke,	
	She doth not wiſh they were to come againe.	
Maide.	But the maides hart a faire white table is,	
	Spotleſſe and pure where no impreſſions be,	
	But the immortall Caraĉters of bliſſe,	20
	Which only God doth write and Angels ſee.	
Wife.	But wiues haue children, what a ioy is this?	
Widoѡ.	Widowes haue children too, but maids haue none.	
Maide.	No more haue Angels, yet they haue more bliſſe,	
	Then euer yet to mortall man was knowne.	25
Wife.	The wife is like a faire manured field:	
Widoѡ.	The widow once was ſuch, but now doth reſt.	
Maide.	The maid, like Paradice, vndreſt, vntild	
	Beares crops of natiue vertue in her breſt.	

[251]

Wife.	Who would not die a wife, as *Lucrece* died?
Widow.	Or liue a widow as *Penelope?*
Maide.	Or be a maid, and so be stellified,
	As all the Vertues, and the Graces be. 5
Wife.	Wiues are warme Clymates well inhabited:
	But maides are frozen Zones where none may
Maide.	But fairest people in the North are bred, (dwell.
	Where Africa breeds Monsters blacke as hell.
Wife.	I haue my husbands honour and his place. 10
Widow.	My husbands fortunes all suruiue to me.
Maide.	The moone doth borrow light, you borrow grace,
	When maides by their owne vertues graced be.
	White is my colour, and no hew but this
	It will receiue, no tincture can it staine. 15
Wife	My white hath tooke one colour, but it is
	An honorable purple died in graine.
Widow.	But it hath bene my fortune to renew
	My colour twice from that it was before,
	But now my black will take no other hewe, 20
	And therfore now I meane to change no more.
Wife.	Wiues are faire Apples seru'd in golden dishes.
Widow.	Widows good wine, which time maks better much
Maide.	But Maides are Grapes desired by many wishes,
	But that they grow so high as none can touch. 25
Wife.	I haue a Daughter equals you my Girle.
Maide.	The Daughter doth excell the Mother then,
	As pearls are better then the Mother of Pearle,
	Mayds loose their value, whe they match with mē

Widow.   The man with whō *I* match'd, his worth was such,
        As now I scorne a Mayd should be my Peare.
Maide.   But I wil scorne the man you praise so much,
        For Mayds are matchlesse, & no mate can beare.   5

        Hence is it that the Virgin neuer loues,
        Because her like, she finds not any wheare:
        For likenesse euermore affection moues,
        Therfore the Mayd hath neither loue nor Peare.

Wife.   Yet many Virgins maried wiues would be,   10
Widow.   And many a Wife would be a Widow faine.
Maide.   There is no Widow but desires to see,
        If so she might, her mayden daies againe.

Wife   There neuer was a Wife that lik'd her lot:
Widow.   Nor Widow but was clad in mourning weeds.   15
Maide.   Do what you will, mary, or mary not,
        Both this estate and that, repentance breeds.

Wife.   But she, that this estate and that hath seene,
        Doth find great odds betweene the Wife & Girle
        Indeed she doth, as much as is betweene   20
        The melting Haylestone, and the sollid Pearle.

Wife.   If I were Widowe, my merry daies were past,
Widow.   Nay, then you first become sweete pleasures guest.
        For Mayden-head is a continuall fast,
        And Mariage is a continuall feast.   25

Maide   Wedlock indeed hath oft compared bin
        To publick Feasts, vvhere meete a publick rout;
        Where they that are vvithout vvould faine go in,
        And they that are vvithin vvould faine go out.

     Or to the Ievvell,vvhich this vertue had,
     That men vvere mad till they might it obtayne,
     But vvhen they had it they vvere tvvife as mad,
     Till they vvere difpoffeft of it againe.   5

Wife. Maydes cannot iudge, becaufe they cannot tell,
     VVhat comforts and vvhat ioyes in mariage be.
Maide. Yes yes,though bleffed Saints in heauen do dvvell
     They do the Soules in Purgatory fee.

Widow. If euery vvife do liue in Purgatory,   10
     Then fure it is that Widows liue in bliffe,
     And are tranflated to a ftate of glory,
     But Maids as yet haue not attaind to this.

Mayde. Not Mayds? To fpotleffe Mayds this gift is giuen
     To liue in incorruption from their birth: 15
     And what is that,but to enherit heauen
     Euen while they dwell vpon the fpotted earth.

     The perfecteft of all created things;
     The pureft gould that fuffers no allay; (fprings
     The fweeteft flower that on th'earths bofome 20
     The pearle vnboard,whofe prize no price can pay

     The Chriftall glaffe that will no venome hold;
     The mirror wherein Angels loue to looke;
     Dianaes bathing fountaine, cleare and cold;
     Beauties frefh Rofe, and Vertues liuing booke. 25

     Of loue and fortune both the Miftreffe borne;
     The foueraigne fpirit that will be thrall to none:
     The fpotleffe garment that was neuer worne;
     The Princely Eagle that ftill flies alone.

She ſees the world, yet her cleare thought doth take
No ſuch deepe print as to be chang'd thereby;
As when we ſee the burning fire doth make
No ſuch impreſſion as doth burne the eye.   5

Wife.   No more (ſweete Maid) our ſtrife is at an end;
Ceaſe now, I feare we ſhall transformed be,
To chattering Pies, as they that did contend
To match the Muſes in their harmonie.

Widow.   Then let vs yeeld the honor and the place,   10
And let vs both be ſutors to the maid
That ſince the Goddeſſe giues her ſpeciall grace
By her cleere hands the Offring be conuaid.

Maide.   Your ſpeech I doubt hath ſome diſpleaſure mou'd,
Yet let me haue the offring, I will ſee: 15
I know ſhe hath both Wiues and Widows lou'd,
Though ſhe would neither Wife nor Widow bee.

IOHN DAVYS.

[180] The Lie.

GOe foule the bodies gueſt
   vpon a thankleſſe arrant,
  Feare not to touch the beſt
 the truth ſhall be thy warrant.
Goe ſince I needs muſt die
  and giue the world the lie.

Say to the Court it glowes
  and ſhines like rotten wood,
Say to the Church it ſhowes
  what's good,and doth noe good.
If Church and Court reply
  then giue them both the lie.

Tell potentates they liue
  acting by others action,
Not loued vnleſſe they giue,
  not ſtrong but by affection:
If potentates reply
  giue potentates the lie.

Tell men of high condition,
  that manage the Eſtate.
Their purpoſe is ambition,
  their practiſe only hate,
And if they once reply
  then giue them all the lie.

Tell them that braue it moſt,
  they beg for more by ſpending
Who in their greateſt coſt
  like nothing,but commending.
And if they make reply,
  then giue them all the lie.

5

10

15

20

25

30

[256]

The Lie.

Tell zeale it wants deuotion
   tell loue it is but luſt.
Tell time it meets but motion
   tell fleſh it is but duſt.
And wiſh them not reply
   For thou muſt giue the lie.

Tell age it daily waſteth,
   tell honor how it alters.
Tel beauty how ſhe blaſteth
   tell fauour how it falters
And as they ſhall reply,
   giue euery one the lie.

Tell wit how much it wrangles
   In tickle points of nyceneſſe,
Tell wiſedome ſhe entangles
   her ſelfe in ouer wiſeneſſe.
And when they do reply
   ſtraight giue them both the lie.

Tell Phiſick of her boldnes,
   tel skill it is preuention
Tel charity of coldnes,
   tell Law it is contention,
And as they doe reply
   ſo giue them ſtill the lie.

Tell Fortune of her blindneſſe,
   tel nature of decay,
Tel friendſhip of vnkindneſſe,
   tel Iuſtice of delay.
And if they wil reply,
   then giue them all the lie.

The Lie.

Tell Arts they haue no foundnes,
    but vary by efteeming,
Tel fchooles they want profoundnes
    and ftand to much on feeming.
If Arts and Schooles reply,
    giue arts and fchooles the lie.

Tell faith it's fled the Citie,
    tell how the country erreth
Tel manhood fhakes of pitty
    tel vertue leaft preferred,
And if they doe reply,
    fpare not to giue the lie.

So when thou haft as I,
    commanded thee, done blabbing,
Becaufe to giue the lie,
    deferues no leffe then ftabbing,
Stab at thee, he that will,
    no ftab thy foule can kill.

A Complaint
Of which all the ſtaues end with the
words of the firſt, like a
Seſtine.

1   5

YE ghaſtly groues, that heare my wofull cries
  Whoſe ſhady leaues do ſhake to heare my paine
Thou ſiluer ſtreame that doſt with teares lament
The cruell chance that doth my greefe increaſe:
Ye chirping birds whoſe cheereles notes declare   10
That ye bewaile the woes *I* feele in minde,
Beare witneſſe how with care *I* do conſume,
And heare the cauſe why thus I pine away.

2

Loue is the cauſe that makes me pine away,   15
And makes you heare the Eccho of my cries
Through griefes encreaſe: And though the cauſe of paine
which doth enforce me ſtill thus to lament
Proceed from loue, and though my paine encreaſe
By dayly cries which doe that paine declare,   20
And witneſſe are of my afflicted minde,
Yet cry I will,till crying me conſume.

3

For as the fire the ſtubble doth conſume,
And as the winde doth driue the duſt away,   25
So penſiue hearts are ſpent with dolefull cries,
And cares diſtract the minde with pinching paine.
But all in vaine I do my cares lament,
My ſorrow doth by ſobs, ſighs, teares, encreaſe:
Though ſobs,ſighes,teares,my torments doe declare,   30
Sobs, ſighes,nor teares moue not her flintie minde.

4

I am caſt out of her vngratefull minde
And ſhe hath ſworne I ſhall in vaine conſume,
My wearie daies my life muſt waſt away,
Conſum'd with paine,and worne with reſtles cries,
So *Philomele* too much oppreſt with paine
By his miſdeed that cauſeth her lament,
Doth day and night her mournfull layes encreaſe,
And to the Woods her ſorrowes doth declare.   1

5

Some eaſe it is,hid ſorrowes to declare,
But too ſmall eaſe to ſuch a grieued minde,
Which by repeating woes doth more conſume:
To end which woes I find at all no way,   1
(A ſimple ſalue to cure ſo great a paine)
But to deaths deafened eares to bend my cries.
Come then ye ghaſtly owles help me lament,
And as my cryes, ſo let your ſhrikes encreaſe.

6   2

For as your ſhrikes (the tunes of death) encreaſe
When ſun is ſet and ſhaddowes do declare.
The nights approach,ſo I from my darke minde
Since my bright Sun is fled,in cries conſume,
My night of woes, and though you flie away   2
Soone as the day returnes and ceaſe your cries,
Yet *I* by day find no releaſe of paine,
But day and night ſo foule a change lament.

7

But while I thus to ſenſles things lament   3
Ruth of my caſe in them thereby d'encreaſe
Which ſhe feeles not, with ſcoffs ſhe doth declare
My pangs to him,who firſt her wanton minde

A Complaint.

From me did win: Since when I ſtill conſume
Like wax gainſt fire, like ſnow that melts away
Before the ſun: Thus thus, with mournful cries
I lyuing die, and dying, liue in paine.   5

8

And now adiew delight, and farewell paine
Adiew vaine hope I ſhall no more lament
Her fained faith which did my woes encreaſe,
And yee to whom my greefes I thus declare,   10
Yee which haue heard the ſecrets of my minde,
And ſeing then my lingring life in paine conſume,
GROVE, BROOK, and BIRDS adiew, now hence away,
By death *I* will, and ceaſe my deadly cries.
                                        F. D.   15

Inscriptions.

YEe wofull Sires, whofe caufles hate hath bread
Greefe to your felues,death to my loue and me,
Let vs not bee dif-ioind when wee are dead,
Though we aliue con-ioind could neuer bee.
Though cruell ftarres deuide vs two one bed
Yet in one tombe vs two entombed fee.
Like as the dart was one, and one the knife
That did begin our loue and end our life.

[183] CLYTEMNESTRA TO
Her Son ORESTES, comming to kill
her for murthering his Father
AGAMEMNON.

HOLD, hold thy hand, vile fon of viler mother,
Death I deferue but ô not by thy knife.
One parent to reuenge wilt thou kill the other,
And giue her death that gaue thee (wretch) thy life.
Furies will plague thy murther execrable,
Stages will play thee,and all mothers curfe thee.
To wound this wombe or breft how art thou able,
When the one did beare thee, and the other nurfe thee?

[184] *AIAX.*

THis fword is mine,or will LAERTES Sonne
Winn this as hee ACHILLES armor wonne?
This fword which you ô *Greeks* oft bath'd haue known
In *Troian* bloud, Ile now bath in mine owne.

This feare-leffe breaft which all mine enemies fierce
Haue left vnpierft, now I my felfe will pierce.
   So men fhall fay, *Aiax* to none did yeeld
   But t' *Aiax* felfe,& *Aiax Aiax* kild.   5

[185] *ROMVLVS.*

NO common wombe was fit mee forth to bring,
    But a pure virgin Prieft, child to a King.
    No mortall father worthie was to breed mee,
Nor humane milke was fierce enough to feed me,   10
Therfore the God of Warre by wonder bred mee,
And a fhee-wolfe by no leffe wonder fed mee.
   In fine, the Gods becaufe earth was too bafe
   T'entombe me dead,did me in heauen place.

[186] FABRITIVS CVRIO, WHO   15
refufed gould of the Samnytes,& difcou-
red to King Pirrhus his Phifition that
offered to poyfon him.

MY famous Country vallues gould farre leffe,
    Then Conqueft braue of fuch as gould poffeffe.   20
    To be o'recome with wealth I doe not vfe,
And to o'recome with poyfon I refufe.
No hand loues more then mine to giue to many,
No hart hates more then mine to take of any.
   With fo firme-fteele vertue my mind hath armed,   25
   That not by gould,nor yron it can be harmed.

Inſcriptions.

[187] Cato Vticen, who ſlew himſelfe becauſe he would not fall into *Cæſars hands*.

CAESAR, thou haſt o'recome to thy great fame
Proud *Germanes*, valient *Gaules*, and *Brittans* rude.
Romes libertie(but to thine eternall ſhame)
And her great Champion thou haſt eke ſubdu'de.
Yet neither ſhall thy triumphes with my name,
Be grac't, nor ſword be with my bloud imbrude.
  Though all the conquer'd Earth do now ſerue thee,
  Cato will dye vnconquered, and free.

[188] An Epitaph vpon the hart of HENRY
the third, late King of France &
Poland : ſlayne 1589 by a
Iacobine Fryer.

Vpon the Tombe of his hart in the Church of Saint C*loud*
neare *Paris*; adioyning the houſe where he was ſlaine.

  ADSTA Viator & dole Regum vicem,
  Cor Regis iſto conditum eſt ſub marmore
  Qui iura Gallis, iura Sarmatis dedit.
  Tectus Cucullo hunc ſuſtulit Sicarius;
  Abi Viator, & dole Regum vicem.

  Thus Paraphraſtically Engliſhed.

WHither thy choyce, or chance thee hither brings
  Stay Paſſenger, and waile the hap of Kings.
This litle ſtone, a great Kings hart doth hould,
That ru'ld the fickle French, and Polackes bould

[264]

Whom with a mightie warlike hoſt attended
With trayterous knife, a couled monſter ended:
So fraile are euen the higheſt earthly things,
Goe paſſenger: and waile the hap of Kings.   5
F. D.

[189] A Dialogue in Imitation of

that betweene HORACE, and LI-
DIA, beginning *Donec gra-*
tus eram tibi &c.   10

1 *Louer.*

VVHile thou diddeſt loue me & that neck of thine
More ſweet, white, ſoft, thē roſes, ſiluer, downe,
Did weare a neck-lace of no armes but mine,
I enuide not the King of *Spaine* his crowne.   15

2 *Lady*

While of thy hart I was ſole Soueraigne,
And thou didſt ſing none but MELLINAES name,
Whom for browne CLOE thou doſt now diſdaine
[I] enuide not the Queene of Englands fame.   20

3 *Louer.*

Though CLOE, be leſſe fayre, ſhe is more kinde,
Her gracefull dauncing ſo doth pleaſe mine eye,
And through mine eares her voyce ſo charmes my minde
That ſo deare ſhe may liue *I*le willing die.   25

4 *Lady*

Though CRISPVS cannot ſing my praiſe in verſe,
I loue him ſo for skill in Tilting ſhowne,
And gracefull managing of Courſiers fierce:
That his deare life to ſaue, ile loſe mine owne.   30

[265]

5 *Louer.*

What if *I* fue to thee againe for grace,
And fing thy prayfes fweeter then before,
If *I* out of my hart blot Cloes face,
Wilt thou loue me againe, loue him no more?

6 *Lady.*

Though he be fairer then the Morning ftarre,
Though lighter then the floting Corke thou be,
And then the *I*rifh Sea more angry farre,   1
With thee *I* wifh to liue,and dye with thee.

[190] *Madrigall.*

Though you be not content
That *I* (poore worme fhould loue you,
As C*upids* power,and your fweete beauty caufe me,   1
Yet (deere) let pitty moue you
to giue me your confent.
To loue my life,as law of Nature drawes me,
And if my life *I* loue, then muft *I* too
Loue your fweete felfe,for my life liues in you.   2

[191] Madrigall
Borrowed out of a Greeke Epigram.

Hee's rich enough whofe Eyes behold thee;
Who heares thee fing a Monarch is:
A Demy-God who doth thee kiffe,   2
And loue himfelfe whofe armes infold thee.

[192] Madrigall.

Vpon her dreaming that ſhe ſaw him dead.

O fayre, yet murdring eies,
Starres of my miſeries, 5
Who while Night clouds your beames,
How much you wiſh my death ſhow in your dreames:
Is't not enough that waking you do ſpill me,
But you a ſleepe muſt kill me?
O kill me ſtill while you your ſleepe are taking 10
So you lend me kind lookes while you are waking.

The ſound of thy ſweete name, my deareſt treaſure,
Delights me more then ſight of other faces,
A glympſe of thy ſweete face breeds me more pleaſure,
Then any others kindeſt words and graces. 15

One gratious word that from thy lips proceedeth,
I value more then others Doue-like kiſſes:
And thy chaſt kiſſe in my conceipt exceedeth,
Others embraces, and loues cheefeſt bliſſes.

[193] Sonnet. 20

WHen traytrous *Photine*, *Cæſar* did preſent
With his great Riuals honourable head,
Hee taught his eyes a ſtreame of teares to ſhed
Hiding in his falſe heart his true content.

And *Hanniball* when Fortunes ballance light, 25
Raiz'd low-brought *Rome* and ſwai'd proud *Carthage*
While all but he, bewail'd their yeelding Towne, (downe,
He laugh't to eaſe his ſwelling harts deſpight.

Thus cunning minds can mask with diuerſe art,
   Griefe vnder fained ſmiles, Ioy vnder teares.
   Like *Hanniball* I cannot hide my feares
   Setting cleare lookes vpon a cloudy hart.
But let mee ioyes enioy, Deer,you ſhall try
Cæſar hid not his ioyes ſo well as I.

[194] *Sonnet.*

While Loue in you did liue,I onely liu'd in you,
   While you for me did burne,for you alone I burned,   10
   While you did ſigh for me, for you I ſigh't and mourned,
   Till you prou'de falſe to me, to you I was moſt true.
But ſince Loue died in you, in you I liue no more,
   Your hart a Seruant new,mine a new Saint enioyeth:
   My ſight offēds your eies,mine eies your ſight annoyeth   1
   Since you held me in ſcorne,by you I ſet no ſtore.
Yet if dead Loue,if your late flames returne,
   If you lamēt your change,& count me your ſole treaſure
   My loue more freſh ſhall ſpring, my flame more bright
                                   (ſhall burne.
   Ile loue none elſe but you,& Loue you without meaſure.   2
If not (Vntrue)farewell, in ſand Ile ſowe no graine,
Nor plant my Loue but where loue yeelds me loue againe.

[195] To Miſtreſſe DIANA.

PHœbus of all the Gods I wiſh to bee:
   Not of the World to haue the ouerſeeing
   For of all things in the Worlds circuit being,
   One only thing I alwaies wiſh to ſee.

Not of all hearbes the hidden force to know,
   For ah my wound by hearbes cannot be cured:
Not in the Sky to haue a place affured,
   For my ambition lies on Earth belowe.   5
Not to bee Prince of the Celeftiall quire,
   For I one Nymph prize more then all the Mufes
   Not with his bow to offer Loue abufes
   For I *L*oues Vaffall am, and dread his yre.
But that thy light from mine, might borrow'd be,   10
And faire *Diana* might fhine vnder me.

[196] Vpon his departure.

Madrigal.

SVre (Deere) I loue you not: for he that loueth
     When hee from her doth part   15
     That's Miftres of his hart,
A deadly paine, a hellifh torment proueth.
     But when fad Fates did feuer
Me farre from feeing you *I* would fee euer,
     I felt in my abfenting,   20
     No paine, nor no tormenting.
For fence of paine how could he finde,
That left his hart and foule behinde.

Epigrams tranſlated out
of Martiall.

Si memini fuerant tibi quatuor,Aelia,dentes
Expuit vna duos tuſſis,& vna duos.   5
Iam ſecura potes totis tuſſire diebus
Nil iſtuc quod agat tertia tuſſis habet.

Foure teeth of late you had,both black and ſhaking,
Which durſt not chew your meate for feare of aking.
But ſince your Cough,(without a Barbers ayde)   10
Hath blowne them out, you need not be afrayd.
   On either ſide to chew hard cruſts,for ſure
   Now from the Tooth-ache you liue moſt ſecure.

[198] *In herm. 15. l.2.*

Quod nulli calicem tuum propinas   15
Humane facis, Herme,non ſuperbe.

A Monſieur Naſo, verolè.

NASO let none drinke in his glaſſe but he,
Think you tis curious pride?tis curteſie.

[199] *De Manuella. 51. l. 1.*   20

Os & libra tibi lingit, Manuella,catellus,
Non miror merdas ſi libet eſſe cani.

I muſe not that your Dog turds oft doth eate,
To a tung that licks your lips,a turd's ſweete meate.

[200] *De Milone.*   25

MILO domi non eſt,peregre Milone profecto
Arua vacant; Vxor non minus inde parit.
Cur ſit ager ſterilis,cur vxor lactitet edam,
Quo fodiatur ager non habet vxor habet.

MILO liues long in France,and while he's there,
  his ground beares nought,his wife doth children beare.
Why fhould th'one barren,th'other fertile be?
His ground lackes plowing vp, fo doth not fhee.   5

[201] *De Codro. Li* .15. 3.

Plus credit nemo, quam tota Codrus in vrbe,
Cum fit tam pauper quomodo? cæcus amat.

CODRVS although but of a meane eftate,
  Trufts more then any Merchant in the cittie,   10
For being old and blind, he hath of late,
Married a wife,yong, wanton, faire,and wittie.

[202] *Ad Quintum.* 117. L.5.

Quæ legis caufa nupfit tibi Lælia,Quinte
Vxorem hanc poteris dicere legitimam.   15

THy lawfull wife faire Lælia needs muft bee,
  For fhe was forft by lawe to marrie thee.

[203] *Nil mihi das viuus, dicis poft fata daturum,*
Si non es ftultus, fcis Maro quid cupiam.

To A. S.   20

RIch Chremes while he liues will nought beftow,
  On his poore Heires, but all at his laft day.
If he be halfe as wife as rich I trow,
He thinks that for his life they feldome pray.

[204] *Semper eris pauper, fi pauper es, AEmiliane,*   25
Dantur opes nullis nunc nifi diuitibus.

To all poore fchollers

FAile yee of wealth, of wealth ye ftill will faile,
  None but fat fowes are now greaz'd in the taile.

[205] *In Cinnam.* 42. *L.* 7.

Primum est vt præstes, si quid te, Cinna rogabo,
Illud deinde sequens, vt cito, Cinna, neges.
Diligo præstantem, non odi, Cinna, negantem,   5
Sed tu nec præstas, nec cito, Cinna, negas.

To his frinds.

MY iust demands soone graunt or soone deny,
  Th'one frendship showes, and th'other curtesie.
But who nor soon doth graunt, nor soone say noe,   10
Doth not true frendship, nor good manners know.

[206] *In Cinnam.* 107. *L.* 5.

Esse nihil dicis, quicquid petis, improbe Cinna, ·
Si nil Cinna petis, nil tibi Cinna nego.

WHat so'ere you coggingly require,   15
  T'is nothing (Cinna) still you cry:
Then Cinna you haue your desire,
If you aske nought, nought I deny.

[207] *De Philone.* 48. *L.* 5.

Nunquam se cænasse domi Philo iurat, & hoc est.   20
Non cænat quoties nemo vocauit eum.

Philo sweares he ne're eates at home a nightes:
He meanes, he fasts when no man him inuites.

[208] 12. *L.* 12.   ·

YOu promise mountaines still to mee,   25
  When ouer-night stark-drunk you bee.
But nothing you performe next day,
Hence foorth bee morning drunk, I pray.

[209] *Ad Peſſimos Coniuges*.35. *L.*8.

C*Vm ſitis ſimiles,pareſque vita:*
 Vxor peſſima,peſſimus maritus,
Miror non bene conuenire vobis.   5

W<small>HY</small> doe your wife and you ſo ill agree,
 Since you in manners ſo well matched be?
Thou brazen-fac'd,ſhe impudently bould,
Thou ſtill doſt brawle,ſhe euermore doth ſcould.
Thou ſeldome ſober art, ſhe often drunk,   10
Thou a whore hunting knaue, ſhe a knowne Punck.
Both of you filch,both ſweare, and damne, and lie,
And both take pawnes, and *Iewiſh* vſurie.
   Not manners like make man and wife agree,
   Their manners muſt both like and vertuous bee.   15

Epigrams.

[210] *A Rule for Courtiers.*

H<small>Ee</small> that will thriue in Court muſt oft become,
 Againſt his will, both blinde and deafe and dombe.

[211] *On a painted Curtizan.*   20

W<small>Hoſoeuer</small> ſaith thou ſelleſt all, doth ieſt,
 Thou buy'ſt thy beautie that ſelles all the reſt.

[212] *In Aulam.*

H<small>Er</small> Sons rich *Aula* tearmes her Leachers all,
 Whom other Dames loues, friends, and ſeruants call.   25
     And ſure me thinks her wit,
     Giues them a name more fit.
For if all mothers then their ſons do call
Whom they haue only borne 9 months in all,
May ſhe not call them ſons with better reaſon,   30
Whom ſhe hath borne 9 times as long a ſeaſon.

[273]

Epigrams.

[213] *For a Looking glasse.*

IF thou be faire, thy beauties beautifie,
With vertuous deeds and manners anſwerable:
If thou be foule, thy beauties want ſupply,
With a faire minde and actions commendable.

[214] *In Aſinium.*

THou ſtill wert wont in earneſt or in ieſt,
To praiſe an Aſſe as a moſt worthie beſt.
Now like an Aſſe thy ſelf thou ſtill commendeſt,   10
Whatſ'ere thou ſpeakſt with thine owne praiſe thou endeſt.
Oh I perceiue thou praiſeſt lernedly,
An Aſſe in *Theſi* and *Hippotheſi.*

[215] *On a Limping Cuccold.*

THou euermore doſt ancient Poets blame,   1
For ſaining V E N V S wife to V V L C A N lame.
I blame the ſtarres and *Hymen* to that gaue
A faire ſtraight wife to thee a foule lame knaue,
And nought doth eaſe my griefe but only this,
Thy V E N V S now hath got a M A R S to kiſſe.   20

[216] *On Crambo a lowzie ſhifter.*

BY want of ſhift ſince lice at firſt are bred,
And after by the ſame encreaſt and fed.
Crambo I muſe how you haue lice ſo many,
Since all men know you ſhift as much as any.   2

[217] *In Quintum.*

Quintus is burnt and may thereof be glad,
For being poore he hath a good pretence,
At euery Church to craue beneuolence
For one that had by fire loſt all he had.   30

Epigrams.

[218] *In Sabam.*

WHy will not S*aba* in a glaſſe behold
   Her face, ſince ſhe grew wrinkled,pale and old?
Doubtles *I* think ſhee doubts that ougly ſight   5
Like Cow-turd IO would herſelfe affright.

[219] *In Aulum.*

AVLVS giues nought, men ſay,though much he craue,
   Yet I can tell to whom the pox he gaue.

F. D.   10

T E N
SONNETS.
By
T. W.

[220] A Dialogue betweene the
Louer and his heart.

L. SPeake gentle heart, where is thy dwelling place?
H. With her whofe birth the heauens thēfelus haue bleſt.
L. What doſt thou there? H. Somtimes behold her face,   5
    And lodge fomtimes within her chriſtall breſt.
        L. She cold, thou hot, how can you then agree?
        H. Not nature now, but loue doth gouerne me.

L. With her wilt thou remaine, and let me die?
H. If I returne, we both ſhall die for greefe.   10
L. If ſtill thou ſtay, what ſhall I get thereby?
H. Ile mooue her heart to purchafe thy releefe.
        L. What if her heart be hard and ſtop his eares
        H. *I*le figh aloud, and make him foft with teares.

L. If that preuaile wilt thou returne from thence?   15
H. Not *I* alone my heart ſhall come with me.
L. Then will you both liue vnder my defence?
H. So long as life will let vs both agree.
        Why then Difpaire, go pack thee hence away,
        I liue in hope to haue a happy day.   20

[221] A Dialogue betweene a
Louer, Death, and Loue.

      Louer.   (preſt.
COme gentle Death D. Who calles? *L.* One that's op-
  D. What is thy will? *L.* That thou abridge my woe,   25
By cutting of my life. *D.* Ceafe thy requeſt,
I cannot kill thee yet. *L.* Alas why foe?
   D. Thou want'ſt thy heart. *L.* who ſtole that fame away?
   D. Loue whom thou feru'ſt, entreat him if thou may.

Louer.

COme *Cupid* come. *C.* who calleth me ſo oft?
*L.*Thy Vaſſall true whom thou ſhouldſt know by night,
*C.*What makes thy cry ſo faint? *L.* My voyce is ſoft,
Quite broke and ſpent with crying day and night.
*C.*Why then what's thy requeſt? *L.* That thou reſtore,
To mee my heart and ſteale the ſame no more.

ANd thou ô Death when I poſſeſſe my heart,
Diſpatch me then at once. *D.* Alas why ſo?
L. By promiſe thou art bound to end my ſmart
D. But if thy heart returne,then what's thy woe?
    *L.*That brought from froſt,it neuer will deſire
    To reſt with mee that am more hot then fire.

[222] That time hath no power to
end or diminiſh his Loue.

TIme waſteth yeares,and months,and dayes,and howers
  Time doth conſume,fame,riches, wit, and ſtrength,
Time kils the greeneſt hearbes, and ſweeteſt flowers
Time weares out youth, and Beauties pride at length,
Time maketh euery ᴛree to die and rot:
Time turneth oft our pleaſures into paine.
Time cauſeth Warres, and wronges to be forgot,
Time cleares the sky that firſt hung full of raine,
Time brings to nought the mightieſt Princes ſtate,
Time brings a flood from new reſolued ſnow,
Time calmes the ſea where tempeſts roared late,
Time eates whatſo'ere the moon doth ſee below:
    Yet ſhall no time vpon my heart preuaile,
    Nor any time ſhall make my loue to faile.

[223] *Loues Hyperboles.*

IF Loue had loſt his ſhaftes, and *Ioue* downe threw
His thunder-bolts, or ſpent his forked fire,
They only might recou'red be a new   5
From out my heart croſſe-wounded with deſire.
   Or if debate by *Mars* were loſt a ſpace,
    It might be found within the ſelfe ſame place.

IF *Neptunes* waues were all dried vp and gone
My weeping eyes ſo many teares diſtill,   10
That greater ſeas might grow by them alone:
Of if no flame were yet remaining ſtill.
   In *Vulcans* forge he might from out my breſt
    Make choyce of ſuch as ſhould befit him beſt.

IF *AEOLE* were depriued of his charge,   15
Yet ſoone could *I* reſtore his windes againe,
By ſobbing ſighes which forth I blow at large
To moue her minde that pleaſures in my paine,
   What man but I could thus encline his will,
    To liue in loue, that hath noe end of ill.   20

[224] An Inuectiue againſt loue.

LOue is a ſowre delight, a ſugred greefe,
A liuing death an euer-dying life.
A breath of reaſons law, a ſecret theefe
A ſea of teares, an euerlaſting ſtrife.   25
    A baite for fooles, a ſcourge of noble wits.
   A deadly wound, a ſhot that euer hits.

Loue is a blinded God, a way-ward boy,
A laberinth of doubts, an idle luſt,
A ſlaue to beauties will, a witleſſe toy,   30

A rauenous bird, a Tyrant moſt vniuſt.
>A burning heate in froſt, a flattering foe,
>A priuate hell, a very world of woe.

Yet mightie *L*oue regard not what I ſay,
Who in a traunce doe lie, reſt of my wits
But blame the light that leades me thus aſtray,
And makes my tongue thus raue by frantick fits,
>Yet hurt her not, leſt I ſuſtaine the ſmart.
>Which am content to lodge her in my hart.

[225] Petrarks Sonnet tranſlated.

*P*ace non trouo, *&* non ho da far guerra.

I Ioy not Peace where yet no warre is found
I feare and hope, I burne yet freeze withall.
I mount to heauen yet lie ſtill on the ground
I nothing hold yet *I* compaſſe all.
>I liue her bond, which neither is my foe,
>Nor friend,nor holds me faſt,nor lets me goe.

Loue will not that I liue, nor let me die,
Nor locks me faſt, nor ſuffers me to ſcape,
I want both eyes and tongue yet ſee and crie.
I wiſh for death, yet after help *I* gape.
>I hate my ſelfe, yet loue another wight
>And feede on griefe in lieu of ſweet delight.

At ſelfe ſame time *I* both lament and ioy,
I ſtill am pleaſ'd, and yet diſpleaſed ſtill:
Loue ſomtimes ſeemes a God ſomtimes a Boy,
Somtimes *I* ſinke, ſomtimes I ſwim at will.
>T'wixt death and life ſmall difference I make,
>All this(deere Dame) endure *I* for thy ſake

[226] HE PROVES HIMSELF

To endure the hellifh torments
of *Tantalus, Ixion, Titius,*
Sifyphus and the B*elides.*

IN that *I* thirft for fuch a Goddeffe grace,   5
As wants remorfe like *Tantalus* I dy,
My ftate is equall to *Ixions* cafe,
Whofe mangled lims are turn'd continually.
    In that my rowling toiles can haue no end,
    Nor loue, nor time, nor chaunce will ftand my frend.   10

IN that my heart confuming neuer dies,
I feele with *Titius* an equall paine,
Vpon whofe heart a vulture feeding lies.
*I*n that *I* rife through hope, and fall againe,
    By feare, like *Sifyphus I* labour ftill   15
    To turne a rowling ftone againft the hill.

IN that *I* make my vowes to her alone,
Whofe eares are deafe,and will retaine no found,
With *Belides* my ftate is all but one,
Which fill a Tub whofe bottome is not found.   20
    Thus in my heart fince loue therein did dwell
    Are all the torments to be found of hell.

[227] *Loues difcommodities.*

VV here heate of loue doth once poffeffe the heart,
    There cares oppreffe the minde with wonders ill.   25
Wit runs awry not fearing future fmart,
And fond defire doth ouermaifter Will.
    The belly neither cares for meate nor drink,
    Nor ouer-watched eyes defire to wink.

FOotſteps are falſe, and wauering too and fro;
  The pleaſing flower of Beautie fades away,
Reaſon retires, and pleaſure brings in woe,
And wiſedome yeeldeth place to black decay.   5
    Counſell and fame, and frendſhip,are contemn'd
    And baſhfull ſhame, and Gods themſelues condemn'd.

WAtchfull ſuſpect is linked with diſpaire,
  Inconſtant hope is often drown'd in feares,
What folly hurts, Fortune cannot repaire,   10
And miſery doth ſwim in ſeas of teares.
    Long vſe of Life is but a lingring foe,
    And gentle Death is only end of woe.

[228] Allegoryof his Loue to a Ship.

THe Souldier worne with warres delights in peace,   15
  The pilgrime in his eaſe,when toiles are paſt,
The Ship to gaine the Port, when ſtormes doe ceaſe,
And I reioyce diſcharg'd from Loue at laſt.
    Whom while I ſeru'd;peace, reſt, and land I loſt,
    With wars,with toyles,with ſtormes,worne,tir'd,& toſt. 20

SWeet Libertie now giues me leaue to ſing,
  What world it was,where loue the rule did beare,
How fooliſh Chaunce by lots rul'd eu'ry thing,
How Error was man-ſaile,each waue a teare.
    The maiſter Loue himſelfe,deep ſighes were winde, 25
    Cares row'd with vowes,the Ship a penſiue minde.

FAlſe Hope the healme,oft turn'd the Ship about,
  And conſtant Faith ſtood vp for midle maſt,
Diſpaire the Cable wiſhed all with doubt,
Held griping griefe the piked Anchor faſt,   30
    Beautie was all the rocks, but I at laſt,
    Haue gain'd the Port,and now my loue is paſt.

[229] *Execration of his paſſed* Loue.

I Curſe the time, wherein theſe Lips of mine,
Did pray or praiſe the Dame that was vnkind.
I Curſe my *I*nk, my Paper, and each line,⠀⠀⠀⠀⠀⠀⠀⠀5
My hand hath writ in hope to moue her minde.
⠀I Curſe her hollow heart, and flattering eyes,
⠀Whoſe ſlie deceits did cauſe my mourning cryes.

I Curſe the ſugred ſpeech and *Syrenes* ſong,
Wherewith ſo oft ſhee hath bewitcht mine eare⠀⠀⠀10
I Curſe my fooliſh will that ſtaid ſo long
And tooke delight to bide t'wixt hope and feare,
⠀I curſe the howre wherein *I* firſt began,
⠀By louing looks to proue a witleſſe man.

I Curſe thoſe daies which *I* haue ſpent in vaine,⠀⠀⠀15
In louing one vngratfull and vnkinde,
I curſe the bow and ſhaftes that bred my paine,
And *Loue I* curſe that ᴀrcher nak'd and blind,
⠀But on that howre that my fond loue did end,
⠀Millions of bleſſings *I* will euer ſpend.⠀⠀⠀⠀⠀⠀⠀⠀20

⠀⠀⠀⠀⠀⠀FINIS.⠀⠀⠀T. W.

[230] A SONNET OF THE SVN.

A Iewell being a ſun-ſhining vpon
the Marigold cloſed a heart of
gould ſent to his Miſtreſſe,⠀⠀⠀⠀⠀⠀⠀⠀⠀25
named Mary.

THe Sun doth make the marygold to flouriſh,
⠀The Suns departure makes it droup againe.
So goulden Maries ſight, my ioyes do nouriſh,
But by their abſence all my ioyes are ſlaine.⠀⠀⠀30
⠀⠀⠀⠀⠀[285]

A Sonnet of the Moone.

The funne, the marigould make it liue and die,
By her the fun fhines brighter, fo may I.
Her fmiles do grace the fun, and light the aire,
Reuiue my heart, and cleare the cloudie Skie,   5
Her frownes the aire make darke the sun to lowre,
The marigould to clofe my heart to die.
By her the fun, the flowre, the aire, and I,
Shine and darken, fpread, and clofe, liue and die,
You are the fun, you are the golden Marie,   10
Paffing the fun in brightneffe, gold in power:
I am the flowre whom you do make to varie.
Florifh when you fmile, droup when you do lowre.
Oh let this heart of gold, funne, and flowre,
Still liue, fhine, and fpringing in your harts bowre. 15

Ch. B.

[231] *A Sonnet of the Moone.*

LOoke how the pale *Queene* of the filent night,
 Doth caufe the *Ocean* to attend vpon her,
And he as long as fhe is in his fight,   20
 with her full tide is redie her to honour:
But when the filuer wagon of the Moone
*I*s mounted vp fo high he cannot follow,
The fea cals home his chriftall waues to mone,
 And with low eb doth manifeft his forrow: 25
So you that are the foueraigne of my heart,
 Haue all my ioyes attending on your will,
My ioyes low ebbing when you doe depart.
When you returne, their tide my heart doth fill.
 So as you come, and as you do depart 30
 *I*oyes eb and flowe within my tender heart.

Ch. B.

[232] 1. Eglogue intituled
CVDDY.

1

A Litle Heard-groome(for he was no bett')   5
　When courſe of yeere return'd the pleaſant ſpring,
At break of day without-en further lett
Caſt with himſelfe his flocke a field to bring,
　And for they had ſo long beene pent with paine,
　At ſight of Sun they ſeem'd to liue againe.   10

2

Such was the flocke all bent to brouſe and play,
But nothing ſuch their Maiſter was to ſee.
Downe hung his drooping head like rainy day,
His cheeks with teares like ſprings bedeawed bee.   15
　His wringed hand ſuch ſilent mone did make.
　Well might you gueſſe he was with loue y'take.

3

Tho while his flocke went feeding on the greene,
And wantonly for ioy of Summer plaid,   20
All in deſpight as if he n'ould be ſeene
He caſt himſelfe to ground full ill appayd.
　Should ſeeme their pleaſance made him more complaine
　For ioy in ſight not felt,is double paine.

4   25

Vnhappy Boy why liu'ſt thou ſtill, quoth he,
And haſt thy deadly wound ſo long ago?
What hope of after hap ſuſtayneth thee?
As if there might be found ſome eaſe of wo.
　Nay better dye ten thouſand times then liue,   30
　Since euery houre new cauſe of death doth giue.

5

The ioyfull Sunne, whom clowdy Winters fpight,
Had fhut from vs in watry fifhes haske,
Returnes againe to lend the world his light,   5
And red as Rofe begins his yeerely taske.
　　His fiery fteeds the fteepy welkin beate,
　　And both the hornes of clyming Bull do heate.

6

But ah no Sun of grace afpires to mee,   10
Clofe hid fhe lies,from whom I fhould haue light,
The clowds of black difdaine fo foggy bee,
That blind I ly(poore boy) bereft of fight:
　　And yet *I* fee the Sun I feeke to find,
　　And yet the more I fee,the more am blind.   15

7

Thrice happy ground,whom fpoyld with winters rage,
The heat of pleafant fpring renewes againe:
Vnhappy I,whom in my fpring of age,
The froft of could Defpaire hath well-nigh flayne. 20
　　How fhall *I* bide your ftormy Winters fmart,
　　When fpring it felfe hath frorne my bloodleffe hart,

8

I fee the beawty of thy flowers renew,
Thy mantle greene with fundry collours fpread,   25
Thou feeft in me a change of former hew,
Paleneffe for white,blacknes for liuely red.
　　What hope of Harueft fruit,or Summer flowers,
　　Since that my fpring is drownd with teares like fhowres.

9

And laſt of all, but lieu'ſt of all to mee,
Thou leany flock, that didſt of late lament,
And witneſſe waſt for ſhepheards all to ſee,   5
(Thy knees ſo weake,thy fleece ſo rough and rent)
   That thou with paine didſt pine away vnfed,
   All for thy Maiſter was with loue miſled.

10

Thou 'ginſt at earſt forget thy former ſtate,   10
And range amid the busks thy ſelfe to feede,
Faire fall thee little flocke both rathe and late,
(Was neuer Louers ſheepe,that well did ſpeede)
   Thou free,*I* bound, thou glad, I pinde in payne,
   I ſtriue to dye, and thou to liue full faine.   15

11

Wo worth the ſtund,wherein I tooke delight,
To frame the ſhifting of my nimble feete,
To cheerefull ſound of Pipe in Moon-ſhine night,
Such pleaſance paſt at earſt now makes me greet.   20
   I ween'd by Night haue ſhun'd the parching ray,
   But night it ſelfe was twiſe more hott then day.

12

Then firſt of all(and all too ſoone for me)
I ſaw thilk Laſſe(nay grau'd her in my breſt)   25
Her chriſtall eyes more bright then Moone to ſee,
Her eies,her eies, that haue robd me of reſt,
   On them I gaz'd, then ſaw *I* to my coſt,
   Through too much ſight mine onely ſight is loſt.

Where beene the dapper *D*itties that I dight,
And Roundlaies, and Virelayes ſo ſoot?
Whilome with Collins ſelfe compare I might
For other Swaine, to ſtriue was little boote,   5
    Such skill *I* had in making all aboue
    But all to little skill to conquer Loue.

What helps it me to haue my piping prayz'd,
Of all ſaue her, whom *I* would only pleaſe?
Nought care I, though my fame to sky be rayz'd   10
For pleaſant ſong that brings my heart no eaſe.
    Wherfore both Pipe and Song I all forſweare,
    And former pleaſance wilfully forbeare.

With that he caſt his looke to Welkin high,
And ſaw the doubled ſhadowes flit away: 15
And as he glaunſt halfe in deſpight awry ,
He ſpide the ſhepheards ſtarre ſhut in the Day;
    Then roſe, and homeward with his flock him went,
    Whoſe voice did helpe their Maiſters caſe lament.

Cuddies Embleme.   20

Queſto per amar ſ'aquiſta.

[233] The Chriſtian Stoick.

The vertuous man is free, though bound in chaines,
    Though poore content, though baniſht, yet no ſträger.
Though ſick, in health of mind, ſecure in danger,   25
    And o're himſelfe, the world, and fortune raignes.

Nor good haps, proud, nor bad, deiected make him,
    To Gods, not to mans will, he frames each action:
He ſeekes no fame, but inward ſatisfaction,
    And firmer ſtands, the more bad fortunes ſhakes him.   30

34] Who giues a gift to binde a friend thereby,
 Doth set or put his gift to vsery.
 And he that giues a gift that is not free,
 Giue where he list, so that he giue not me.   5
   For bought and sold is friendship strange,
   Who liues by selling liues by change.
   And he that loues to change his friend,
   Will turne to nothing in the end.

[235] *The Anatomie of* Loue.   10

NOw what is Loue, *I* pray thee tell?
 *I*t is that Fountaine and that Well,
Where Pleasure and Repentance dwell:
It is perhaps that sounding Bell,
That tolls all in, to heauen or hell;   15
   And this is Loue, as I heare tell.

Now what is Loue, I preth thee say?
*I*t is a worke on holy day;
It is December matchd with May
When lusty bloods in fresh array: 20
Heare ten months after of their play:
   And this is Loue, as *I* heare say.

Now what is Loue, I preth thee fayne?
*I*t is a sunne shine mixt with Raine;
It is a gentle pleasing paine;   25
A flower that dies and springs againe.
It is in faith that Would full fayne,
   And this is Loue, and not a stayne.

Yet what is loue *I* preth thee say?
*I*t is a pretty shaddow way,   30
As well found out by night as day,

It is a thing will foone decay
Then take the vantage while you may,
 And this is Loue as *I* heare fay.

Now what is Loue, *I* preth thee fhow?
A thing that creeps and cannot goe.
A Prize that paffeth too and froe
A thing for one a thing for moe.
And he that proues fhall find it foe
 And this is fome fweet friend I trow.

1

[236] In vaine *I* liue, fith forrow liues in me,
In vaine liues forrow,fince by her I liue,
Life workes in vaine, where Death will Maifter be,
Death ftriues in vaine where life doth vertue giue,
 Thus each of vs would worke an others woe,
 And hurts him felfe in vaine, and helpes his foe.

1

[237] *A* Poeme.

If wrong by force had Iuftice put to flight,
Yet were there hope fhe might returne againe,
If lawleffe warre had fhut her vp from fight,
Yet lawfull peace might foone reftore her traine.
 But now alas,what hope of hope is left?
 When wrongfull death hath her of life bereft?

The Sun that often falls, doth often rife.
The Moone that waineth, waxeth full with light:
But he that death in chaines of darkneffe ties,
Can neuer breake the bands of lafting night,
 What then remaines but teares of loffe to waile,
 In which all hope of mortall helpe doth faile?

[292]

Who then fhall weepe? nay who fhall teares refraine?
If common harmes muft moue the mindes of all.
To few are found that wrongfull harts reftraine,
And of too few,too many Death doth call   5
    *The*fe common harmes I wail among the reft,
    But priuat loffe denies to be expreft.

38] IF Stepdame Nature haue beene fcant,
    In dealing Beauties gifts to mee;
    My wit fhall helpe fupply that want,   10
And skill in ftead of fhape fhall bee.
My ftature I confeffe is fmall,
And therefore nill *I* boaft of warre:
My name fhall fill the Heauens and all,
This skin fhall ferue to hide that skar.   15
My heade to beare the Helme vnfit,
My hands vnapt to murther men;
But little heads oft hold much wit,
And feeble hands can guide a pen.

39] Death is my doome, awarded by difdaine,   20
A lingring death that will not let me dye,
This length of life is lengthning of my paine,
And length of paine gets ftrēgth of paine thereby:
    And ftrength of paine,makes paine of lōger laft,
    Ah who hath ty'de my life to paine fo faft.   25

And yet I feeme,as if *I* did but faine,
Or make my greefe much greater then *I* need,
When as the care to hide my burning paine,
With fecret fighes,conftraines my hart to bleed.
    Yet well I wote,be kild I fhall not be,   30
    Vntill by death a proofe hereof you fee.

[293]

But if this lodge,the witnes of my woe,
Whofe ftony walls enteard my plaints contain
Had fence to feele and tongue my paine to fhow,
Which hee inclofd,*I* vtter all in vaine,
 You foone fhould know that moft I make my mone,
 Alone,if he that loues can be alone.

VVhy fhould I feeke to make my fhame be knowne,
*T*hat foolifh loue is caufer of my paine,
(Forgiue me *L*oue) the fpeech is not mine owne,
But fo they fpeake that thee and thine difdaine.
 And I my felfe confeffe my skill to fmall,
 To pleade for loue,and cleere my felfe withall.

VVhat reafon can my fimple wit deuife,
VVhy bootleffe greefe fhould thus my minde afflict,
I loue the thoughts,that loue it felfe defpife.
I feeke for that I neuer looke to finde.
 Oft haue I heard,or which *I* thinke I dye,
 Thine angry tongue all kinde of loue defye.

Yet is my life vpon thy promife ftaid,
By which thou haft affur'd me of thy loue;
And though thereby my heate be not allayd,
No ftay of flight,where gaine is ftill aboue.
 Yet fince thy hart can yeeld to loue no more,
 I reft content, although *I* die therefore.

  Quis deus oppofuit noftris fua numina votis.

240] Though late my hart, yet turne at laſt,
And ſhape thy courſe another way,
Tis better looſe thy labour paſt,
Then follow on to ſure decay.   5
    VVhat though thou long haue ſtraid awry?
    *I*n hope of grace for mercie cry.

Though waight of ſinne doth preſſe thee downe,
And keepe thee grou'ling on the ground,
Though black deſpaire, with angry frowne,   10
Thy wit and iudgment quite confound,
    Though time and wit haue beene miſpent,
    Yet Grace is left if thou repent.

VVeepe then my hart, weepe ſtill and ſtill.
Nay melt to flouds of flowing teares,   15
Send out ſuch ſhrieks as heau'n may fill,
And pierce thine angry Iudges eares,
    And let thy ſoule that harbours ſin,
    Bleede ſtreames of blood to drowne it in.

Then ſhall thine angry *I*udges face,   20
ᴛo cheerefull lookes it ſelfe apply,
Then ſhall thy ſoule be fild with grace,
ᴀnd feare of death conſtraind to fly.
    Euen ſo my God: oh when? how long?
    I would, but Sin is too too ſtrong.   25

I ſtriue to riſe, Sin keepes me downe,
I fly from Sin, Sinne followes me.

My will doth reach at glories crowne,
Weake is my ſtrength it will not be.
  See how my fainting ſoule doth pant,
  O let thy ſtrength ſupply my want.

FINIS.

Additional Poems
in the Edition of 1611 (*C*)

Addit.per Cha.Beſt.Arm.

[241] An Epitaph on *Henry* the fourth
the laſt French King.

THat we ſhould more bewaile the hap of kings,
   Great Henry Bourbons death occaſion brings,   5
To Henry Valois next crownd King of France,
Next both in bloud, in name, in reigne, in chance.
Perils his youth, wars did his manhood ſpend,
His old age peace, till murder his life did end:
His conqueſts glory,his wiſedome peace did win,   10
His faith heauen, Chriſt pardon for his ſinne.

    [242] *An Epitaph on Queene Elizabeth.*
ELiza that great maiden Queene lies heere,
   Who gouern'd England foure and fortie yeare,
Our coines refinde in Ireland tamde, Belgia protected,   15
Friended France,foiled Spaine,and Pope reiected:
Princes found her powerfull, the world vertuous,
Her ſubiects wiſe and iuſt,and God religious:
God hath her ſoule,the world her admiration,
Subiects her good deeds,Princes her imitation.   20

    [243] *Vnions Iewell.*
Diuers rare gems in thee O vnion ſhine:
Firſt ſeauen Margarites in thy Iewell ſtand:
Matildaes three, three Ianes of regall line,
Two royall Maries, two Elizaes,and   25
One Isbell, Anne,Sibill,and Margery,
All royall gems, ſet princely ſhine in thee,

But firſt in it doth Agaſia ſhine,
Who first with Durſtus it began to make.
Then Margret,next of our King Edgars line,
VVhom Malcolme King of Scots,to wife did take.
 VVhoſe grandchild Mawde our Empreſſe did conioine
 Scots,Saxon, Norman bloud in our Kings line.

For their child Mawde,our firſt Henry did marry,
Of them Matild our ſaid Empreſſe did ſpring:
By whoſe ſecond husband our Kings did carry   1
Name of great Plantagenet,then Scots King
 Firſt Alexander did Sibilla wed,
 VVho ſprong from our VVilliam conquerors bed.

The third Matild their firſt king Dauid maried,
Earle VValdoffes daughter,neece to great K VVilliam: 1
Iane our King Iohns daughter thither was caried
By their ſecond Alexander,after came
 Their third King Alexander who did marry
 An other Margret, daughter of our third Harry.

From them two did another Margret ſpring,
VVho by Norwaies Prince a fourth Margret had,   2
Scots infant Queene whom firſt Edward our king:
To haue married to his ſonne,would haue bene glad.
 So Scotlands Peares would too: her death ſayd nay,
 VVhich onely this great vnion then did ſtay.   2

Though that moſt noble and victorious king.
This naturall vnion could not then aduance,
Another he as great t'effect did bring
VVhen he his ſonne maried to the heire of France
 Isbell,by whom ſince all our kings haue claimed   3
 The crowne of France,which ſome of thē haue gained.

[300]

Though this our second Edward did preuent,
That he from Scotland did not take his wife,
His daughter Iane performed his intent
VVith second Dauid spending there her life.   5
He did the child of second Edward marry
As third Alexander did of our third Harry.

Without issue they died,then Margery,
Their first King Roberts daughter Bruse by name,
Scots Queene by birth,must needs remembred be: 10
By whom Lord Stewart did encrease his fame.
  From them second Robert,& Iames Stewart from him
  Third Robert namde,whence first Iames did begin.

A valiant Prince who spent his youthfull prime,
In martiall deeds,with our fift Henry in France: 15
To whom our sixt king Henry in his time,
Iane our third Edwards grandchild did aduance.
  In mariage,she of Henry Bewford sprong,
  Somersets Earle was vertuous,faire and yong.

Fifth Margaret Richmonds Countes forth did bring   20
Our seuenth Henry,who one diuision ended,
With Eliza, heire of our fourth Edward king:
From both whom great'st Margret of all descended:
  From whom and fourth Iames,fift Iames Scottish king,
  And from him Mary Scots last Queene did spring.   25

Fourth Iames being dead,Margret did Douglas marry,
They a daughter Margret had,Earle Lyneux wife:
Whose sonne Lord Darnley married their last Mary,
Of whom comes Charles Iames finisher of strife.
  Who with Anne makes vnion by the childlesse death,   30
  Of our Queenes Mary, and Elizabeth.

The rareſt pearles, and richeſt Margarits all,
Which euer did in any Iewell ſtand:
The rareſt Iewell too,and moſt Angelicall,
Almoſt made vp by God and Natures hand, 5
   By men to be finiſht to this Iſle ſent,
   Then to be worne for her beſt ornament.

[244] *A Panegyricke to my ſoueraigne*
Lord the King.

GReat King,ſince firſt this Ile by Ioues owne hand, 10
  Was ſet apart within great oceans armes,
And was appointed by her ſelfe to ſtand,
Fenc't round about with rocks from forren harmes:
   She into ſundry parts hath oft bene torne,
   And greateſt wounds by her owne blowes hath borne. 15

But all the fractions now which man did make,
Since it in one whole number nature gaue,
Are added vp, and brought to one great ſtake,
And being all ſum'de vp, one totall haue.
   For Brittaine now to all the diuidend, 20
   In one whole quotient all doth comprehend.

For thou the Monarch of this weſterne Ile,
Now all her ſhiuered parts haſt brought together:
Spreading thy Empires wings eight hundred mile,
In length, and foure in breadth, there ſtaying neither. 25
   But ore old oceans breſt thy arme doſt ſtretch
   Through Ireland,making it to India reach.

To Iuda thou the tribes haſt brought againe,
Which by themſelues did in Samaria dwell:
Iordane by thee whoſe ſtreame did run amaine,
Is now dride vp,that euery tribe may well   5
    To other go:thou haſt broke downe the wall,
     Which Adrian made, and which we picticke call.

Thou vertues orbe where fame is ſtill aſcendent,
And neuer can her higheſt auge attaine,
Conquerour of all hearts,all flattries tranſcendent,   10
Who hold'ſt it loſſe to take,to giue great gaine.
    Of bounteous deeds the euer-running ſpring,
     To many wealth,to all doſt gladneſſe bring.

The Muſes dearling who with golden Pen,
And ſilu'red tongue thy princely mind canſt tell,   15
In whom learning a Princes richeſt Iemme,
Both humane,and diuine abounding dwell.
    The great contriuer of this triple Ile,
     To one imperiall diadem and ſtile.

The royall product of the princely doue,   20
VVhich Englands Noah from peaces Arke ſent forth,
After warres deluge,who oliue branch of loue.
Doſt bring with thee in thy returne from North:
    How ioyfully did Brittaine reach her hand,
     To take thee int' the Arke of this her land?   25

With great Eliza glory of her owne,
Wonder of future times,true Churches nurſe,
The ancient faiths reuiuer,on whom were ſhowne,
Heauens bleſsings,all mens praiers, no mans curſe.
    Fortunes fauours, natures wealth, Gods high grace,   30
     The Muſes lodge,all vertues dwelling place.

Our Sun did fet with great Elizabeth,
Before night thou a new day-light didft bring,
Our fommers peace did clofe at her cold death,
Without warres winter thou renewd'ft our fpring.   5
    All our liues ioyes with her dead feemd to bee,
    Before intombde they were reuiude by thee.

Center of royall births,in whom do meete,
Lines drawne from all the noble conquerors bloud,
Which euer in any part with warlike feete,   10
Of this great Iles circumference haue ftood,
    With thy faire Queene,a fea whither do runne,
    Streames of all royall bloud of Chriftendome.

Both royall plants whence princely branches fpring,
VVhereon grow our beft fruits of hope and ioy   15
Great of-fprings both, of many a noble King,
An antidote fh' againft this lands annoy.
    In whofe milde lookes hath princely maieftie,
    A marriage made with modeft courtefie.

She vertues booke bound in a golden couer,   20
Wherein nature hath writte with Gods owne quill,
All beauties learning,where thou her true louer,
Maift reade fweete lectures of delight at will.
    And on the frame of whofe diuineft feature,
    All graces fhine that can be in a creature.   25

Sprung of a double, knit to a triple King,
Late quadruple,the holy number,Three,
Gratefull to God did feeme more apt to bring,
Peace to this land,with loue and vnitie.
    Plant royall fet by Iuno in this land,   30
    Whofe anceftors by Mars heere once did ftand.

Sacred beautie her makes feeme angelicall,
Thee heauenly wifedome to the ftarres do raize,
Minerua her, Apollo thee do call
Their dearlings,both trueft theames of all praife.   5
   Together liue and loue, and long do raigne,
   To our,to your,to Gods ioy, bliffe,and gaine.

[245] *To my Lord the Prince.*

DEarling of thefe,of future times the glory,
   Branch royall fprung from many a regall ftemme,   10
On whofe faire ftru&ture, written is the ftory
Of natures chefeft skill, worlds choifeft Iemme,
Wits richeft Cabinet, vertues beft aray,
Centre where lines of all hearts loues do meete.
Sweete ground whereon the Mufes loue to play,   15
Ripe in wit, though greene in yeares,of forme moft fweet
Scotlands faire fruit, Englands great hope, Frances loue,
Irelands awe, Cambriaes ioy,great Brittains fame,
Abridgement of all worth, the mighty Ioue,
Long lengthen your good daies,and ftill your name,   20
And when you fhall haue honoured long this land
Grant you a glorious Saint in heauen to ftand.

[246] *To the excellent Lady Elizabeth her Grace.*

FAire vertues Iemme fet in moft royall gold,
   The worthieft owner of the faireft manfion,   25
Rich prize for which nature and fortune hold
VVith Mufes and graces Great contention:
All which by agreement this partition make,
None of themfelues worthy of all difcerning,
Nature your beauty, Graces your vertues take,   30
Fortune fhares your honour, Mufes your learning.

[305]

Map of perfe&tion, who deferue to be,
And are the worthieſt marke the world can yeeld,
For all great Chriſtian Princes loues, they ſee
Such vertues wheat,growing in beauties field:
Long may you liue, a holy and happy life,
A royall maide firſt, then a royall wife.

[247] De lapſu hominis in *Adam.*

PAuper amabilis & venerabilis eſt benedictus,
Diues inutilis,inſatiabilis,eſt maledictus,
Qui bona negligit,& mala diligit, intrat abyſſum.
Nulla potentia, nulla pecunia liberat ipſum.
Irremeabilis,inſatiabilis,illa vorago,
Hic vbi mergitur,horrida cernitur omnis imago.
Vir miſerabilis Euaque flebilis hoc ſubierunt,
Hic cruciamina, per ſua crimina,cum meruerunt.
Iuſſa Dei pia, iuſſa ſalubria ſi tenuiſſent,
Vir neque fœmina,nec ſua ſemina,morte periſſent,
Sed quia ſpernere iuſſaque ſoluere non timuere,
Mors grauis irruit, hoc merito fuit, & periere.
Janua mortis paſsio fortis crimen eorum,
Attulit orbi ſemina morbi,totque malorum.
Jlla parentes,atque ſequentes culpa peremit,
Atque piarum deliciarum munus ademit.
Flebile fatum dans cruciatum,danſque dolorem,
Illa merenti perdere tanti regis honorem.
Eſt data ſæuam cauſa per Euam perditionis,
Dum meliorem ſperat honorem voce draconis,
Hoc male credens, nos quoque lædens crimine magno,
Omnia triſti ſubdidit iſti ſæcula damno.
Stirps miſerorum plena dolorum poſtea creuit,
His quoque damnis pluribus annis ſubdita fleuit.

[248] De restitutione hominis per Christum.

SEd *Deus omnipotens, qui verbo cuncta creauit,*
  Sic cecidisse dolens homines quos semper amauit,
Ipse suum verbum transmisit ad infima mundi,   5
Exulibus miseris aperire viam redeundi.
Filius ergo Dei descendit ab arce superna
Nunquam discedens à maiestate paterna,
Qui corpus sumens animatum, numine saluo
Procefsit natus sacræ de virginis aluo.   10
Verus homo, verusque Deus, pius & miserator,
Verus saluator, nostræque salutis amator,
Sponte sua moriens mortem moriendo peremit
Et sic perpetua miseros à morte redemit,
Namque pia de morte refurgens, vt Leo fortis,   15
Restituit vitam prostrato principe mortis.

[247] *Of the fall of man in* Adam.

THe poore mā belou'd, for vertue approu'd, right blessed is he,
  Where couetous chuff who neuer hath enough, accursed shalbe.
Who goodnes reiecteth, & euill affecteth, shall fall in the pit,   20
No plenty of pence shall free him from thence, no power nor wit.
Both vnrepassable and vnsatiable, that gulph will appeare,
Imbogd he shall be, where nought he shall see, but horror & feare.
Adam vnstable, and Eue variable, the very first time,
By falling from God, deserued this rod, (O horrible crime,)   25
For had they adhered to God, & him feared, by keeping his reede
Thē death had not come on, the mā or the womā, or any their seed.
But when as the man, from Gods will began, basely to reuolt,
For his grieuous sinne, death came rushing in, and on him laid holt,
This was the great crime, which at the first time, by craft of the de- 30
Did bring in the seed, of sicknes and need, & all other euill: uill,

[307]

This was the fin,which firft did begin,our parents to kill,
And heauenly foode,prepard for our good, did vtterly fpill.
Vnhappy the fate,which firft fuch a ftate, fuch forrow did bring,
To him that had loft, fo much to our coft,our heauenly king.   5
The credulous Eue, twas fhe that did giue,the caufe of fuch euill,
Hoping that honor,wold come more vpõ her,deceiued by the deuil.
Beleeuing of him,did make her to fin,to all our great loffe,
For mankind e're fence,receiued from hence,an horrible croffe.
For all the nations,through all generatiõs,which after have bene   10
With grief of their heart,haue tafted the fmart of that primitiuefin.

[248] *Of the reftoring of man by Chrift.*

BVt Ioue omnipotent,all things by his word who created,
Grieuing man to be falne,whofe loue was in him fo innated
Sent from aboue his word, for man to prepare a returning   15
Thence,where elfe had he lien,through all eternity burning.
So Gods onely begotten fonne, came downe to redeeme vs,
Yet did he ftill himfelfe, his fathers glory beteeme vs.
A body formde with a foule, to his diuinity taking.
And to be borne of a virgine, his humanity making.   20
Borne very God,very man, he a man God, mercifull,holy,
Purchafed our faluation, was our Sauiour wholy.
For by his willing death, he deaths felfe wholy defeated,
And fo vs all from eternall death, by death rebegetted
From death again rifing, he deaths prince mightily maimed,   25
Whereby his owne from death, to eternall life he regained.

FINIS.

Additional Poems
in the Edition of 1621 (*D*)

[249] *Epithalmion vpon the spousals* of W.A.
and I.A.

He who firſt did inſtitute holy wedlock,
Knitting man and woman in happy bedlock,   5
Putting on their concupiſence a holy fetlock,
    Not to be broken:
Grant O grant, ye grace to loue one another,
Like a Siſter, Chriſtian, and a brother,
So make the weaker of you a mother,   10
    Loues happy token.

[250] *Another of the ſame.*

Loue is foolery if it be not founded,
And on heauēly beauty chiefely grounded
All deformity from the firſt ſin runneth,   15
Al true beauty from our God only cōmeth
*W*ith loues puritie him then only praiſe ye,
That by mercy he to himſelfe may raiſe ye,
Hee's the fountaine of all true perfect beauty:
And beſt meriteth all harts, loue, and duty,   20
 Then ſend vp to him al your ſighs & gronings
 Then poure out to him all your teares and mournings,
 And fixe only on him your ioyes and gladneſſe,
 For to ioy in earthly things is madneſſe.

VARIANT READINGS AND MISPRINTS

VARIANT READINGS AND
MISPRINTS

THE following list aims to include every verbal variant
from *A* (1602) in *B* (1608), *C* (1611), and *D* (1621), and
from the additional poems of *B* and *C* in *CD* and *D*
respectively, as well as all the significant misprints in
ABCD. Mere differences in spelling (like *desire-desier*,
ift-if't, *of-off*, *on-one*, *Phœbus-Phœbus*) are not listed unless, for one reason or another, they seem to have a spe-
cial interest; but wherever the spelling in verse-lines
adds an extra syllable it is noted. In general no atten-
tion is paid, furthermore, to capitalization, hyphena-
tion, or punctuation; to cases of faulty spacing, unless a
misleading or a doubtful wording results, or unless they
are corrected in my own text; to wrong fonts of type[1] or
blurred or broken letters (like *t*'s and *e*'s that, especially
in the text of *B*, resemble *r*'s and *c*'s respectively); to
apostrophes turned the wrong way, letters or words out
of alignment, printer's lead-marks, or changed inden-
tion. This list, finally, does not record the section-head-
ings and section-endings added in *D*, or the errors made

---

[1] In the texts that I *reprint* italic colons have been corrected to
roman at 43.11, 17, 66.18, 83.11, 111.11, 137.19, 149.3, 154.6, 155.21,
162.18, 163.4, 6, 18, 171.15, 183.23, 197.21, 206.14, 248.7, 250.6, 272.22,
286.11, 21, 293.23, 295.21, 299.18, 300.22, 24, 301.22, 27, 302.3, 13,
303.6, 23, 306.5. Letters in wrong font are usually retained (as at
240.18, 241.25, 244.15, 246.17, 250.5, 8, 253.4, 12, 16, 264.19, 21,
281.13), but a few (148.10, 152.21, 195.4, 222.12, 254.8, 270.4) have
been corrected in the text, where they would have been almost intoler-
able, and have been entered in the Variant Readings.

in *ABCD* in folio-numbers, key-words, signature-marks, and head-lines; for all these matters are enumerated in the bibliographical descriptions of *ABCD* in volume II. Readings at the left of the brackets are those of my own text: variations from them in any of the original editions are given at the right of the brackets, the orthography always being that of the first edition cited.

The following list is based upon the White-Rosenbach copy of *A* and the Huntington copies of *BCD;* but when the readings assigned to *ABCD* do not appear in the Bodleian copy of *A* and the Harvard copies of *BCD,* a note is added with those copies distinguished by asterisks, as "*Not in A*,*" "*Not in D*.*"

3. 4 Caerdiffe] Cardiffe *BCD: pages* 3–4 *are mutilated in A, a few letters and words being torn off. They are supplied in the text from A**

   5 *D adds:* Lord Cham-/berlaine of his Maiesties houshold, one of his Maie-/ sties most Honorable Priuie Counsell, and/ Knight of the most noble order of the/ Garter.

   6 high and noble] braue Heroike *BCD*

   8 outward] eutward *C apparently* (*not in C**)

  10 in²] *Om. CD*

  15 Thou] Or *BCD*

  16 Thou that deseru'st] Who hast deseru'd *BCD*

  17 t' other] th' other *BCD*

  20–21, 23–25 *om. BCD*

4. 7–8 friend Anomos] friends Anonymoi *BCD*

  11 former] rest *BCD:* name] names *BCD*

  15 both] *Om. BCD*

  18 disliked] mislked *D*

  20 publishing] published *D*

5. 3 Iubeo] Iubio *D*

  9 Lawyers] er *blurred out in B* (*not in B**)

5. 17 that] *Om. CD*
 21 will] wilt *D:* it] *Om. CD*
 23 Cum] Tum *B*
 26 our] out *D*
 29 Ph.] Philip *BCD*
 32 Anomos] *The first* o *is imperfect and blurred in A,*
  Anonymos *BC,* Anonymus *D*
6. 13 neither] neuer *D*
7. 2 neuer yet published] *Om. BCD*
 5 Maister] M. *BCD:* *after this line D inserts* I.
  Pastorall
8. 12 your] you *B*
9. 11 seuer'd] seuered *BCD*
 13 Ph] Phil *D*
 14 *Before this line D inserts* II. Pastorall
10. 6 among] amongst *CD*
11. 5 vndershade] vnder shade *D*
 9 that] the *CD*
 17 mayst] mayest *C*
12. 2 to] vnto *D*
 6 be] to be *CD*
 13 of] of of *C*
 14 Sir] S. *D*
 15 Fiction] A Fiction *BCD:* *before this line D in-*
  serts III. Poem
13. 13 apace] a pace *D*
14. 4 Shaftes] shaft *D*
 6 the] thy *BC*
 7 the] thy *D*
 8 knowest] knowst *CD*
 26 Anomos] *Om. BCD*
15. 2 *Before this line D inserts* III. Pastoral
 3 Astrea] *Final* a *inverted in C:* 3–6 made . . . 15]
  Om. BCD
 8 help] helps *D*
 10 needst] needs *D*

15. 21 Not] Nor *CD*
    22 holds] hol *B* (ho *B**)
16. 5 minde] min *B:*   *speech tags inexactly placed here and later in BC*
    17 three] there *BCD*
    27 thine] shine *BCD*
17. 2 oft] of *D:*   enclowdes] in clouds *BCD*
    14 do] to *D*
    17 Pembroke] Pembreoke *D*
18. 2 *Before this line D inserts* IIII. Pastorall: ¶] *Om. BCD*
    10 I¹] *Om. D*
    23 others] other *D*
19. 16 Klaius] *This tag appears both at the bottom of C3 and (misprinted* Kia ius*) at the top of C3ᵛ in B*
    18 Ee'n] Eu'n *CD*
    21 vpon] vpou *A*
    23 Strephon] Strephou *D*
    26 Nor] No *D*
20. 6 me:] mei *B*
    22 mee] *Om. C*
21. 2 Strephons Palinode] Strephons Palinde *BC*, V. Pastorall./ Or Strephons Palinode *D*
    9 his] hi *B* (*not in B**):   knees] knee *D*
    16 deserts] desires *CD*
    19 suspended] spended *C*
22. 21 their] your *D*
23. 21 now] not *D*
25. 2 I. Eglogve] VI. Pastorall *D*
    17 sighings] sighing *CD*
26. 3 boystrous blasts] blustring windes *BCD*
    6 soone as] when fresh *BCD*
    7 thy] the *BCD*
    16 defaste] defact *C*, defac't *D*
    17 youth] earth *C*, soule *D*
    26 Soone-] some- *BC*, some *D*

26. 30 soone] soone as *D*
27. 15 Hot] No *D*
    19 A way] Away *BCD*
    21 Summer] Summers *CD*
    23 flower] flowers *CD*
    27 thy] they *BCD*
28. 3 Is] As *C*
    16 Earth] wretch *D*
    21 paines] paine *C*
    24 fruitfull] fruitfuil *C*
29. 12 Star] Sarre *C*
    23 thy] the *D*
    28 In] Iu *C*
30. 4 And] Aud *C*
    10 are gone from] abandon *BCD*
    28 iournie's] iourne's *D*
    29 doost] doest *CD*
    30 Tethis] Thetis *CD*
31. 11 decay] dechy *B*
    13 neuer] neuet *D*
32. 2 haue] hath *D*
    9 flowret] flower *CD*
    11 Yee] And *BCD:*   had] haue *BCD*
    12 with'red] withered *BCD*
    17 happy fauour] happyf auour *A*
    21 iuice] ioyce *D*
    25 Yee] You *BCD*
    30 so do] do so *BCD*
33. 15 thou] thon *C*
    19 griefe] griefes *CD*
34. 4 weight] wight *B*
    8 die] eie *C*
    18 his] this *C*
    20 gan] can *C*
    21 As] And *D:*   their] his *BCD*
35. 2 whenas his] when floods of *BCD*

35. 3 weary . . . for] stormes of weary sighes more calme
BCD
   4 began] went on BCD
   6 clouds] cloude D
   10 Francis Dauison] F.D. BCD
36. 2 III. Eglogve] An Eglogue BC: D *has* VIII. Pastorall
   6 arreed] arred D
   7 raft] reft BCD
   10 to] do CD
   14 flowrets] flowers CD
   23 too] to o A
37. 4 thy] the D
   8 alderliefest] al derliefest B, all-derliefest CD
   12 and] the D
   16 vncouth] vncoth BCD
   18 tree] rree B (*not in* B*)
   23 thy] my D
   24 in] it D
   27 guise] giu e C (*not in* C*)
   28 fingers] finger' B, finger's C: hoarsely] horsely D
38. 4 sits] fits CD
   6 Tway] T'way BCD: our] for D
   19 thee] thou CD
39. 30 Willy] Sidney BC, Willey D
40. 4 he] we C
   13 Ne] Me CD
   15 the] his D
   19 flockt] flock BCD
41. 4 No] Mo D
   6 That] Th at A
   7 turned] turnd CD
   26 greatest] *Om.* D
   28 Girlonds] Garlands BCD
42. 2 whereof] *Om.* BC
   3 so] *Om.* BC

42. 8 thy] our *D*
    10 bankes] banke *C*
    20 disfigur'd] disfigured *D*
    28 Amazed] Amazd *C*
    30 and] aud *B*
43. 16 now] *Om. D*
44. 2 Collin] Callin *B*
     7 my] our *D*
    13 *Line om. in C*
45. 2 II. Eglogve] IX. Pastorall *D*
    12 Daphnee] Daphne *BCD throughout*
    19 loue] loues *BCD*
46. 15 lads] lad's *BCD*
47. 17 when that] when as *D*
    29 straines] straine *C*
48. 3 doth] can *CD*
     5 faith's] faiths *B*
     7 Shepheard] a *upside down in A*
    14 the] thy *D*
    17 whilst] whist *C*
    23 e'en] euen *CD*
    24 shalt] shall *D*
49. 18 thinkes] thiukes *A*
    19 Daphnee] Daphnes *BCD*
    27 Ignoto] *Om. BCD*
50. 2 IIII. Eglogve] X. Pastorall *D*
     3 Concerning olde Age] *This phrase comes after* want-
       ing (*line 4*) *as a separate line in D*
     9 youthly] youthfull *D*
    12 asswage] asswae *D*
    15 wee] me *D:*   twight] t' wight *B*
    19 beene] be *CD*
    21 Selfe] Se fe *C* (*not in C**):   thou] thon *C*
    22 eath] earth *D*
    23 truth] truh *D*
51. 2 ill] lll *P*

51. 5 too] to *CD*
    10 blissefull] blesfull *CD*
    13 bladders] bladder *CD*
    16 yherried] y'herried *BCD*
    17 thy] thee *D*
52. 4 wrigs] waggs *BCD*
    21 seeme] seemes *CD*
53. 6 holli-day] holy-day *BCD*
    10 Anomos] *Om. BCD*
    11 Deest] The end of the Pastorals *D*
55. 2 *BC omit* and *before* Madrigalls *and add* and Epigrams. *The title is not in D*
57. 3 Sonnet. I] IIII. Sonet *D*
    10 Loues] Louers *BCD*
    12 Ennabling] Enabled *D*
    17 wondrous¹] wondrons *A*
58. 2 Sonnet. II] V. Sonnet *D*
    11 tears that] *Torn and blurred, as are also certain words in lines 16–18, in A (not in A*)*
59. 2 Sonnet III] So   III *A (blurred, but correct in A*),* VI. Sonnet *D*
    4 fairest Eies] *Blurred in A (not in A*),* fairest eie *CD*
    5 the] e *inverted in D (not in D*)*
    8 The cherriest] Those cherrie *BCD*
    9 which] *Om. CD*
    17 All these] *Badly blurred in A (not in A*)*
60. 2 Sonnet. IIII] VII. Sonet *D*
    8 Britton] Maiden *BCD*
    12 adamātines] Adamantine *CD*
    14 thence] then *D*
61. 2 Elegie. I] I. Elegie *D*
    3 renounceth] re *blurred in A*
    11 thoughts] thought *CD*
    14 song] mind *D*
62. 4 dulled] dullen *CD*
    12 colours] colour *D*

62. 14 taste] soule *D*
    15 mine] my *D*
63. 2 Sonnet. V] VIII. Sonnet *D*
   16–17 *BCD have:*

> And onely liue, and liuing mercy cry,
> Because her glory in my death will dy.

64. 2 Ode. I] I. Ode *D*
    5 Passion] Passions *D*
65. 2 Madrigal I] V. Madrigall *D*
   12 in] at *BCD:*   libettie] libettie *A*
   13 would'st] wilt *BCD*
   15 Madrigal II] VI. Madrigall *D*
   21 this . . . true] I can this only reason giue *BCD*
   22 I . . . you] in you I liue *BCD*
66. 2 Madrigal III] VII. Madrigall *D*
    4 seldome] slowly *BCD*
    5 hath murthered] soone murthers *BCD*
   10 a sweete Kisse] doue-like kisses *BCD*
   11 blisse] blisses *BCD*
   12 Would] Will *BCD*
   13 it would] they will *BCD*
   14 Madrigal IIII] VIII. Madrigall *D*
   16 lippes I kist] *Badly blurred in A. In BCD lines 16–19 run:*

> Since *I* your cherry lips did kisse,
> Where *Nectar* and *Ambrosia is.*
> My hungry maw no meate requires:
> My thirsty throate no drink desires.

   22 Then] O *BCD:*   (Deare)] then *BCD*
   23 O] And *BCD*
   26–27 *BCD have:*

> By cherries twayne his life he cherrisht,
> By cherries twaine at length he perisht.

67. 2 Ode II] II. Ode *D*

67.   3–4 *The title in BCD is* Vpon her protestation of kinde
      affection, hauing tryed his sinceare fidelitie
    12 so louely] well-form'd and *BCD*
    13 long hart-binding] hart ensnaring *BC*, heart en-
      snared *D*
    18 most pleasing] enchaunting *BCD*

68.   2 Ode II] *So incorrectly* Ode 2 *in BC,* III. Ode *D*
    11 Sprit] Sp'rit *BC*, Spirit *D*
    19 plentie] pleasure *D*

69.   2 Elegie II] *Om. D:*   Letter] Letters *BCD*
    14 their²] they *CD*
    17 rase] race *CD*
    18, 19 *Between these lines BC insert* 3, *D inserts* Another

70.   7 might] may *BCD*
    17 great] gteat *A*
    21 not] not to *BCD*
    23 blist] blest *CD*
    25, 26 *Between these lines BC insert* 4, *D inserts* Another
    30 her faire] faire her *D:*   booke] looke *BCD*

71. 24 minutely] minuitly *D*
    27, 28 *Between these lines BC insert* 5, *D inserts* Another
    28, 29 my hart] me *BCD*
    30 although] altough *B*

72.   2 months] moneths *D:*   nay²] and *BCD*
    9 for . . . I] you do make me *BCD*
    15 alwayes] alweie *BCD*
    17, 18 *Between these lines BC insert* 6, *D inserts* Another
    18 that . . . do] (vnkind) when I *BCD:*   consither]
    consider *CD*

73.   6 hath merited] doth merit *BCD*
    7 To loue that *L*oue, which once it [I *CD*] did inherit
    BCD
    13 so] thus *BCD*
    15 grace, and] kindnesse *BCD:*   *between 15 and 16*
    BC insert 7, D inserts Another
    29 sweetest] sugred *BCD*

74. 8 you do] do you *BCD*
    10 In stead in] In stead of *BCD*
    14 side] besides *D*
    15 vndeseru'd] vnderu'd *C*, undeserued *D:*   despight] spight *D*
    20 letters] letter *BCD*
    23, 24 *Between these lines BC insert* 8, *D inserts* Another
    28 trie it on, &c.] on rebellious hearts and E es [eies *CD*] *BCD*
    31 curelesly] curelesle *C*, curelesse *D*
75. 5 *D adds* Finis
    6 Ode IIII] IIII. Ode *D*
    7 sweete] *Om. BCD*
    8 by his absence in Italie] *Comes between* Being *and* depriued *in BCD:*   desires] desireth *BCD*
    13 life's] liefs *BC*, lifes *D*
    18 *Line om. in D*
    21 wherefore] whereof *D*
76. 12 My blisse] Mbl isse *B*
    14 an] and *B*
    16 his] this *D:*   onely] one ly *A*
    18 Balme] Blame *BCD*
    21 poyson] poson *D*
    23 Doth make my] Make my poore *BCD*
77. 9 pretended] presented *BCD*
78. 2 Madrigal V] IX. Madrigall *D*
    6 th'] the *BCD*
    7 Babble] Bable *CD*
79. 2 Sonnet. VI] IX. Sonet *D*
    10 Two] To *BCD*
    11 To] Two *C*
    12 my . . . deedes] vvith hatefull deeds my loue *BCD*
    15 maske] make *CD*
    17 ift] if 'it *D*
    18 due] *Om. C*, worth *D*
80. 2 Sonnet. VII] X. Sonet *D*

80. 5 if] that *BCD*

     14 your . . . loue] loue is your fault *BCD*

     15 iust] much *D*

     17 no] not *D*

     18 Ode.] *Perhaps* Odf *A*

81. 2 Ode V] V. Ode *D*

     16 *In BCD this line wrongly ends the first stanza*

     17 still] deere *BCD*

     20 that] *Om. BCD:*   you loue] delight *BCD*

82. 2 *Before this title BC insert* Ode VI, *D inserts* VI. Ode: Prosopopœia] Presopopæia *D*

     9 the] th' *CD*

     16 Ode VI] Ode VII *BC*, VIII. Ode *D*

83. 5 infused] refused *D*

     11 hop't] hopt *B*, hopp't *C*

     26 you] still *BCD*

84. 2 Ode VII] Ode VIII *BC*, VIII. Ode *D*

     9 behavour] behaviour *D*

     13 Only you and you want pitty *BCD*

     14 both] most *BCD*

     15 Madrigall VI] X. Madrigall *D*

85. 6 Madrigall. VII] XI. Madrigall *D*

     11 doth meane] intends *BCD*

     13 his . . . mistrusts] that part which least his foe mistrusts *BCD*

86. 2 Sonnet VIII] XI. Sonet *D*

     3 commending] comming *D* (*not in D**)

     7 Inconstancy] vnconstancy *D*

     8 praiseles] praises *CD*

     12 to . . . say)] (as you say) to sing *BCD*

     18 *After this line BCD add, evidently by mistake,* My then greene Hart so brightly did enflame [eflame *D, not D**]

87. 2 Madrigall VIII] XII. Madrigall *D*

     16 Madrigal IX] XIII. Madrigall *D*

     17 Answere] Answers *CD*

87. 21 Ti's] Tis *BCD*
88. 2 Ode VIII] Ode IX *BC*, IX. Ode *D*
    11 th'] the *CD*
89. 2 Madrigal X] XIIII. Madrigall *D*
    3 timerous] time rous *A*
    12 Madrigal XI] Madrigal 11 *C*, XV. Madrigall *D*
    14 and] and most *D*
90. 2 *Before this title D inserts* III. Canzonet
    3 woman-] women- *D*
    14 nor¹] not *D*
    15 Madrigal XII] XVI. Madrigall *D*
    16 from] fom *A:*   him] hlm *B*
    19 To] T *D*
91. 5 Madrigal XIII] XVII. Madrigall *D*
    6 Beauty] Beanty *A*
92. 2 *Before this title D inserts* IIII. Canzonet
    4 Shut] Shun *CD*
    6 inflames] inflame *D*
    8-11 *Arranged in BCD in two long lines*
    14 H] Hart *BC*, Hatt *D*:*   Thou] Tou *D*
    16-19 *BCD run thus:*

    Let one ioy fill vs, as one greefe did harme vs,
    Let one death kill vs, as one loue doth warme vs.

93. 2 Elegie. III] II. Elegie *D*
    3 not] *Om. D:*   Ladies] Lady *C*
    4 Deere] Deeare *D*
    6 Ist] I'st *BCD:*   -hol'd] -hold *B*
    9 Ist] I'st *D*
    14 golde or pearle] pearle or gold *CD*
    22 Though] Tho ugh *A*
94. 4 Hath] Both *BCD*
    5 moe] more *D*
    10 A Quatrain] Or Quatrain *preceded by* V. Canzonet
       D
    13 it] me *D*

95. 2 Sonnet IX] Sonnet X *BC*, XII. Sonet *D*
    15 deepe wit] deep ewit *A*
96. 2–98.20 *Om. in D*
    8 Olympiaes] Olympias *C*
    10 fetcht] fetch *B*
97. 3 Kingdoms] Kingdome *C*
    4 mighti'st] mightiest *BC*
98. 20 In] Iu *C*
99. 2 *Before this title D inserts* VI. Canzonet
    7 most] more *BCD*
    9 th' other] to' other *D*
    17 Fra.] Francis *BC*, F. *D:*   Davison] D. *D*
101. 2 Sonnet. I] XIII. Sonet *D*
    17 lines] liues *C*
102. 2 Sonnet. II] XIIII. Sonet *D*
    3 in] and *D*
    8 rise] arise *D*
    16 doome] iudge *BCD*
    17 in, if] if, in *BCD:*   bee regarded] scales be wayed *BCD*
    18 With equall loue my loue must be repayed *BCD*
103. 2 Sonet. III] XV. Sonet *D*
    17 haue] of *D:*   soueraingntie] soueraigntie *BCD*
    19 *BCD add:*

    How they make my poore hart at once to dwell,
    In fire and frost, in heau'n and in hell

104. 2 Sonnet. V] Sonnet IIII *BC*, XVI. Sonet *D*
    3 Comparisons] comparison *D*
    8 these] there *CD*
    11 Lifes] Liues *D*
    12 but] bnt *D:*   Suns] Snns *A apparently*
    16 equal'd are] equal'd dare *B*
105. 2 Ode I] X. Ode *D*
    23 *Line om. in BCD*
106. 2 out] our *C apparently*

106. 5 doth] d *blurred in A* (*not in A**)
      8 Sonnet VI] Sonnet V *BC*, XVII. Sonet *D*
      16 those] these *D*
107. 2 Sonnet IIII] Sonnet VI *BC*, XVIII. Sonet *D*
      7 Joyntly] Jovntly *A apparently:*   their] rheir *B*
      8 gracious] graeious *A:*   Face] Faee *B*
      14 Starres] Sarres *B*
108. 2 Sonnet. VII] XIX. Sonet *D*
      5 banisht] rauisht *CD*
      6 with] by *D:*   doo] doth *D*
      11 be blest] beare rest *BCD*
      17 Garments] garment *D*
109. 2 Sonnet. VIII] XX. Sonet *D*
      3 Torments] Torment *BCD*
      9 Eares] Eeares *A*
      13 oppression] oppressions *BCD*
110. 2 Ode II] XI. Ode *D*
      12 I] is *BCD:*   languish] anguish *CD*
      19 loue] life *CD*
      24 hate] hates *BCD*
111. 2 I] *Om. BCD*
      5 gaine] giue *CD*
      14 no.] *Possibly* no: *in A*
      18 perseuer] preseruer *C*, perseruer *D*
      21 no⁴, no.] no., no *A*
112. 2 Sonnet. IX] Sonnet VII *BC*, XXI. Sonet *D*
      14 eares] eare *BCD*
      17 nor] no *D*
113. 2 Sonnet. X] Sonnet VIII *BC*, XXII. Sonet *D*
      3 loue] liue *CD*
      5 plaine] paine *C*
      9 distain] disdaine *B*
114. 2 Sonnet XI] Sonnet IX *BC*, XXIII. Sonet *D*
      3 words] word *D*
      4 plants] plaints *BD*
      10 cause] much *D*

114. 14 yeeld] take *D*
   15 but²] in *CD*
115. 2 Sonnet. XII] Sonnet X *BC*, XXIIII. Sonet *D*
    7 tempestuous] tempestious *B*
  18 and] my *D:*   run] rue *CD*
116. 2 Elegie] III. Elegie *D*
    3 *Between 3 and 4 B inserts the stanza-number* 1, *C inserts* 6
    4 on] and *BCD*
    8 fare] feare *BCD*
  14 like] as *D*
  17 *Between 17 and 18 B inserts the stanza-number* 2, *CD om. all space*
  18–118.24 *Om. in CD*
117. 8 *Between 8 and 9 B inserts the stanza-number* 3
  12 laue] leaue *B*
  13 light] life *B*
  14 *Between 14 and 15 B inserts the stanza-number* 4
  15 heart-] harts *B*
  19 loue] lone *B*
  21 eu'n] eu n' *B*
  28 *Between 28 and 29 B inserts the stanza-number* 5
118. 9 which] with *B*
  11 Though] Through *B*
  12 *Between 12 and 13 B inserts the stanza-number* 6
  24 to] *Om. B*
  27 too] to *D*
119. 3 flattering] flattring *D*
    4 *Between 4 and 5 BC insert the stanza-number* 7, *D om. all space*
    8 by] with *D*
  14 Hares] heartes *CD*
  18 engaged] engag'd *BC*
  20 *Between 20 and 21 BC insert the stanza-number* 8
  22 fight] sight *C*
  28 glosse] grosse *C*, glasse *D*

119. 29 doth] do *D*
    30 Tygres] Tygers *BCD*
120. 2 Allegeance] alleageance *C*
    3 self-deuided] selfe denied *D** (*not in D*)
    5 that] thar *D*
    9 childishly] chiidishly *C*
    10 *Between 10 and 11 BC insert the stanza-number* 9, *D om. all space*
    13 vnreaue] bereaue *D*
    21 *Between 21 and 22 BC insert the stanza-number* 10, *D om. all space*
    27 *Line om. in CD*
121. 2 Sonnet. XIII] Sonnet XI *BC*, XXV. Sonet *D*
    15 then] that *BCD*
    17 moue] loue *CD*
122. 2 Sonnet. XIIII] Sonnet XII *BC*, XXVI. Sonet *D*
    5 No] Not *D*
    6 thing] *Om. D*
    10 Prayr'es] Prair's *C*, prayers *D*
    17 leaue] leane *D*
123. 2 *Before this title D inserts* III. Device
    8 than] then a *D*
    9 W.D.] *Om. D*
125. 3-4 *Om. in BCD* (*the entire title-page is not in D*)
127. 2 III] Three *BCD:*   2-3 for a . . . following] *Om. D*
    7 Sonnet I] XXIX. Sonet *D*
    11 men to] to men *D*
    15 Castall] Castell *CD*
    18 for] me *BCD*
    20 Peacockes] Peacock *CD:*   pride] prides *CD*
128. 2 Sonnet. II] XXX. Sonet *D*
    5 knowst] knowest *C*
    12 Hers] Here *CD*
    16 write] writ *D*
129. 2 Sonnet. III] XXXI. Sonet *D*

130. 2 Ode I] Ode *C*, XII. Ode *D*
131. 2 *Before this title D inserts* XIIII. Canzonet
     5 mee] the *C*
132. 2 Ode. II] XIII. Ode *D*
133. 2 *Before this title D inserts* LI. Canzonet
    14 for] of *BCD*
    20 with²] it *D*
134. 3 requite] require *C*
     7 Accept] Accep *D:*   Prisner] prisoner *CD:*   as] at *A*
     8 *Before this title D inserts* XV. Canzonet
    20 ruth] truth *CD:*   either] neather *BC*
135. 4 within] in *BC*, from *D:*   her sacred] his troubled *D* (*not in D**)
     8 ruth] truth *D:*   may] might *BD*, migh *C*
    10 the] a *BCD*
    11 *Instead of this title D inserts* XVIII. Madrigall
136. 2 *Before this title D inserts* VI. Device: Phalev-ciaks] Phaleuciak *C*
     5 wisht] wish *D*
    16 *Before this title D inserts* XVII. Canzonet
    17 Sweet] Sweeete *B*
137. 2 *Before this title D inserts* XIX. Madrigall
    16 *Before this title D inserts* XVIII. Canzonet
138. 11 But] Bnt *D* (*not in D**)
    14 *Before this title D inserts* XIX. Canzonet
    21 How] Aow *D* (*not in D**):   refraine] tefraine *A*
    22 seeke the] seekethe *C*
    23 wound] wonnd *A*
139. 7 to] lo *D* (*not in D**)
    13 *After this line BCD insert the title* Desire and hope, *preceded in D by* XIIII. Ode
    14 and] aud *D*
140. 17 so] no *BCD*
    18 heate] feare *C*, *om. D*
    19 Madrigal III] Elegie. III *C*, IIII. Elegie *D*

140. 20 *Before this line BCD insert the title* Her praise is in her want

141. 2 the] thy *C: before this line BCD insert the title* Her outward Iesture deceauing [deceiued *D*] his inward hope, *preceded in D by* XX. Canzonet
     9 thoght] though *C*

142. 2 II] *Om. D: * Phalevciacks] Phaleuciacke *CD*, *preceded in D by* VII. Device.
     3 selfe] life *D*
     6 eue] euen *CD*
     19 Phaleuciacks] Phalenciacks *D*

143. 2 *After this title BCD insert* Desire hath conquered Reuenge, *preceded in D by* XXXII. Sonet
     17 *Before this title D inserts* XXI. Canzonet

144. 7 such] so *BC*
     13 alwaies] alwaie *C apparently* (*not in C**)
     18 Content] consent *C*
     21 Phœnix] Pheœnix *D*
     27 fame] time *CD*

145. 6 *Line om. in D*
     7 *Before this title D inserts* XXXIII. Sonet
     8 causers] causer *D*
     11 treason] reason *D*
     12 of] to *D*
     17 disperse] dispearst *D*
     18 harbour] harbuor *D*

146. 2 Ode IIII] XV. Ode *D*
     4 for] to *BCD*
     15 inioy'd] enioyn'd *D*
     16 what] who *D*

147. 2 *Before this title D inserts* XXIII. Canzonet
     3 groūd] gronnd *D*
     4 dries] driues *D*
     13 burnt] burne *D*

148. 8 Ode V] XVI. Ode *D*
     10 When] Whẹn *A*

[333]

148. 13 thy] my *CD*

149. 2 *Before this line BCD insert the title* The Louers
[Louer *CD*] absence kils me, her presence cures me,
preceded in D by XXIIII. Canzonet

    19 griefe] girefe *A*, *the* fe *out of alignment in B and
dropped in B**

    23 death] drath *A*

150. 3 If] IE *A*:   *before this line BCD insert the title*
The kinde Louers complaint in finding nothing but
folly for his faithfulnesse, *preceded in D by* XVII.
Ode

    5 your] you *CD*

151. 3 breathe] breath *BCD*

    7 springs] spring *CD*

    20 *Before this line BCD insert the title* Vnhappy Eies,
preceded in D by XVIII. Ode

152. 8 Coy] C *blurred in A*

    19 haue] hath *CD*

    20 *Before this line BCD insert the title* Cupid shootes
light, but wound [wounds *CD*] sore, *preceded in D by*
VI. Poem

    21 didst] di*d*st *A*

    24 mee] me me *D*

153. 4 that] thar *D*

    9 numme] nnmme *A*

    14 all wayes] alwaies *CD*

    19 sting] string *B*

    22 health] wealth *D*

154. 1 *After the head-line BCD insert the title* A true De-
scription of Loue, *preceded in D by* VII. Poem

    2 Paraphrastically translated out of Petrarkes 103
BCD

    4 S'] S. *D*

    18 thee] these *BCD*

155. 3 blastes] st *blurred out in C*

    8 fraight] fraught *CD*

155. 13 death, and] *Smudged in C**
    14 *Before this line BCD insert the title* Faire Face, and
       hard Hart, *preceded in D by* XXV. Canzonet
    16 hear'st] flear'st *CD*
    18 though in] thou ghin *A*
156. 15 *Before this line BCD insert the title* Disdaine at var-
       ience with Desire, *preceded in D by* XIX. Ode
157. 15 *Before this line D inserts* XXVI. Canzonet
    17 Nor] Not *BCD* (*not in D**):   eu'ry] euery *CD*
    20 harmeful] harmelesse *CD*
    25 Which] With *B*
158. 20 *Line om. in D*
159. 2 *Before this title D inserts* VII. Poem
     5 Troyans] Troyians *D*
    15 Marses] Mars his *BCD*
    16 praises] pra ses *B:*   shall] will *D*
    22 eu'ry] e u'ry *A*
160. 11 Is] *Om. B**
161. 5 sought by] soughtby *A*
    10 the] thy *CD*
    16 bee] by *CD*
    19 hope[1]] feare *CD*
162. 2 *Before this title D inserts* XXVII. Canzonet
     4 thy] my *CD*
     5 ti's] 'tis *BCD*
    13 brooke] broke *BCD*
163. 2 *Before this title D inserts* XXVIII. Canzonet
     3 My] Myy *D* (*not in D**):   which] with *BC*
    14 Tide] tides *CD:*   driues] driue *D*
    19 follow] followes *CD*
164. 2 *Before this title D inserts* XX. Ode
    23 wanton] wantou *D*
165. 18 *Before this title D inserts* XXI. Ode
166. 4 An happy] vnhappy *CD*
    16 eu'ry] euery *CD*
    18 then] now *CD*

167. 2 *Before this line BCD insert the title* In praise of the
  Sunne, *preceded in D by* XXIX. Canzonet
  10 power] powet *B*
  19 nothing] noting *D* (*not in D**)
168. 2 Ode XI] XXII. Ode *D*
  9 deepe] deeepe *A*
169. 2 *Before this line BCD insert the title* Death in Loue,
  preceded in D by XXX. Canzonet
  15 brauer] b auer *B* (*not in B**)
  19 and] a d *C*
170. 2 *Before this line BCD insert the title* Breake heauy
  Hart, *preceded in D by* XXXI. Canzonet
  10 harbour] labour *CD*
  19 heauy] Beauie *C*
  20 *Before this line BCD insert the title* Desires gouern-
  ment [gonernment *B*], *preceded in D by* XXXII.
  Canzonet
171. 8 twixt] t'wixt *BCD:*   *before this line BCD insert
  the title* Loues Properties, *preceded in D by* XXXIII.
  Canzonet
172. 2 A] *Om. C:*   *before this title D inserts* XXXIIII.
  Canzonet
  3 care] eare *A*
  13 loue] liue *D*
  16 *Before this line BCD insert the title* The Passionate
  Prisoner, *preceded in D by* XXXV. Canzonet
  23 beate¹] heare *D*
173. 2 *Before this title D inserts* XXXVI. Canzonet
  13 the²] and *CD*
174. 2 Ode XII] XXIII. Ode *D*
  10 thoughtst] thoughts *BC*
  12 a nobler] another *BCD*
  18 the] thy *BCD*
175. 9 with all] withall *BCD*
  12 but] bur *B**
  14 still] *Om. C*

[336]

175. 19 neuer] nener *B**

176. 2 II] III *BC, om.* D, *which inserts before the title* VIII
Device

    5 Wisdome] W *blurred out in A*

    6 *Line om. in C*

   11 shore] the shore *D*

   12 arise] rise *CD*

   14 noui] uoui *B:*   14–15 *om. D*

177. 3 *Before this line BCD insert the title* A defiance to dis-
dainfull Loue, *preceded in D by* XXIIII. Ode

    9 my] thy *D*

178. 2–20 *om. D*

   14 thee] the *BC*

   17 lighter is] lighteri s *B*

   21 Ode XIIII] XXV. Ode *D*

180. 2 *Before this title D inserts* IX. Device

   24 Anomos] *Om. BCD*

181. 2 other] *Om. C:*   2–3 *om. D*

    6 Ode I] XXVI. Ode *D* (*preceding, not following, lines*
4–5)

   15 worthies] worrhies *D*

182. 2 *After this line BCD insert the title* A comparison Betwixt the strength of Beasts, the wisedome of Man,
and the beautie of a Womans face [heart *D*], *preceded in D by* XXVII. Ode

    4 Horse his] Horses *D*

    7 weele] wheele *D*

   10 Poore] From *D*

   13 resists] resist *B*

   15 Ode. III] XXVIII. Ode *D*

   21 knockt] knocks *CD*

   22 Who's there] Who'st here *A*, Whose there *BCD*

183. 5 ope] op't *CD*

   19 wightly] weighty *D:*   in] on *BCD*

   21 fury] fuery *D:*   rekes] reekes *BCD*

   22 host] Hhoast *D*

183. 24 it] of *CD*
184. 2 *Before this title D inserts* XXIX. Ode
      4 doth] do *BCD*
      5 whereby] where *CD*
      8 -foote] -hoofe *D*
     11 waters] water *D*
     14 that] thet *D*
     19 T.S.] *Om. D*
185. 2 Anacreons] Anacrons *B*, Anacoreons *C*:   *before*
        this title D inserts XXX. Ode
     14 For] And *D*
     20 That sore] These sore *C*, Therefore *D*
     21 R.G.] *Om. BCD*
186. 2 *Before this line BCD insert the title* Naturall com-
        parisons with perfect Loue, *preceded in D by*
        XXXVII. Canzonet
      6 sourse, &] surges *D*
     14 Incerto] *Om. BCD*
     15 *Before this title D inserts* XXXVIII. Canzonet
     18 which] with *BCD*
187. 14 set] seat *D*
     15 breeds] breede *BC*
     20 Anomos] *Om. BCD*
188. 2 *Before this title D inserts* XXXIX. Canzonet
      5 Vials] Viols *CD*
     20 downes] gownes *BCD*
     21 dare] dares *D*
189. 2 *Before this title D inserts* X. Device
      5-6 when . . . is all] *Om. CD*
      9 Elegicall] Elegiacall *BC*
     14 Which] With *BCD*
190. 2 Hexameters] An Epigram in Hexameters *D*
191. 2 An other] Another Epigram *D*
      3 arriuall] arriull *C*
      4 Bœtia] Bœotia *D*
     11 a^r] *Om. BCD*

192. 2 Others] Other Epigrams *D*
    16 couldst] couldest *CD*
193. 3 *Line om. in D*
    5 him] them *D*
    9 sorrowfull] sorrrwful *D*
    12 climes] mounts vp *D* (*with an inverted* c *instead of* o):
       the¹] *Om. D*
    13 declines] fals downe *D:*   -ward] -warn'd *CD*
    16 resounded] resouuded *B*
195. 2 *Before this title D inserts* XL. Canzonet
    3 wastest] wasteth *BC*
    4 liuest] líuest *A*
    11–12 by thee² . . . rise] *Om. C*
    12 by] to *D*
    19 measur'de] measured *CD*
196. 2 *Before this title D inserts* IX. Poem: A] Or a *D*
    20 pleasure] pleasnre *C*
197. 10 not] not what *BCD* (*not in B**)
    14 *Before this title D inserts* XI. Device: A] Or a *D*
    16 me] my *D*
    18 mee] my *D*
    21 *BCD prefix* Body *and have no stanza-division*
    27 *BCD prefix* Bodie
198. 2 *Before this title D inserts* XII. Device
    5 Slanderous] Sclanderous *B*, Scandalous *CD*
    23 Anomos] *Om. BCD*
199. 2–3 *om. D*
201. 2 *Before this title D inserts* XLI. Canzonet
    4 ties mēs] tiesmēs *A:*   Gardiõs] Gordions *CD*
    14 these] those *CD*
    26 doth] with *B*, will *CD*
202. 4 fel] *Blurred out of D* (*not D**)
    10 dying] dyings *C:*   pleasure] pleasures *D*
    20 I.D.] *Om. D*
203. 2 *Before this title D inserts* XXXIIII. Sonet
    4 his] the *D*

203. 5 were] weare *D*
      6 auaile] assaile *BCD*
    11 pris'ner] prisoner *CD*
    13 hart, thy] hartt, hy *B* (*not in B**):   pittie] pittty *D*
    15 fettering] fettring *C*
    17 t'is] tis *BCD*

204. 2 Sonnet. II] XXXV. Sonet *D*
     5 Traytor] Troytor *B* (*not in B**)
     9 reuealed] reuaeled *B* (*not in B**)
    13 plants] plaints *BCD*
    16 dide] di'de *C*

205. 2 Sonnet III] XXXVI. Sonet *D*
     3 and] and of *BC*
    11 my] by *B*
    15 Throgh] Through *BCD*. *The final period as well as the hyphen in line 18 are trimmed off in A and A**

206. 2 Sonnet IIII] XXXVII. Sonet *D*
     7 Riuall] riuals *CD*
     8 dazeled] dazled *CD*
     9 dart] r *blurred out of C*
    17 dide] di'de *BCD*

207. 2 Sonnet V] XXXVIII. Sonet *D*

208. 2 Sonnet. VI] XXXIX. Sonet *D*
     3 of] at *BCD*
    12 such] su ch *A*
    16 then] the *BCD*:   the] then *BCD*

209. 2 Sonnet. VII] XL. Sonet *D*
     6 behold] hehold *A*
     8 portray her] portraiture, which *BCD*:   wanting] wanted *CD*

210. 2 Sonnet. VIII] XLI. Sonet *D*:   *after this line CD add the title* To the Sun of his mistris beauty eclipsed with frownes
     4 lightning] lighening *B*
    11 Shine] O shine *CD*

211. 2 Sonnet. IX] XLII. Sonet *D*
    5 you I] I you *BCD*
    6 with the] to *B*, to the *CD*
   12 disdaine] d sdaine *C*
   13 tis] t'is *C*
   15 tis] t'is *BCD*
   17 you] your *BCD*
212. 2 Sonnet X] XLIII. Sonet *D:*   *after this line CD insert the title* The Hearts captiuitie
    8 requireth a] requires a far *BCD*
   17 Melophilus] I.D. *BCD*
213. 2 *Before this title D inserts* XLII. Canzonet: A] Or a *D*
    3 let] le *D*
    4 whose] vuhose *B* (*not in B**)
   15 water] waters *D*
   20 eu'ry] euery *D*
   21 murmuring] mnrmuring *D*
   24 This . . . was] Or a Hymne that was *D:* Amphitryte] *Followed by a comma in BCD. In C the entire phrase comes at the top of sig. I2ᵛ before No. 152, rather than at the end of No. 151 on sig. I2. Hence in D it comes wrongly after* XLIII. Canzonet, *the title inserted before 214.2:* Thamesis] Thamasis *D: the final* d *and* e *in lines 24–25 are trimmed off in A* (*not in A**)
214. 2 *See the foregoing note*
   20 the] a *CD*
   23 Th. Campion] *Om. BCD*
215. 2 his] her *BCD:* *before the title D inserts* XLIIII. Canzonet
    4 flowne] flowue *D*
   10 with] within *CD*
   15 Th.] Tho. *BCD*
216. 2 *Before this title D inserts* XLV. Canzonet
   13 speake] k *inverted in D* (*not in D**)

216. 15 Th:] Tho. *CD*
217. 2 *Before this title D inserts* XIII. Device
    15 my] your *BCD:*   yours] mine *BCD*
218. 2 An Elegie] An [V. *D*] Elegie of a womans heart *CD*
    15 yet] ytt *A*
    22 Yeeld] eelde *C*
    25 shame] shames *D:*   as] *Om. D*
    29 H.W.] *Om. D*
219. 2 *CD insert the title* A Poesie to proue affection is not
    loue, *preceded in D by* X. Poem
220. 9 perfit] perfect *BCD*
    14 W.R.] *Om. D*
    15 *CD insert the title* In praise of two, *preceded in D by*
    XX. Madrigall
    17 feater] better *BCD*
    19 sings full] singsf ull *A*
221. 2 *Before this title D inserts* XXI. Madrigall
    8 these] those *BCD*
    11 the] to the *CD*
    13 did] do *BCD*
    15 knowledge] knoweldge *D*
    17 learnes] taught *BCD*
    24 T. Sp.] *Om. BCD*
222. 2 *Before this title D inserts* XLVI. Canzonet: Small]
    Om. D
    3 Sickness] sickensse *D*
    12 might] might *A*
    14 prize] price *BCD*
    22 do part] doe depart *C*, depart *D*
    23 Th. Sp.] Th: Spilman *BC*, *om. D*
223. 2 A Sonnet in the grace of wit, of tongue, of face *C*,
    XLVII. Canzonet./ In the grace of wit, of tongue,
    and face *D*
    12 mine Eye] mineey *C*
224. 2 *CD insert the title* For her heart onely, *preceded in D
    by* XLIIII. Sonet

224. 7 cheeks] cheeke *BCD*
    10 thy] they *CD:*   will²] will not *CD*
    13 loue] lnue *C*
225. 2 *CD insert the title* That time and absence proues,/
      Rather helps then hurts to loues, *preceded in D by*
      XXXI. Ode
    4 thy] my *D*
    6 thou canst] you can *BCD*
   11 Affections] Affection *C*
   16 within] withiu *D*
226. 2 *BCD insert the title* The true Loue [loues *CD*] knot,
     preceded in D by XXII. Madrigall
    7 though] through *CD*
   16 Ay] By *CD*
   18 turne¹] runne *CD:*   againe] again e *A*
   26 Ignoto] *Om. D*
227. 2 Sonnet] XLV. Sonet *D*
228. 2 Sonnet] XLVI. Sonet *D*
229. 2 Sonnet] XLVII. Sonet *D*
    7 hight] high *CD*
   14 the] he *A* (*not in A**)
   17 I.S.] *Om. D*
230. 2 A Madrigal] XXIII. Madigall (*sic*) *D*
    5 eu'ry] euery *BCD*
   11 A Poeme *BC*, XI. Poem *D*
   12-13 When I to you of all my woes complaine *BCD*
   15-16 With scornefull smiles you answere me againe,
       That Louers true must beare & hold their peace
       BCD
   18 *BC add* F.D.
231. 2 Sonnet] XLVIII. Sonet *D*
    5 Ioue] loue *D* (*and perhaps C*)
232. 2 *Before this title D inserts* XLVIII. Canzonet
    3 to²] too *BCD*
    5 loue] lone *C*
   10 you] ye *BCD*

232. 11 women] woneu *C* (*not in C**)
    13 turne] run *D*

233. 2 Loues embassie in an Iambicke Elegie *CD, preceded in D by* VI. Elegie
    3 my] *Om. CD*
    12 suffreth] suffereth *BCD*

234. 2 Sonnet] XLIX. Sonet *D:*   *CD insert the title* Loues seuen deadly sinnes
    6 no] uo *C*
    7 And] 3. And *BCD:*   by] my *BCD*
    9 to] 4. To *CD*
    10 4.] *Precedes line 9 in BCD:*   consent] content *CD*
    17 H.C.] *Om. CD*

235. 2 Sonnet] L. Sonnet *D*
    4 sisters] and Sisters, the Ladie Margaret Countesse of Cumberland, and [*CD om.* and] the Lady Anne Countesse of Warwicke *BCD*
    5 yee] you *CD*
    7 more truely] morely *B* (more ttuly *B**)
    15 you] one *B* (*not in B**)

236. 2 Ode] XXXII. Ode *D*
    4 Th'] The *CD*
    25 before] beforc *C:*   *in D 25–28 are transferred to fol. LI*[v]*, where they appear before the title supplied for No. 234. See the note on 291.2, below*
    29 Finis] *Om. BCD*

239. 2 *CD add* By [Sir *D*] Iohn Davis, *D omitting* neuer yet [before *C*] published, *and prefixing* I. Poem
    9 Nor] Not *CD:*   t'were] twere *CD*
    14 another] an oher *B*

240. 8 or] of *D*
    10 affects] effects *CD*
    13 Discouers] Discouer *CD:* costs] coasts *CD:* doth] to *D*

241. 14 seeme] see me *B*
    17 dying] *Om. CD*

241. 29 want's] wants *CD*
    30 Iohn Davys] *Om. CD*
242. 2 *Before this title D inserts* I. Device
    14 fortune] fortunes *D*
    26 God] GGd *D*
    27 for] *Om. CD:*   me] *Om. D*
243. 2–3 noe sooner] not sooo/ ner *B*
    5 haue] *Om. D.*
    7 fortune] Fortunes *D*
    13 wheeles] Wheele *D*
    15 chariot] Chariots *CD*
    29 send] lend *D*
244. 5 doth] do *CD*
    16 these] this *C*
    22 part] prat *B apparently*
    26 in] in your *D*
245. 4 she] he *CD*
    6 haue] make *D*
    7 other] others *C*
    12 huswifrie] huswifery *CD*
    13 were] are *D*
    17 A] *Om. D*
    21 Snufkin] Snuftkin *CD*
246. 13 most^1] must *D:*   do] doth *D*
    18 to] *Om. CD*
    20 31] 30 *C*
    21 pleas'd] pleasz'd D
    32 Finis. I.] Sir I. *D*
247. 2 *Before this title D inserts* II. Poem
    4, 10 offring] offering *CD*
    11 bright.] *The period is above the line in B (no period at all in B*)*
    15 presūpteous] presumptuous *CD*
    17 girle] maide *CD*
    24 set] sent *CD*
248. 8 fall] fals *D*

248. 21 your] you *C*
    24 obserues] preserues *CD*
249. 13 euer] ouer *B apparently (not in B*)*
    14 what's] what's *B (not in B*),* whats *CD*
    19 what] whats *D*
    25 make] makes *CD*
    27 net] yet *D*
251. 7 Wife] *Om. D*
252. 9 Africa] Atfica *B*
    19 it] is *C*
253. 20 *CD prefix* Maid
    27 vvhere] were *C*
254. 8 dvvell] dvve*l* *B*
    21 prize] price *CD*
255. 7 shall] *First* l *pulled above the line in B*
    18 Iohn Davys] *Om. D*
256. 1 *Before this title D inserts* I. Canzonet
258. 5 to] so *CD*
    8 it's] its *CD,* its *B* with the apostrophe in the space between the stanzas*
259. 1 Complaint] compiaint *C:*   *D prefixes* IIII. Poem
    7 do shake] would helpe *D:*   heare] ease *D*
    9 my] with *D*
    11 feele] beare *D*
    12 consume] coosume *D*
    28 cares] case *D*
    29 by] my *C:*   sighs, teares] and sighs *D*
    30, 31 *D changes as follows:*

    It nought auailes my torments to declare,
    Since that my teares cannot her flinty mind

260. 2–261.14 *Practically rewritten in D as follows:*

4

To pitty moue; I am cast out of mind,
So hath she sworne I shall in paine consume,
My weary dayes, my life must wast away,
Consum'd with deadly paine and restlesse cryes.

[346]

So *Philomele* too much opprest with paine,
By his misdeede that causeth her lament,
Both day and night her mournefull layes encrease;
And pind, in paine her sorrowes doth declare.

5

It is some ease hid sorrowes to declare,
But too small ease to such a grieued mind,
As by repeating cryes doth more consume,
To end that which he finds at all no way,
But carefull sighs mingled with ruthfull cryes,
(A simple salue to cure so great a paine)
Come then ye gastly owles, helpe me lament,
With fearefull shrikes, and as your shrikes increase.

6

When as the Sunne departing doth encrease,
The doubbled shadowes which as signes declare,
The night drawes neere: so I to ease my mind,
Here will augment my plaints; so to consume
My loathed life: and though you flye away,
Soone as the day returnes and cease your cryes,
Yet I vnhappy wretch opprest with paine,
But day and night am forced to lament,

7

So foule a change: But while I thus lament,
My griefe with teares: The more for to increase
My woe; with scoffs: my state she doth declare,
To him who first, from me her wanton mind;
By gifts did win: since when I still cnnsume [*sic*]
Ay more and more; ne find I any way,
To ease my mind: but thus with mournefull cries,
I liuing dye, and dying liue in paine.

8.

And now adue delight and farewell paine,
Adue vaine hope; I shall no more lament,
Her fained faith whichdid [*sic*] my woes increase,
And ye to whom my griefes I thus declare,

Ye which haue heard the secrets of my mind,
And seene my lingring life in paine consume,
Adue ye woods, and waters hence away,
By death I must, and cease my ruthfull cries.

[L'Envoy]

Ye which heare not my cries nor know my paine,
Yet do my chance lament, let pitty increase:
Your griefe by teares declare: To ease your mind,
Witnesse how I consume, and wast away.

260. 13 minde] mmde *B*
26 day] daies *C*
261. 10 yee to] yeeto *B, followed by a printer's lead-mark*
15 F.D.] *Om. D*
262. 1 *Before this title D inserts* II. Device
2 Thisbe] Thesbe *D*
5-6 dis-ioind, con-ioind] *The hyphens apparently occur in B but have dropped out completely in B**
7 deuide] denide *CD*
17 the other] tother *D*
18 giue] giues *D*
19 murther] murthers *D*
263. 2 feare-lesse] fearfull *D:*   mine] my *D*
16, 17 discou-/ red] disco-/ red *B*
26 That not] atn ot *C*
264. 2 Vticen] Vtican *CD*
12 An] To the *CD*
16 Cloud] Clou. *B*
17 the] to the *CD*
23 Thus] This *D:*   Paraphrastically] Paraphasti-
cally *C*
24 Whither] Whether *CD*
265. 7 *Before this title D inserts* V. Poem: A] Or *D*
19 Cloe] Cole *CD*
20 enuide] *The spacing in BC shows that* I enuide *is
the correct reading, as in D*
22 Cloe] Cole *CD*

[348]

266. 4 thy] my *CD*
    5 Cloes] Coles *D*
   12 Madrigall] I. Madrigall *D*
   21 Madrigall] II. Madrigall *D*
267. 2 Madrigall] III. Madrigall *D*
   11 while] when *D*
   20 Sonnet] Sonnets *C*, I. Sonet *D*
268. 7 Cæsar] Casar *B*
    8 Sonnet] II. Sonet *D*
   11 sigh't] sigh *D*
   24 *Before this line D inserts* III. Sonet
269. 12, 13 IIII. Madrigall./ Vpon his departure *D*
270. 1 *Before this title D inserts* Of Epigrams
    3 Æliam] Aelian *CD*
    4 *Aelia] Aelia B*
    5 vna¹] vnta *D*
   22 Non] Mon *C*
   23 doth] do *D*
   28 lactitet] lact tet *C*, lacttet *D:*   edam] eadem *D*
271. 8 cæcus] cœcus *CD*
    9 a] *Om. CD*
   21 while] whiles *CD*
   26 Dantur] Danter *D:*   nisi] nifi *D*
272. 2 42.] 42. 42. *D*
    5 præstantem] præctanter *D*
    6 negas] e *inverted in D*
    8 soone¹] so one *CD*
   11 nor] and *CD*
   14 nego] negos *CD*
   16 nothing] noting *D*
   20 domi] dōmi *B apparently (not in B*)*
273. 28 then] them *CD*
275. 6 -turd] -turnd *CD*
277. 1–4 *C has this phrase as a section-heading, not a sepa-rate half-title, preceded by the words* Sonnets, Odes, Elegies, and/ other Poesies./ *Om. D*

279. 1 A] IIII. Device./ Or a *D*
       5 there] heere *D*
      12 releefe] reliefes *D*
      19 *D prefixes* L.
      20 *D prefixes* H.
      21 A] V. Device./ Or a *D*
280. 4 shouldst] should *D:*   night] right *CD*
       7 Why] What *D*
      13 L.] D. *CD*
      15 *Before this title D inserts* XXVII. Sonet
      22 pleasures] pleasure *D*
281. 2 *Before this title D inserts* VII. Canzonet
      15 Aeole] Aeole. *B apparently*
      21 *Before this title D inserts* VIII. Canzonet
      30 to] of *CD*
282. 3 flattering] flattring *D*
       6 rest] reft *CD*
       9 her] me *CD*
      11 *Before this title D inserts* VIII. Canzonet
      19 that I] let me *D*
      21 and²] I *CD*
      25 selfe same] the selfe *D*
283. 1 *Before this title D inserts* IX. Canzonet
      14 againe] agine *D*
      16 the] a *CD*
      18 eares] teares *C*
      22 of] in *D*
      23 *Before this title D inserts* X. Canzonet
284. 14 *Before this title D inserts* XI. Canzonet
      18 discharg'd] dischargd'd *C*
      24 man-] -main *D*
      25 winde] w inde *with* d *imperfectly impressed B*
      29 wished] twisted *CD*
      32 the] the the *D*
285. 2 Execration] Execreation *C:*   *before this title D inserts* XII. Canzonet

285. 6 moue] please *CD*
    7 flattering] flattring *D*
    12 tooke] ooke *D:*   and] aud *B*
    14 louing] *The* i *is inverted in D*
    15 those] the *D:*   which] that *D*
    19 did] doth *D*
    21 Finis. T. W.] *Om. D*
    22 *Before this title D inserts* XIII. Canzonet, *omitting* A Sonnet
    24 a] in a *CD*
    28 makes] make *D* (*not in D**):   it] ît *B*
    30 their] her *CD*
286. 2 make it] makes *CD*
    4 grace] glad *CD:*   aire] aires *D* (*not in D**)
    15 springing] spring *CD*
    16 Ch. B.] Cha. Best *C, om. D*
    17 *D has* XXVIII. Sonet./ Of the Monne (*sic*)
    21 her¹] his *CD*
    24 mone] moue *CD*
    32 Ch. B.] Cha. Best *C, om. D*
287. 2 *D inserts before this title* VII. Pastorall, *omitting* I
    5 bett'] bett *D*
    16 hand] hands *D*
    17 might] may *CD*
    18 *D om.* 3
    19 Tho] The *C*
    22 ground] gronnd *B*
288. 10 aspires] appeares *D*
    19 whom] who *CD*
289. 5 witnesse] winesse *C*
    10 Thou] Now *D:*   at] as *D*
    14 pinde] pine *CD*
    20 now makes] does gar *D*
    25 nay . . . brest] yea more then saw her too *D*
    27 that . . . rest] through which I am vndoo *D*
290. 3 Roundlaies] Roundelaies *D*

290. 9 I would only] onely I would *D*
 13 wilfully] vtterly *D*
 22 *Before this line D inserts* II. Canzonet
 26 *One page ends with this line in C, another begins with line 27; hence D has no space between 26 and 27*

291. 2 *Before this line D supplies the heading* XLIX. Canzonet, *followed by 236.25–28 and by the title (also in B* and C)* Of loue gift
 5 Giue] Giues *D*
 10 *Before this title D inserts* L. Canzonet
 15 tolls] rolls *B apparently*
 17, 23, 29 preth thee] prethee *D*
 22 this] thls *B*

292. 5 preth thee] prethee *D*
 11 *None of the editions unmistakably indicates a new poem here:* sith] such *CD*
 17 A Poeme] XII. Poem *D*

293. 8 *Before this line CD insert the title* A Poeme in the nature of an Epitaph of a friend, *preceded in D by* XIII. Poem, *and in both divided into two six-line stanzas:* haue] hath *D*
 20 *Before this line CD insert the title* Loues contentment, *preceded in D by* XIIII. Poem
 30 be kild] beleeu'd *D*
 31 hereof] thereof *CD*

294. 3 enteard] vnheard *D:* contain] conta in *B,* containe *B**
 7 he] here *D*
 18 or] for *C,* on *D*
 25 although] althongh *B*

295. 2 *Before this line C inserts the title* A repentant Poeme, *preceded in D by* XV. Poem
 6 awry] away *C*

296. 6 Finis] *Om. CD*

299. 1 *Om. in D*
 3 French King] King of France *D*

299. 9 age] a e *C:*   till] tili *D* (*not in D**)
     20 *D adds* Cha. Best
     21 *Before this title D inserts* XVI. Poem
300. 19, 20 Margret] Margaret *D*
     29 the] th' *D*
     31 France] e *blurred out in C*
301. 3 not] not not *C*
     22 fourth] fourh *D*
     23 Margret] Margaret *D*
302. 8 *Before this title D inserts* XVII. Poem: A] Or *D*
     26 dost] doth *D*
305. 2 her] *Om. D*
      5 all] all our *D*
      8 *Before this title D inserts* LI. Sonet
     18 Cambriaes] Cambraies *D*
     23 *Before this title D inserts* LII. Sonet
306. 8 *Before this title D inserts* A Deviso
     16 meruerunt] *The first* e *is blurred in C*
     26 perdere] *The final* e *is inverted in C*
307. 8 discedens] descedens *D*
     13 moriens] mor ens *C*
     17 *In D the long lines in Nos. 247 and 248 are printed as two*
308. 27 Finis] *Om. D*

INDEX OF FIRST LINES

INDEX OF FIRST LINES

References are to poem-numbers. When poems do not appear
in all four of the original editions *ABCD*, their first lines are
followed by letters in parentheses — as *(ABC)*, *(CD)*, *(D)* —
showing in what editions they do occur. Lines in brackets
are readings that are to be found in an edition later than *A*,
and only such bracketed readings are included as are necessary
to make the index readily usable for *BCD* no less than for *A*.
Authority for the bracketed lines or phrases will be found in
the appropriate entries of the Variant Readings and Misprints.

INDEX OF FIRST LINES

INDEX OF FIRST LINES

INDEX OF FIRST LINES

INDEX OF FIRST LINES

INDEX OF FIRST LINES

INDEX OF FIRST LINES

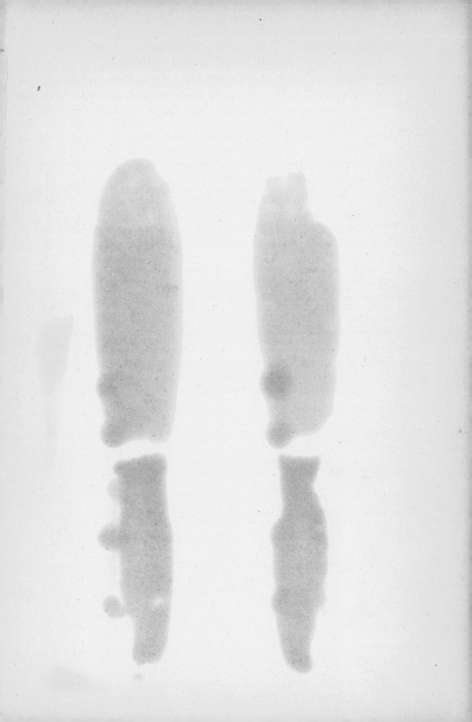

DATE DUE	

GAYLORD   PRINTED IN U.S.A.